FOR DUMMIES
COMPUTER
BOOK SERIES
FROM IDG

Windows® 95 For Kids & Parents™

W9-AZW-437

In the Beginning . . .

To Do This . . .	Do This . . .
Find a hidden Start button	Place your pointer at the lower-left corner of the screen
Install a new program	Pop in disk or CD-ROM and follow directions onscreen
Open a program	Click the Start button, glide up to Programs, and double-click the program's name
Open a file	Double-click its icon

Oops! Fixing a Mistake

To Do This . . .	Do This . . .
Get help anywhere	Press F1 or the Help Key
Undo a mistake	Choose Edit⇨Undo
De-select an icon	Click anywhere but on the icon
Find out what a button does	Let the mouse hover over it for a few seconds
Take a file out of the Recycle Bin	Double-click the Bin and drag the file out

Finishing Touches

To Do This . . .	Do This . . .
Save a file	Choose File⇨Save
Save a file with a new name	Choose File⇨Save As
Print a file	Choose File⇨Print

Working with Program Windows

To Do This . . .	Do This . . .
Minimize a window to a taskbar button	Click the Minimize button
Maximize a window from a taskbar button	Click the taskbar button for the window
Restore a window to its previous size	Click the Restore button
Change the size of a window	Drag the window's border outline or grip
Move a window	Drag the window by its title bar
Close a window	Click the Close button
Move from one window to another	Click the window's name in the taskbar
Find a file or folder	Click the Start button, glide to Find, and then click Files or Folders
Shut down Windows 95	Click the Start button, glide to Shut Down, and then click Yes

Fun with Files, Folders, and Text

To Do This . . .	Highlight the Item and . . .
Cut text	Choose Edit⇨Cut
Copy text	Choose Edit⇨Copy
Paste text	Choose Edit⇨Paste

Information to Keep Handy

Serial number of your computer: _____

Serial number of your copy of Windows 95: _____

Microsoft Technical Support: _____

Amount of internal memory on your computer: _____

Your computer's microprocessor type: _____

Technical Support number for your computer: _____

Your Internet Service Provider (ISP): _____

Your ISP dial-in number: _____

Your ISP password: _____

...For Dummies: #1 Computer Book Series for Beginners

Windows® 95 For Kids & Parents™

Cheat Sheet

Web Sites Just for Kids

Site Name	Address	What You Get
Children's Television Workshop Online	www.ctw.org	Play with Bert, Ernie, Oscar, and the rest of the gang
CollegeBound.net	www.cbnet.com	Great resource for checking out colleges, scholarships, and more
Convomania	www.mania.apple.com	A special site for kids with disabilities or who are chronically ill
Homework Help	www.startribune.com/stonline/html/special/homework	Help with tough homework questions
NetPlay Game Club	www.netplay.com	Classic games go online
Smithsonian Institute	www.si.edu/newstart.htm	The world visits your computer through fabulous exhibits
White House for Kids	www.whitehouse.gov/WH/kids/html	Say hello to the President and tell him what you think
Yahooligans	www.yahooligans.com	The easiest search engine for kids
Yuckiest Site on the Internet	www.nj.com/yucky	Way cool science stuff

Web Sites Just for Parents

Site Name	Address	What You Get
American Academy of Pediatric Dentistry	www.aapd.org	Get the facts and your questions answered here
CyberInvest.Com	www.cyberinvest.com	Tips and help for the new investor
Family.com	www.family.com	Fun stuff to do with your kids
Kids Parties Connection	www.kidsparties.com	Gift ideas, entertainers, and party locations
The Monster Board	www.monsterboard.com	Largest online classified site in the world
Thunderbeam Online Software Store	www.thunderbeam.com	Low prices and great info on software for kids
Yahoo!	www.yahoo.com	Terrific search engine
Windows95.com	www.Windows95.com	Insider Windows 95 tips
Zip2 Yellow Pages	www.zip2.com	Telephone numbers and driving directions all in one place

...For Dummies: #1 Computer Book Series for Beginners

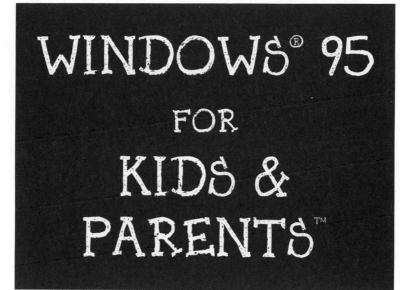

WINDOWS® 95 FOR KIDS & PARENTS™

by Lisa Price and Jonathan Price

Foreword by Sam Mead

IDG Books Worldwide, Inc.
An International Data Group Company

Foster City, CA ♦ Chicago, IL ♦ Indianapolis, IN ♦ Southlake, TX

Windows® 95 For Kids and Parents™

Published by
IDG Books Worldwide, Inc.
An International Data Group Company
919 E. Hillsdale Blvd.
Suite 400
Foster City, CA 94404
www.idgbooks.com (IDG Books Worldwide Web site)
www.dummies.com (Dummies Press Web site)

Library of Congress Catalog Card No.: 98-70107

ISBN: 0-7645-0277-8

Printed in the United States of America

10 9 8 7 6 5 4 3 2 1

1E/QZ/QS/ZY/IN

Distributed in the United States by IDG Books Worldwide, Inc.

Distributed by Macmillan Canada for Canada; by Transworld Publishers Limited in the United Kingdom; by IDG Norge Books for Norway; by IDG Sweden Books for Sweden; by Woodslane Pty. Ltd. for Australia; by Woodslane Enterprises Ltd. for New Zealand; by Longman Singapore Publishers Ltd. for Singapore, Malaysia, Thailand, and Indonesia; by Simron Pty. Ltd. for South Africa; by Toppan Company Ltd. for Japan; by Distribuidora Cuspide for Argentina; by Livraria Cultura for Brazil; by Ediciencia S.A. for Ecuador; by Addison-Wesley Publishing Company for Korea; by Ediciones ZETA S.C.R. Ltda. for Peru; by WS Computer Publishing Corporation, Inc., for the Philippines; by Unalis Corporation for Taiwan; by Contemporanea de Ediciones for Venezuela; by Computer Book & Magazine Store for Puerto Rico; by Express Computer Distributors for the Caribbean and West Indies. Authorized Sales Agent: Anthony Rudkin Associates for the Middle East and North Africa.

For general information on IDG Books Worldwide's books in the U.S., please call our Consumer Customer Service department at 800-762-2974. For reseller information, including discounts and premium sales, please call our Reseller Customer Service department at 800-434-3422.

For information on where to purchase IDG Books Worldwide's books outside the U.S., please contact our International Sales department at 650-655-3200 or fax 650-655-3295.

For information on foreign language translations, please contact our Foreign & Subsidiary Rights department at 650-655-3021 or fax 650-655-3281.

For sales inquiries and special prices for bulk quantities, please contact our Sales department at 650-655-3200 or write to the address above.

For information on using IDG Books Worldwide's books in the classroom or for ordering examination copies, please contact our Educational Sales department at 800-434-2086 or fax 817-251-8174.

For press review copies, author interviews, or other publicity information, please contact our Public Relations department at 650-655-3000 or fax 650-655-3299.

For authorization to photocopy items for corporate, personal, or educational use, please contact Copyright Clearance Center, 222 Rosewood Drive, Danvers, MA 01923, or fax 978-750-4470.

About the Authors

Lisa and Jonathan Price are parents and award-winning authors who have been writing about family computing since their family started 16 years ago. They are the authors of *Discover Microsoft Home Essentials,* published by IDG Books Worldwide, Inc., and many other computer books. Their articles have appeared in *Family Fun, Family PC, Harper's, Home Office Computing, Macworld, Reader's Digest,* and *TV Guide.*

Lisa is Features Editor on Thunderbeam, a site devoted to helping parents and grandparents find the best software for their kids. Jonathan consults with major computer hardware and software companies on improving their manuals and online help; he also teaches at New Mexico Tech and University of California at Santa Cruz.

Lisa and Jonathan give workshops and talks around the world, focusing on high-tech writing and family software. They invite you to visit their Web site (www.theprices.com/circle/) where you can find out what else they are up to. Please e-mail them with your thoughts and suggestions at LisaSPrice@aol.com and JonPrice@aol.com.

ABOUT IDG BOOKS WORLDWIDE

Welcome to the world of IDG Books Worldwide.

IDG Books Worldwide, Inc., is a subsidiary of International Data Group, the world's largest publisher of computer-related information and the leading global provider of information services on information technology. IDG was founded more than 25 years ago and now employs more than 8,500 people worldwide. IDG publishes more than 275 computer publications in over 75 countries (see listing below). More than 60 million people read one or more IDG publications each month.

Launched in 1990, IDG Books Worldwide is today the #1 publisher of best-selling computer books in the United States. We are proud to have received eight awards from the Computer Press Association in recognition of editorial excellence and three from *Computer Currents*' First Annual Readers' Choice Awards. Our best-selling *...For Dummies*® series has more than 30 million copies in print with translations in 30 languages. IDG Books Worldwide, through a joint venture with IDG's Hi-Tech Beijing, became the first U.S. publisher to publish a computer book in the People's Republic of China. In record time, IDG Books Worldwide has become the first choice for millions of readers around the world who want to learn how to better manage their businesses.

Our mission is simple: Every one of our books is designed to bring extra value and skill-building instructions to the reader. Our books are written by experts who understand and care about our readers. The knowledge base of our editorial staff comes from years of experience in publishing, education, and journalism — experience we use to produce books for the '90s. In short, we care about books, so we attract the best people. We devote special attention to details such as audience, interior design, use of icons, and illustrations. And because we use an efficient process of authoring, editing, and desktop publishing our books electronically, we can spend more time ensuring superior content and spend less time on the technicalities of making books.

You can count on our commitment to deliver high-quality books at competitive prices on topics you want to read about. At IDG Books Worldwide, we continue in the IDG tradition of delivering quality for more than 25 years. You'll find no better book on a subject than one from IDG Books Worldwide.

John Kilcullen
CEO
IDG Books Worldwide, Inc.

Steven Berkowitz
President and Publisher
IDG Books Worldwide, Inc.

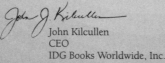

Eighth Annual Computer Press Awards ≥1992

Ninth Annual Computer Press Awards ≥1993

Tenth Annual Computer Press Awards ≥1994

Eleventh Annual Computer Press Awards ≥1995

IDG Books Worldwide, Inc., is a subsidiary of International Data Group, the world's largest publisher of computer-related information and the leading global provider of information services on information technology. International Data Group publishes over 275 computer publications in over 75 countries. Sixty million people read one or more International Data Group publications each month. International Data Group's publications include: **ARGENTINA:** Buyer's Guide, Computerworld Argentina, PC World Argentina; **AUSTRALIA:** Australian Macworld, Australian PC World, Australian Reseller News, Computerworld, IT Casebook, Network World, Publish, Webmaster; **AUSTRIA:** Computerwelt Osterreich, Networks Austria, PC Tip Austria; **BANGLADESH:** PC World Bangladesh; **BELARUS:** PC World Belarus; **BELGIUM:** Data News; **BRAZIL:** Annuário de Informática, Computerworld, Connections, Macworld, PC Player, PC World, Publish, Reseller News, Supergamepower; **BULGARIA:** Computerworld Bulgaria, Network World Bulgaria, PC & MacWorld Bulgaria; **CANADA:** CIO Canada, Client/Server World, ComputerWorld Canada, InfoWorld Canada, NetworkWorld Canada, WebWorld; **CHILE:** Computerworld Chile, PC World Chile; **COLOMBIA:** Computerworld Colombia, PC World Colombia; **COSTA RICA:** PC World Centro America; **THE CZECH AND SLOVAK REPUBLICS:** Computerworld Czechoslovakia, Macworld Czech Republic, PC World Czechoslovakia; **DENMARK:** Communications World Danmark, Computerworld Danmark, Macworld Danmark, PC World Danmark, Techworld Denmark; **DOMINICAN REPUBLIC:** PC World Republica Dominicana; **ECUADOR:** PC World Ecuador; **EGYPT:** Computerworld Middle East, PC World Middle East; **EL SALVADOR:** PC World Centro America; **FINLAND:** MikroPC, Tietoverkko, Tietoviikko; **FRANCE:** Distributique, Hebdo, Info PC, Le Monde Informatique, Macworld, Reseaux & Telecoms, WebMaster France; **GERMANY:** Computer Partner, Computerwoche, Computerwoche Extra, Computerwoche FOCUS, Global Online, Macwelt, PC Welt; **GREECE:** Amiga Computing, GamePro Greece, Multimedia World; **GUATEMALA:** PC World Centro America; **HONDURAS:** PC World Centro America; **HONG KONG:** Computerworld Hong Kong, PC World Hong Kong, Publish in Asia; **HUNGARY:** ABCD CD-ROM, Computerworld Szamitastechnika, Internetto online Magazine, PC World Hungary, PC-X Magazin Hungary; **ICELAND:** Tolvuheimur PC World Island; **INDIA:** Information Communications World, Information Systems Computerworld, PC World India, Publish in Asia; **INDONESIA:** InfoKomputer PC World, Komputek Computerworld, Publish in Asia; **IRELAND:** ComputerScope, PC Live!; **ISRAEL:** Macworld Israel, People & Computers/Computerworld; **ITALY:** Computerworld Italia, Macworld Italia, Networking Italia, PC World Italia; **JAPAN:** DTP World, Macworld Japan, Nikkei Personal Computing, OS/2 World Japan, SunWorld Japan, Windows NT World, Windows World Japan; **KENYA:** PC World East African; **KOREA:** Hi-Tech Information, Macworld Korea, PC World Korea; **MACEDONIA:** PC World Macedonia; **MALAYSIA:** Computerworld Malaysia, PC World Malaysia, Publish in Asia; **MALTA:** PC World Malta; **MEXICO:** Computerworld Mexico, PC World Mexico; **MYANMAR:** PC World Myanmar; **NETHERLANDS:** Computer! Totaal, LAN Internetworking Magazine, LAN World Buyers Guide, Macworld Netherlands, Net, WebWereld; **NEW ZEALAND:** Absolute Beginners Guide and Plain & Simple Series, Computer Buyer, Computer Industry Directory, Computerworld New Zealand, MTB, Network World, PC World New Zealand; **NICARAGUA:** PC World Centro America; **NORWAY:** Computerworld Norge, CW Rapport, Datamagasinet, Financial Rapport, Kursguide Norge, Macworld Norge, Multimediaworld Norge, PC World Ekspress Norge, PC World Nettverk, PC World Norge, PC World ProduktGuide Norge; **PAKISTAN:** Computerworld Pakistan; **PANAMA:** PC World Panama; **PEOPLE'S REPUBLIC OF CHINA:** China Computer Users, China Computerworld, China InfoWorld, China Telecom World Weekly, Computer & Communication, Electronic Design China, Electronics Today, Electronics Weekly, Game Software, PC World China, Popular Computer Week, Software Weekly, Software World, Telecom World; **PERU:** Computerworld Peru, PC World Profesional Peru, PC World SoHo Peru; **PHILIPPINES:** Click!, Computerworld Philippines, PC World Philippines, Publish in Asia; **POLAND:** Computerworld Poland, Computerworld Special Report Poland, Cyber, Macworld Poland, Networld Poland, PC World Komputer; **PORTUGAL:** Cerebro/PC World, Computerworld/Correio Informático, Dealer World Portugal, Mac*In/PC*In Portugal, Multimedia World; **PUERTO RICO:** PC World Puerto Rico; **ROMANIA:** Computerworld Romania, PC World Romania, Telecom Romania; **RUSSIA:** Computerworld Russia, Mir PK, Publish, Seti; **SINGAPORE:** Computerworld Singapore, PC World Singapore, Publish in Asia; **SLOVENIA:** Monitor; **SOUTH AFRICA:** Computing SA, Network World SA, Software World SA; **SPAIN:** Communicaciones World España, Computerworld España, Dealer World España, Macworld España, PC World España; **SRI LANKA:** Infolink PC World; **SWEDEN:** CAP&Design, Computer Sweden, Corporate Computing Sweden, Internetworld Sweden, it.branschen, Macworld Sweden, MaxiData Sweden, MikroDatorn, Nätverk & Kommunikation, PC World Sweden, PCaktiv, Windows World Sweden; **SWITZERLAND:** Computerworld Schweiz, Macworld Schweiz, PCtip; **TAIWAN:** Computerworld Taiwan, Macworld Taiwan, NEW ViSiON/Publish, PC World Taiwan, Windows World Taiwan; **THAILAND:** Publish in Asia, Thai Computerworld; **TURKEY:** Computerworld Turkiye, Macworld Turkiye, Network World Turkiye, PC World Turkiye; **UKRAINE:** Computerworld Kiev, Multimedia World Ukraine, PC World Ukraine; **UNITED KINGDOM:** Acorn User UK, Amiga Action UK, Amiga Computing UK, Apple Talk UK, Computing, Macworld, Parents and Computers UK, PC Advisor, PC Home, PSX Pro, The WEB; **UNITED STATES:** Cable in the Classroom, CIO Magazine, Computerworld, DOS World, Federal Computer Week, GamePro Magazine, InfoWorld, I-Way, Macworld, Network World, PC Games, PC World, Publish, Video Event, THE WEB Magazine, and WebMaster; online webzines: JavaWorld, NetscapeWorld, and SunWorld Online; **URUGUAY:** InfoWorld Uruguay; **VENEZUELA:** Computerworld Venezuela, PC World Venezuela; and **VIETNAM:** PC World Vietnam.   3/24/97

Dedication

We dedicate this book to our two wonderful boys, Ben and Noah, and to their grandparents, Bob & Elsie Deuchar and Bob & Ruth Price, sometimes better know as our parents.

Author's Acknowledgments

First and foremost, we thank our great kids, Ben and Noah, who uncomplainingly did a little extra around the house, like cooking dinner, mowing the lawn, and running errands while Mom and Dad worked under an extremely tight schedule. We especially appreciate their good humor considering this entire book was written during their football season. Because of their unselfishness, we never missed a deadline or one of their football games.

We'd also like to thank our wonderful agent, Margot Maley of Waterside Productions, who brought us this book in the first place. Her professionalism and sympathetic ear is greatly appreciated.

Publisher's Acknowledgments

We're proud of this book; please send us your comments about it by using the IDG Books Worldwide Registration Card at the back of the book or by e-mailing us at feedback/dummies@idgbooks.com. Some of the people who helped bring this book to market include the following:

Acquisitions, Development, and Editorial

Project Editor: Mary Goodwin

Acquisitions Editor: Ellen Camm

Product Development Manager: Mary Bednarek

Media Development Manager: Joyce Pepple

Permissions Editor: Heather H. Dismore

Copy Editors: Gwenette Gaddis, Rowena Rappaort

Associate Technical Editor: Joell Smith

Technical Editor: Kevin Spencer

Editorial Manager: Elaine Brush

Editorial Assistant: Paul Kuzmic

Production

Project Coordinator: Regina Snyder

Layout and Graphics: Lou Boudreau, Angela F. Hunckler, Brent Savage, Janet Seib, Michael A. Sullivan

Proofreaders: Christine Berman, Kelli Botta, Joel Draper, Betty Kish, Nancy Price, Rebecca Senninger, Janet M. Withers

Indexer: Liz Cunningham

Special Help

Jason Ely

General and Administrative

IDG Books Worldwide, Inc.: John Kilcullen, CEO; Steven Berkowitz, President and Publisher

IDG Books Technology Publishing: Brenda McLaughlin, Senior Vice President and Group Publisher

Dummies Technology Press and Dummies Editorial: Diane Graves Steele, Vice President and Associate Publisher; Mary Bednarek, Acquisitions and Product Development Director; Kristin A. Cocks, Editorial Director

Dummies Trade Press: Kathleen A. Welton, Vice President and Publisher; Kevin Thornton, Acquisitions Manager

IDG Books Production for Dummies Press: Beth Jenkins Roberts, Production Director; Cindy L. Phipps, Manager of Project Coordination, Production Proofreading, and Indexing; Kathie S. Schutte, Supervisor of Page Layout; Shelley Lea, Supervisor of Graphics and Design; Debbie J. Gates, Production Systems Specialist; Robert Springer, Supervisor of Proofreading; Debbie Stailey, Special Projects Coordinator; Tony Augsburger, Supervisor of Reprints and Bluelines; Leslie Popplewell, Media Archive Coordinator

Dummies Packaging and Book Design: Patti Crane, Packaging Specialist; Kavish + Kavish, Cover Design

◆

The publisher would like to give special thanks to Patrick J. McGovern, without whom this book would not have been possible.

◆

Contents at a Glance

Foreword .... *xxi*

Introduction *1*

Part I: Getting Started 7

Chapter 1: Diving into Windows 95 Head First 9
Chapter 2: Poking Around Your Desktop 33
Chapter 3: Taking Apart a Window 53
Chapter 4: Playing with the Look and Feel 87

Part II: Working and Playing with Windows 95 109

Chapter 5: Cutting, Copying, and Pasting 111
Chapter 6: Messing Around with Documents, Folders, and Floppies 127
Chapter 7: Playing with the Free Programs in Windows 95 147
A Sneak Peek at Windows 98 .... I-1
Chapter 8: Playing with Games, Music, and Video 171
Chapter 9: Sharing Software with the Rest of the Family 189

Part III: Opening a Window to the Internet 207

Chapter 10: Surfing the World Wide Web with Internet Explorer 209
Chapter 11: Cruisin' the Online Services — Microsoft Network
and America Online 229

Part IV: The Part of Tens 253

Chapter 12: Ten Easy Answers to First-Timers' Questions 255
Chapter 13: Oof! Ouch! The Ten Most Common Error Messages
and What to Do about Them 261
Chapter 14: Ten Useful and Fun Web Sites for Windows' Families 267

Part V: Appendixes 273

Appendix A: Um, It Won't Work the Way I Want It to Work 275
Appendix B: About the CD-ROM 289
Appendix C: An A-to-Z of Nerdisms 299

Index *305*

License Agreement *326*

Installation Instructions *328*

Book Registration Information .... *Back of Book*

Cartoons at a Glance

By Rich Tennant

page 273

page 253

page 7

page 109

page 207

Fax: 978-546-7747 • E-mail: the5wave@tiac.net

Table of Contents

Foreword .... *xxi*

Introduction *1*

About This Book 1
How to Use This Book 2
How This Book Is Organized 3
Part I: Getting Started 3
Part II: Working and Playing with Windows 95 3
Part III: Opening a Window to the Internet 3
Part IV: The Part of Tens 3
Part V: Appendixes 4
Icons Used in This Book 4
But, Are We There Yet? 5

Part I: Getting Started 7

Chapter 1: Diving into Windows 95 Head First 9
Windows Aren't Just Something in Your House 9
Your Friends Know Why Windows 95 Is Cool 10
Windows 95 — Are You in There? 11
Turning on Your Computer and Mousing Around 12
Poking Around — Clicking Icons and Unfolding Folders 16
On Your Mark, Get Set, Go! 19
Ordering Fast from the Menus 22
Two-for-One: Having Several Programs Open at Once 26
Tapdancing on the Keys 26
Printing the Proof to Show Your Friends 27
Safe Not Sorry: Saving What You've Done 28
But I've Got to Use the Computer Now! 29
Stop: Turning Your Computer Off without Breaking Anything 30

Chapter 2: Poking Around Your Desktop 33
Playing Around with the Taskbar 35
A real Start-a-rama 36
It's not the X-Files — it's Documents 37
Setting things up 37
Help! I've fallen and I can't reach the remote! 39
Run for your life 41
Shut up about Shut Down, will ya? 41
Honey, I shrank the program 42
Getting the right corner 43

Hey, It's My Computer! 44
Don't Talk Trash. It's a Recycle Bin 47
    Making up a silly example to throw away 48
    Throwing stuff away (and getting it back) 49
Short(cut) and Sweet 50

Chapter 3: Taking Apart a Window 53

Every Button in Your Window Is Hot 54
    Button, button, who's got the button? 55
    Making a button do what you say 56
    But when do I use the other mouse button? 57
    How many clicks is enough? 58
    Magic buttons! Make a window big! No, make it small!
        Make it go away! 58
        Getting down with the Minimize button 59
        Pumping things up with the Maximize button 60
        Giving a window a chance at a come back:
          The Restore button 60
        X marks the spot: The Close button 61
Staying Inside the Border 62
Working with the Bars in Your Windows 64
    The title bar: Why you care 64
    The menu bar: A salad bar for commands 65
    Toolbars and their many buttons 66
    The ruler of the known universe 67
    The status bar (if you're totally, like, lost) 68
    Hear ye! Hear ye! The scroll bars 68
Chatting with Your Program Using Dialog Boxes 70
    Text boxes: Where you get to type the text in the dialog box 71
    List boxes — regular size 72
    Drop-down list boxes 73
    Check boxes 74
    Command buttons 74
Making a Window Dance 75
    Making a window stand up and beg 75
    Changing a window's stripes 76
    Switching windows 78
    Moving a window around 79
    Changing a window's size or shape 79
    Setting up two windows next to each other 80
    Finding a missing window 81
    Laying out windows 82
        Making a splash 82
        Laying out windows like tiles on the bathroom floor 84

Chapter 4: Playing with the Look and Feel 87

Why You Should Care about the Control Panel 88
Unveiling the Control Panel 88
Get Back! Repapering Your Computer's Back Wall 91
Creating Your Own Background 92
    Choosing a ready-made color scheme 93
    Making up your own color scheme: Way cool 94
Making Everything Bigger or Smaller 95
Squinting? Helping Someone with Special Visual Needs 96
Save That Screen! 98
Font-for-All 99
Mousing Around 102
Making the Keyboard Easy for Heavy Fingers 103
Making Your Computer Louder 105
    Pumping up the volume 105
    Sounding off 106

Part II: Working and Playing with Windows 95 .... *109*

Chapter 5: Cutting, Copying, and Pasting 111

First You Select It, Then You Make a Change 111
    Selecting some text 112
    Selecting a patch of a painting 112
Off with the Old, On with the New 113
    Wipe out! Deleting text forever 113
    Deleting an entire line 114
    Getting rid of a few letters 114
The Electronic Holding Area 114
    Move over! 115
    Checking what's on the Clipboard 118
Double up! Copying and Pasting 120
Little Scraps — No Mess! 122
Make a Big-Time Mistake? Don't Panic! 123
Adding Chips, Clips, and Other Art 125
    How do you use clip art? 126
    What you can and can't use clip art for 126

Chapter 6: Messing Around with Documents, Folders, and Floppies 127

Getting Up Close and Personal with Windows Explorer 128
Taking a Quick Look at My Computer 129
Finding a Document in a Haystack 131
It's My Folder 132
Protecting Your Files and Your Setup 133

I Want Them All! Selecting a Bunch of Documents or Folders 135
     Surrounding a bunch 136
     Click and grab a bunch 137
     Selecting All 138
Moving a Document or a Folder 138
     Slow: The traditional and ugh! long way 138
     Faster: Drag, drop, and forget it 138
     Fastest: One-handed drag and drop 139
Renaming a File or Folder 140
Trash It 140
Flipping Floppies 142
     Formatting a new floppy disk 142
     Formatting a used floppy 142
     Copying to a floppy 144

Chapter 7: Playing with the Free Programs in Windows 95 147

Writing with WordPad 150
     Gimme something to write on — fast! 150
     Don't throw that away! Saving what you've done 151
       Saving 101 152
       Saving a WordPad document for a friend — or for school 153
     Playing with the size of the type 153
     Putting your names in lights — together 154
     Making smiley faces 155
     Showing off with WordPad 156
     Correcting a massive error 157
     Opening a file in WordPad 157
     Get that on paper! Wow — your own printout 158
Drawing with Flare Using Paint 160
     Opening your Paint can 160
     Step back, Leonardo! You're exploring the Paint tools 160
     A neat trick: Replacing one color with another 163
     Really getting into Paint 164
       Magnifying 164
       Labeling 164
       Moving or cutting chunks 165
       Want to see more of your picture? 165
       Using your picture in another program 165
       Hate the whole picture? 165
     Put your picture up on the screen — and call it wallpaper! 166
Total It Up with Your Calculator 166
     Opening your number cruncher 166
     Crunching your numbers 167
     Going exponential 168

A Sneak Peek at Windows 98 .... I-1

Chapter 8: Playing with Games, Music, and Video............................ **171**

Let the Games Begin! 171
    Hearts 172
    Solitaire 174
    FreeCell.. 176
    Minesweeper 177
Let's Party with Some Tunes!... 178
    You have to have this junk on your computer 178
        A CD-ROM drive 178
        A sound card 180
    Listening to audio CDs 180
    Do it your way — makin' your own hit list 181
        Labeling the CD and its songs 181
        Playing only the songs you want to hear 183
        Ordering your songs around 183
        Getting funky with the Sound Recorder 184
    Ready for the big time? Recording sounds 185
Putting It All Together on Video with the Media Player 186

Chapter 9: Sharing Software with the Rest of the Family **189**

Software for Family Projects 190
Enhancing Your Surroundings 191
    Trying out new rooms with interior design software 191
        Remodeling with 3D Home Architect 191
        Spiffing up a room with 3D Home Interiors 192
    Refinancing or buying a new home 192
    Planning and ordering the garden together: LandDesigner 193
Making Up Menus and Cooking Together 195
Inside Fun 196
    Picking the right dog 197
    Board games go electronic 198
Punt, Pass, and Climb 198
    Tracking and perfecting sports 198
    Working together on fitness and nutrition 199
Having a Party 199
Picture Perfect 201
    Using your camera 201
    Scanning to capture printed pictures electronically 201
    Making albums, calendars, cards, and more using
        electronic snapshots 201
Fantastic Encyclopedias 203
Taking a Trip 204
Testing Before You Buy or Browse 205
    Arranging to watch a software demo 205
    Where to find downloadable demos 205

Part III: Opening a Window to the Internet 207

Chapter 10: Surfing the World Wide Web with Internet Explorer 209

Browsing for Stuff on the Internet 209
Getting the Right Address 212
    Dit dit dot dot 212
    Slashing through the Web 213
Getting Ready to Use Internet Explorer 213
Starting Internet Explorer 214
Wandering in Cyberspace 216
    Click-click-clicking along 216
    Tooling around with the toolbar 217
Print It! 219
Searchin' and Surfin' 220
Playing Those Old Favorites 222
    Getting where you want to go — fast 224
    Cleaning up after your favorites 224
    Going back in time 225
Using Electronic Mail to Talk to Grandma (or Your Friends) 226
    Reading your mail 226
    Writing back 227
    Sending a new message 227

Chapter 11: Cruisin' the Online Services — Microsoft Network and America Online 229

Zipping All over the Internet with MSN 230
    Setting up to use MSN 230
    Whose network is this? Customizing MSN 233
    Jumping jack! 234
    Dancing on stage . . . it's showbiz! 238
    Chatting, blabbing, and conversing 239
        Getting on the horn at Chat Central 240
        What do you want to talk about? 240
    Finding more than you expected 241
    Playing around on an MSN bulletin board 242
Surfin' America Online 245
    Signing on to (and off of) America Online 246
    E-mailing your friends and relatives 248
    Reading Grandma's reply 249
    Chatting up a storm on AOL 250

Part IV: The Part of Tens 253

Chapter 12: Ten Easy Answers to First-Timers' Questions 255

Where's the Start Button, and What's It Good Fer? 255
How Do You Start a Program? 256

How Do You Find a File, Folder, or Program? 256
How Do You Install a New Program? 256
Can You Add Programs to the Start Menu? 257
How Do You Neaten Up All Those Icons? 257
How Do You Change the Name of a File or Folder? 258
How Do You Copy a File onto a Floppy Disk? 258
How Do You Copy a Floppy Disk? 259
Do You Have Any Room Left on Your Hard Disk? 260

**Chapter 13: Oof! Ouch! The Ten Most Common Error Messages
and What to Do about Them 261**

A:\ is not accessible. The device is not ready 262
Cannot find this file 262
Destination disk drive is full 262
This filename is not valid 263
Not enough memory 264
Open with 265
There was an error printing to LPT1 265
Deleting this file will make it impossible to run this program 265
Unable to locate the server 266
Windows 95 wasn't properly shut down 266

**Chapter 14: Ten Useful and Fun Web Sites
for Windows' Families 267**

Online Help for Windows 95 268
Yahoo!: Finding What You Need 268
Yuckiest Site on the Internet — Alive or Dead 268
TeenVoice = Teen Talk 269
Bonus.com: Leave the Searching to Them 269
Convomania 269
Discovery Channel: Go on a Virtual Field Trip 270
Smithsonian Institute: Visit a Museum 270
Family Education Network: Let's Talk 270
The Monster Board: Getting a New Job 271

Part V: Appendixes *273*

Appendix A: Um, It Won't Work the Way I Want It to Work 275

Hold the Phone! You're on with Microsoft Technical Support 275
Does Your Machine Have the Power to Run Windows 95? 277
Aaaachew! What to do If You Get a Virus 277
Getting Help for Common Problems 279
    Yikes! Get me outta here 279
    Nothing's moving 279
    I can't find my pointer 280
    You can't find a program or file 282
    You don't have a mouse with a right button 283

The computer says you don't have enough memory 283

You're having printing problems 284

Saving difficulties 285

You try to print your screen, but nothing happens! 285

How come I didn't get all the programs Windows 95
     said came with it? 286

Fixing Things that Really Bug You 286

Getting rid of a dialog box — quickly 287

Scrolling through files and documents takes so long! 287

You're sick of the standard beeps and boops 287

How can I find out about some cool tips? 287

Appendix B: About the CD-ROM **289**

System Requirements 289

How to Use the CD 290

What You'll Find 291

Edutainment programs for kids 292

Elmo's Preschool Deluxe 292

Living Books Sampler 292

Orly's Draw-A-Story 293

Madeline Classroom Companion: 1st and 2nd Grade 293

Schoolhouse Rock! 1st & 2nd Grade Essentials 294

3D Atlas 98 294

Schoolhouse Rock! 1st - 4th Grade Math Essentials 294

Mighty Math Demo 295

Logical Journey of the Zoombinis 295

Higher Score for the SAT/ACT 296

Not for Mom and Dad only 296

Betty Crocker Cookbook 296

HomeBuyer 2.0 297

Land Designer 3D 4.5 297

If You've Got Problems (Of the CD Kind) 298

Appendix C: An A-to-Z of Nerdisms **299**

Index *305*

License Agreement *326*

Installation Instructions *328*

Book Registration Information .... *Back of Book*

Foreword

· ·

More than 20 years ago, my dad and I walked into a computer store and bought our first computer. It was an Atari 800, and at the store, we were amazed at what it could do. It had a word processor, could run a basic spreadsheet, and, of course, there were the games. Hustling home with it, we set it up and got down to trying to use it ourselves.

First, we couldn't get anything to print on the printer; we moved on to just using the software. Function keys? Commands? Carrots? Where was the multi-use machine we saw at the computer store?

My Dad split for the kitchen. I moved on to the games and (surprise!), with some help from a particularly lame manual, got them working. But from then on, the computer was used for little else.

I could have killed for a *...For Kids and Parents* book on making that Atari 800 work. There's nothing more frustrating that paying a bunch of money for an overachieving doorstop. (That's what flatirons are for.) Luckily, the people at IDG Books Worldwide, Inc. (publishers of the *...For Dummies* series) figured out that even though "Make it intuitive" has been the computer industry's mantra, people need a bit more help. They've been publishing entry-level guides for computer users now for many years.

This book, *Windows 95 for Kids and Parents,* comes just in time to give you all the inside secrets of using the latest Microsoft operating system. Authors Lisa and Jonathan Price, veteran computer industry writers, but more importantly, computer-owning parents, deliver the goods on what's really neat about the system, and what your family will find most useful. In the book you'll find out everything from how to play your favorite music CDs while checking your e-mail to making your reports look great with formatting. And the best part is that whether you're a veteran from the days of DOS or a newbie, you'll find this book a handy resource.

This book is not something that should be used as reading on vacation. Instead, keep it within reach of your computer like I do. That way you can quickly figure out how to tile your windows — especially handy when working on several documents simultaneously. Want to use a password to protect certain files on the machine? It's here. There's tons on using your computer to surf the Web and blocking unsavory sites.

One thing's for certain — read this book and you and your family will find you'll be using your computer for a lot more than just playing games or sending e-mail. And perhaps, just maybe, your computer will become — dare I say it? — intuitive. Well, at least it won't become a doorstop yet, anyway.

— Sam Mead

Author of the *Family PC Guide to Cool PC Projects* and online editor for *Family Fun* magazine

Introduction

· ·

Congratulations! You took the plunge and moved up to Windows 95. Now you'll be able to run all of the very latest programs and games.

If this is your first computer, you're probably feeling a little intimidated if you're an adult or incredibly excited if you're a kid. Not to worry. Windows 95 does that to people. Windows 95 can be complicated and techie at times, but it can also be downright easy and even sensible at others.

Like the title says, this book is written for kids and parents. We concentrate on the basics that regular folks need to know and skip the stuff that's only important if you want to work in a windowless cubby hole, stuffing yourself with brownies and cola. (If you want to know everything there ever was to know about Windows 95 now and in the future, put this book back on the shelf and look for one with three times the page count of this one that has no pictures, no jokes, and lots of text.)

About This Book

For some reason, the manual that comes with Windows 95 (if you're lucky enough to get a manual at all) is mostly written for Martians who landed in Roswell, New Mexico, 50 years ago and have peacefully lived side by side, unnoticed, with other New Mexicans. These Martians really do understand the lingo of all computer manuals, and when they're not busy scaring the general population with flashing lights on alternate Julys, they sneak into the Manual Hall of Fame and voraciously read manuals from cover to cover.

Luckily, you won't have to read this book from cover to cover to find out what you need to know. Each chapter is self-contained. We never go on some techie tangent unless we really can't help ourselves. In that case, we give you fair warning with a Nerd Alert icon, so you can skip the passage if you really hate that stuff.

What you do find in this book is easy step-by-step instructions on how to do the following things, plus much more:

✔ Get around in Windows 95

✔ Use the right mouse button to show shortcut menus

✔ Play around with the taskbar

✔ Open, close, save, and print files

✔ Draw pretty pictures

✔ Listen to and record music

✔ Mess around with cool games

This book covers everything you need to know about Windows 95 to do the stuff you really want to do. We don't get into DOS, Windows 95's grandfather, but occasionally we bring you up to date on changes from Windows 3.1 to 95.

Many different programmers have had a hand in the operating system of your computer in the years since computers have evolved from huge main frames with dip switches to tiny little four-pound laptops. With each new operating system, like Windows 95, programmers make their money by inventing new ways to do ordinary tasks, like copying a file. Often the programmers think of many ways to do the same thing. So as not to tear our hair out (and to save your eyesight and time), we let some of the older and longer ways to do things go by way of the self-correcting typewriter. We concentrate on the easiest ways to accomplish your tasks.

How to Use This Book

When you have a question about something, please look through the Table of Contents or Index until you find the topic that covers it. You can go directly to the section of the book that addresses your question and start reading right there — we don't require that you read every part of this book.

In emergencies, you may want to go directly to Appendix A, which is a kind of troubleshooting guide. And if a computer term leaves you scratching your head, look it up in the glossary.

How This Book Is Organized

This book contains four major parts, plus a few appendixes, including a technospeak-blasting glossary.

Part I: Getting Started

This part takes you on a tour of Windows 95. We show you how to customize your windows by resizing and moving them around, how to redecorate them by changing the look and feel of your desktop, and we even give you some clues on how to find a missing window. By the end of this part, Windows 95 will be as homey as a custom-built job, with you as the creator!

Part II: Working and Playing with Windows 95

Windows 95 has some neat games that are perfect for diversions between your homework assignments. We give you some gaming tips, and we also show you how to pump up the volume with the Media Player. Oh, yes, we almost forgot! This part also covers the basics of cutting, copying, and pasting words and pictures with the help of the marvelous Clipboard. And just for good measure, we explain the differences between My Computer and Windows Explorer.

You also see a yellow section in Part II. That's our preview of Windows 98. Remember it's just a preview — the final features in Windows 98 may differ from what I show you.

Part III: Opening a Window to the Internet

Windows 95 comes prepackaged with Microsoft Internet Explorer and MSN, which serve as your gateway to the vast reaches of the Internet. We go over the ins and outs of getting an Internet service provider (ISP) and using parental controls. We also talk a little about some other items you may experience online, including America Online and Netscape.

Part IV: The Part of Tens

Top ten lists are very popular at the end of the year, but you don't have to wait until December for these lists, which include the answers to first timer's questions, what to do about those pesky error messages, and great Web sites for families.

Part V: Appendixes

Appendix A is the all important troubleshooting guide. Not that we think you'll need it, of course. But isn't it nice to know that if by some minuscule chance something should go wrong, this Appendix can hold your hand, wipe your brow, and offer some advice.

Appendix B tells you all about the demos on the CD that comes with this book.

Appendix C offers a glossary where you can find translations into real everyday English of super computer terms.

Icons Used in This Book

We use this icon to make your life with Windows 95 a little easier.

This alerts you to programs that have placed demos of their product on the CD that accompanies this book.

Surf the Web with the help of these interesting sites.

Probably more than you want to know.

Definitely more than you want to know.

We try to steer you away from danger.

We tell you what to do if you make a mistake.

Parents, your kids may need your help setting something up when you see this icon. Kids — you don't need to bother with this stuff.

Fun for the whole family awaits in these sections.

But, Are We There Yet?

Yup, you're there. You really read through this introduction? Really, really really?? Cool! You deserve a cookie. Oh, not those Cyber ones on the Internet, but a real big gooey chocolate chip one. And remember, this isn't a text book, so mark it up. Doodle on it, highlight the stuff you like and cross out the rest. Have fun and remember to never, never, never kick the computer when it does something stupid; refer to this book instead.

6   Windows 95 For Kids & Parents _____

Part I
Getting Started

In this part . . .

1f you want to start blasting through a bunch of software programs at the speed of a *Star Wars* hyper-processor, go ahead, but skip this part. Read on, though, if you're the type who likes to get everything in order first. Start at the beginning and take a tour of Windows 95. Discover how to arrange your windows to fit your person-ality and why that taskbar thing is always at the bottom. When you finish this part, you'll know how to zip around Windows 95 at warp speed!

Chapter 1

Diving into Windows 95 Head First

• •

In This Chapter

▶ Starting Windows 95

▶ Looking around

▶ Starting a program

▶ Ordering from a menu

▶ Working with folders and icons

▶ Saving your work

▶ Printing

▶ Turning off the computer

• •

Blockhead: How many windows does it take to run a computer?

Smarty: Ninety-five. But you have to get a kid to turn the computer on first.

You've heard your friends talking about all the great stuff they can do with Windows 95 — such as playing games and getting their homework finished (and finished well!) in half the time. Now you finally have a chance to figure out what your friends have been up to all this time with Windows 95. Time to get flying.

Windows Aren't Just Something in Your House

Now that you have Windows 95, you can turn your computer from a piece of plastic, metal, and glass into a center of fun, bright lights, hot sound, and, yes, occasionally, education. What the heck is Windows 95, then?

It's a superprogram that makes the computer come alive. After Windows 95 wakes up inside the computer, that chunk of wires and chips can begin to do something interesting. Windows 95 is an operating system, and everything else is, well, just a program. A program lets you take all that computing power and apply it to something useful or silly, like a budget or a game. But without Windows 95, you'd be looking at a big boat anchor.

Your Friends Know Why Windows 95 Is Cool

Windows 95 is awesomely popular with kids, right up there with the Big Three: Coke, Pepsi, and Mountain Dew. Why has something so geeky as a computer program become so popular? We can think of about 1,000 reasons, but here are just a few:

- ✔ **Windows 95 is fun.** Just like your favorite baseball or soccer team, Windows 95 has its own logo, with red, yellow, green, and blue windows coming at you through space, as shown in Figure 1-1.

Figure 1-1:
Look, up in the sky! It's a bird, it's a plane — no, it's the Windows 95 logo.

- ✔ **In Windows 95, pictures jump up and down, characters zip around in games, and video rolls.** Windows uses cool tools like the Media Player to make the computer into a TV that you can control, as if you were playing a movie on your VCR. (See Figure 1-2.)

- ✔ **It's got its own rock song —** *Start Me Up,* **from the oldest rock 'n' roll band in history, the Rolling Stones.** (Microsoft only had to pay $12 million for the rights.) If you don't know who the Rolling Stones are, just trust us that this is a big deal.

Figure 1-2:
Windows 95 lets you run music or video using a program that works like your CD-player or VCR. Rad!

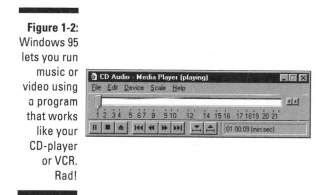

✔ **It's the leader.** In the computer world, Windows 95 is McDonald's, and everyone else is Taco Bell. Windows is MTV, and everyone else is the evening news.

✔ **It's tomorrow.** If you want to get a part-time job down at the local rock station, just tell them you know Windows and watch as doors open for you.

Windows 95 — Are You in There?

Don't know if the computer has Windows 95? Ask your folks. Here's how: Just sit in front of the computer and yell, as loud as you can, "Oh my gosh, look at this!" Or take this book in to show your parents. Ask them to read the next paragraph. (If you know your computer already has Windows 95, go to "Turning on Your Computer and Mousing Around" or anywhere else in the book that interests you.)

Hey, parents — when you see this icon, an adult needs to step in for a moment and help out. Right now, you just need to confirm that the family computer already has Windows 95 installed. If you bought your computer after August 1995 (when Windows 95 was launched) and before the blitz began for Windows 98, the computer probably came with Windows 95 already installed. If you just bought Windows 95 and need to install it, now's the time. Put the CD-ROM in the drive and follow the instructions from the Installation Wizard, a robot-like creature that talks you through the whole process. To get the most out of Windows 95, you need the following:

✔ 16 megabytes of RAM

✔ A CD-ROM drive

✔ A Pentium processor

But you can (just barely) get by with 8 megabytes of RAM and a 386 or 486 computer. Your local computer dealer can easily increase the RAM in your computer but can't so easily upgrade your chip from 386 to 486 or 486 to Pentium.

Optional, but neat:

- ✔ A sound card
- ✔ Speakers

By the way: If you can stand it, the kids love having the speakers turned on, so if you have any, you may want to show them how to power the speakers, and how to keep the volume down to a low drone.

Now that you're introducing your kids to your personal computer, you may want to lay down some laws about what areas are off limits. Depending on the age, make sure they understand never to throw away any of your files. Also, alas, you may need to set up a new routine, in which you regularly back up files, just in case.

Turning on Your Computer and Mousing Around

Getting Windows 95 rolling is so easy, even your little brother (or the little kid down the block) can do it. Windows 95 starts up when you turn on your computer, so that's what you need to do now.

Maybe Windows is already running. If so, you may see something like Figure 1-4 on the screen. If that's the case, you don't have to lift a finger. Someone has been nice enough to start Windows 95 and leave it running for you already. But if you need to fire up Windows 95 yourself, just follow these steps, and you'll be staring at Windows before you know it:

1. Figure out where the monitor's ON button is and push it.

Look for the ON button somewhere on the front of the monitor or on the side near the top.

If your monitor has a bunch of buttons (either on the front or behind a pop-up panel), showing on/off switches or plus and minus signs, don't mess with them. They probably control contrast and brightness, and a bunch of other stuff like image position and size, just like on your TV.

When you press the screen's ON button, you may see a little light come on next to it, proving that the screen is powering up.

2. If you have speakers attached to the computer, turn those on.

You want to to hear the boing sound that means "Windows is getting started" — at least once.

What? No speakers? Or maybe you don't have a *sound card* — the gizmo you need deep inside the computer to make the sounds. Start saving up — you need about $100, minimum, to buy one. Or ask Uncle Ed if you can have the sound card and speakers that came with that computer he keeps in his hall closet.

3. Push the computer's ON button.

You may open your CD-ROM drive by mistake — just push the button again to close it. Don't force it shut by hand because it breaks way easier than you think!

After a moment, you hear grinding noises from inside the computer — don't worry. That's just the *hard disk* spinning, and it's supposed to do that. (A hard disk is a platter like those old records your folks have on the bookshelf, with Peter, Paul, and Mary, or The Who on them.) This hard disk has Windows 95 on it. The computer plays Windows from the hard disk to get started.

Then your screen may flash and run text over the background, and flash again. Exactly what happens on-screen depends on what your folks have done with the computer, but none of it matters, as long as you keep humming and tapping your finger, waiting.

What's this? Do you see a bunch of text on the screen ending in something like "Press any key"? Did you hear a beep, too? Well, if your computer asks you to press any key, all you gotta do is press that big bar at the bottom of the keyboard (just so you know, that big bar is called — the *spacebar*). The computer just needs your okay to go on starting up Windows.

If you are asked for a password, or warned that Windows 95 has had some kind of problem or error, call Mom or Dad. Most of the time these scary messages don't mean much, but better be cautious and get a parent to take the next step.

After a few more moments, you see a colored background appear with little pictures called *icons* (you can read more about icons in "Poking Around — Clicking Icons and Unfolding Folders," later in this chapter). You may also see the Welcome to Windows 95 box, as shown in Figure 1-3 — unless, of course, someone has already turned the welcome off (see the sidebar "Saying 'Hasta la vista' to the Welcome box" in this chapter to find out how to make those tips disappear forever).

You know all those lectures about how you have to get along together as a family? Well, you can't believe the fights that break out over the computer. No, maybe you can. But one thing that causes a lot of fights is changing the way the computer is set up. Maybe someone else really likes those tips that come up when you start Windows. So, before you zap the tips forever, or make any other change like that, ask! Check with anyone else who uses the computer. Get an okay. You wouldn't paint your front door pink without getting at least a casual "Yeah, sure!" from the rest of the family — or would you?

Tip of the day
(There are a dozen!)

Take a tour, play the game
Hover, and watch silly videos

Figure 1-3:
Microsoft
welcomes
you with
a tip of
the day.

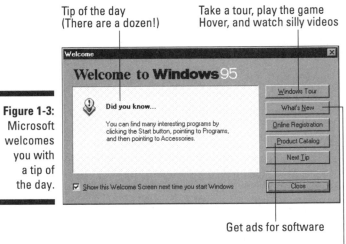

Get ads for software

Find out what's different from Windows 3.1

If nothing happens for a few minutes, or you get some annoying message that you can't understand, and you don't end up with the colored screen or the Welcome box, perhaps something's gone wrong. Ask your parents for help. If they're busy, check out Appendix A. Good luck!.

4. Move your mouse to make the arrow move around on-screen.

If you haven't used a computer mouse before, turn its tail toward the screen, and, holding the rest of the thingamajig with the palm of your hand, move the mouse around. See how the arrow on the screen moves at the same time?

5. If you want to take a brief tour of Windows, click the button called Windows Tour and then follow directions.

6. Get rid of the Welcome box by clicking the X in the top-right corner.

To click, slither the mouse around so that the tip of the arrow is pointing at the target and then press the left-hand mouse button quickly and let go.

X is the way to close a window. In a moment, the Welcome box disappears.

7. Scope out the screen, which looks more or less like Figure 1-4.

Your background picture is probably more interesting than the one we show here because Microsoft provides a spectacular blue picture. (We show you how to switch to another image for the background in Chapter 4.)

Because the whole screen is where you do your work, Microsoft calls the screen the *desktop*. Of course, this desktop doesn't have any gum wrappers, CD boxes, or crumpled-up notes from school. This desktop is more like a big table on which Windows lays out various programs, each in its own, uh, window. That's right, you have windows on top of the desk, and the wastebasket, too (it's called the Recycle Bin). Well, if you can toss old T-shirts on your desk, why can't Microsoft fill your electronic desktop with pictures, windows, trash baskets, and enough colors to make 31 flavors of ice cream?

Icons for stuff you can do in Windows   The background on your screen may be a picture

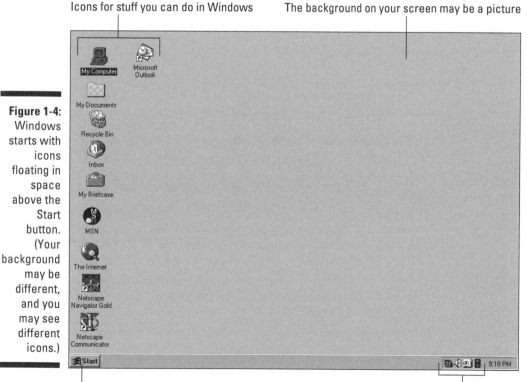

Figure 1-4:
Windows starts with icons floating in space above the Start button. (Your background may be different, and you may see different icons.)

Start programs here   The taskbar helps you keep track of what you're doing

Saying "Hasta la vista" to the Welcome box

If you never want to see one of these tips again — and if you are sure nobody else in the family cares — click the little box at the bottom of the Welcome screen — the one that says Show this Welcome Screen next time you start Windows. Then click OK. That Welcome box won't bother you or anyone else ever again.

Poking Around — Clicking Icons and Unfolding Folders

Do you hog the remote when you're watching *Real World* on MTV or Nick at Nite, flipping through the channels, making that TV do exactly what you want it to do? Well, you'll love Windows 95. You can use the mouse to click and click and click, making Windows jump and juke and jive.

What can you click? Right on your desktop, you see a bunch of little pictures, called *icons,* that were meant to be clicked. You can make Windows do all kinds of stuff by clicking icons. Here's how they work:

1. Click the My Computer icon twice, really fast.

The icon looks like a computer, and it usually lives up in the top-left corner of your screen, although it may have drifted off somewhere else on your screen.

Clicking twice very fast is called *double-clicking.* Double-clicking tells Windows that you are really, really serious about using whatever you're clicking. Double-clicking tells Windows you want to open an icon, to start a program, or to see what is inside of a window.

After a moment, a window opens and looks like the one shown in Figure 1-5. By double-clicking this icon, you tell Windows 95 that you want to open the My Computer window — and it does it!

The My Computer window shows what's on your computer, or what can be added. Inside the window, you see plenty more icons — double-clicking any of these icons makes Windows 95 do something else.

The icon for your hard disk (usually)

Figure 1-5: Double-clicking the My Computer icon made this window appear. My Computer shows what's on your computer. Surprise!

2. **Double-click the icon for the hard disk (usually called C) to see what information is stored there.**

   You see a list of folders, like those big manila folders your parents have in their desks. Each electronic folder contains programs, or stuff that helps the programs do their work, or the results of someone's work using one of the programs. If you want to look inside these folders now, turn to Chapter 6.

3. **To put away the My Computer window (or any window, for that matter), click the X in the top-right corner.**

   The window disappears, but the icon stays on the desktop so you can use it again.

When you look at all these icons, the drawings and labels may help you figure out what these buttons do. But most icons are pretty confusing. Table 1-1 gives you the buzz on what some of the most common icons mean. (Depending on how your folks installed Windows 95, you may or may not have all these icons, plus some others.)

Table 1-1	Common Icons on Your Desktop	
Icon	*Name*	*What It Does*
	My Computer	Shows you what's on your computer (stuff such as programs, letters, and pictures).
	Inbox	Where your electronic mail lands, if you get any. (Your folks have to do a lot of setup to make this work. You can read more about e-mail in Chapters 10 and 11.)
	My Briefcase	Holds stuff you want to move over to your laptop computer when you go on a business trip. What? You don't have a laptop and you aren't planning any business trips anytime soon? Well, forget this.
	Recycle Bin	The trash. When you're tired of a game or anything else on your computer, you toss it into this bin to get rid of it. You may be able to recover it, if you act fast, as described in Chapter 2.
	Microsoft Network	Microsoft's answer to America Online. A big site on the Web with lots of info; also, the software that gets you there. (Your folks may not have installed this, so the icon may not be on your screen.) Read about it in Chapter 11.
	The Internet	One way to get onto the Internet, the free-for-all world of Web sites. Uses Microsoft's program, Internet Explorer, to get onto the World Wide Web. Won't work unless your folks have signed up with a service that actually makes the connection. Check it out in Chapter 10.

TECHNICAL STUFF

Don't read this — no really, don't!

Don't waste you time with this sidebar if you don't care what's new in Windows 95. But if you're wondering how Windows 95 differs from some other computer junk you've used, read on.

If you've been used to ancient PC machines at school, or an old Apple II, you are going to be knocked out at all the graphics and the way you can use a mouse to do stuff, instead of always typing, typing, typing.

If you've been using a Macintosh, well, Windows 95 is as close as the PC world gets to the Mac. You'll know right off how to use a lot of things, such as windows, icons, and buttons. Deep down, there are big differences, but your experience as a Mac person will see you through.

If you're familiar with Windows 3.1, well, you're going to find some major changes in Windows 95:

- ✔ Your program groups now show up on the Start menu, which you can read about in "On Your Mark, Get Set, Go!" in this chapter. The Start menu replaces the Main window.

- ✔ The File Manager has become something called Windows Explorer, which lives on the Start menu.

- ✔ The Control Panel now lives underneath Settings in the Start Menu.

- ✔ The Run command shows up on the Start menu.

- ✔ Windows 95 has fewer calories and tastes better than Windows 3.1. Really.

On Your Mark, Get Set, Go!

Programs are the beef inside the cheeseburger, the disk inside the CD case. Programs take all the power in your computer and apply it to doing something fun, or, if not fun, maybe something you have to get done (your book report, for example).

You've heard of word processing programs that help you write and programs that let you draw. Whenever you play Nintendo or Sega, you're running a program. So how do you get Windows to run a program for you?

Good news! You can start every program the same way in Windows 95. Just follow these easy steps:

1. Use your mouse to slide the pointer down to the bottom of the screen.

If it was hidden, the taskbar appears. The taskbar is a fun little bar across the bottom of the screen, as shown in Figure 1-6. It helps you do your work — that's why they call it the taskbar. If you want to find out how to hide it yourself, or keep it on top of everything else, check out Chapter 2.

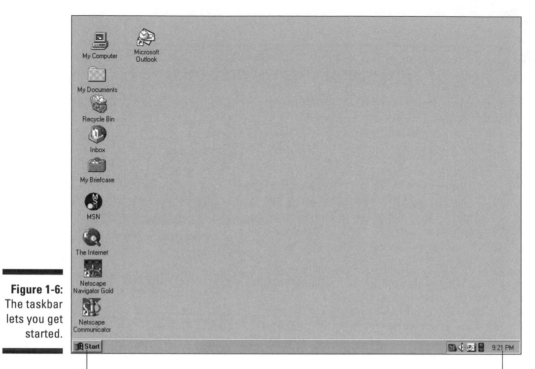

Figure 1-6:
The taskbar
lets you get
started.

Where you start   The time of day

2. **Slide the pointer along the taskbar to the left to point to the Start button.**

3. **Click Start.**

   The Start menu pops up, as shown in Figure 1-7. (Yours won't look exactly like this, because you may have different programs than we do, or someone may have asked Windows to make everything smaller. But, hey, it looks sort of like this.)

   (Read "Ordering Fast from the Menus" in this chapter to get the 411 on menus.)

Figure 1-7:
The Start
menu helps
you do lots
of stuff,
such as
start a
program.

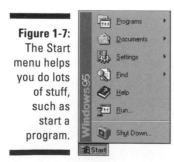

You can start more than programs from the Start menu

The Start menu grows on you. The main thing you use it for, at the beginning, is to start a program, using the Programs option. After you create something on the computer, you can open it again from the Start menu, using the Documents list, which shows stuff you have been working on. Other options let you adjust Windows' settings, find something on your computer, and get advice and help. The last item on the start menu is seriously important: This is the way to close down your computer, so nothing gets damaged when you finally turn it off.

---

4. Click Programs.

You could just as easily rest the pointer on top of Programs and wait a second to get the same effect. But clicking is more fun.

Another menu zips out to the side, showing programs and little folders that hold whole groups of programs.

Yes, here, you find menus upon menus. They come out like a waterfall, so Microsoft calls them *cascading menus*.

5. Locate the program that you want to work with.

You may have to do some digging to find the program you want. For example, say that you want to start a neat program called Media Player. It turns your computer into a sound machine.

To open Media Player, you have to go to the top of the Programs menu and click Accessories.

Wow! Another menu appears: The accessories are just little programs that are fun or helpful. They're called accessories because, like putting on a new belt or an earring, they add a spark of pizzazz to Windows 95.

You then click Multimedia, to see programs that play music, video, or animation, and then you click Media Player.

The Media Player program opens up in all its glory, as shown in Figure 1-8.

Congratulations! You've opened a Windows program. Want to see what it can do? Skip on down to the next section, and find out how to order your computer around!

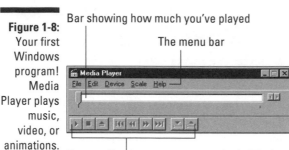

Figure 1-8:
Your first
Windows
program!
Media
Player plays
music,
video, or
animations.

Bar showing how much you've played

The menu bar

Buttons like those on your tape deck, CD player, or VCR

Ordering Fast from the Menus

Whenever you open a program, you see a row of words at the very top of the program window. These words say weirdo stuff like File, Edit, and Tools. But those aren't just ordinary words — they are actually *menus*.

The menus on your computer are a lot like those menus you see over the heads of the clerks at fast-food restaurants, or on their cash registers, if you've gotten behind the counter. Menus let you place an order — that is, boss your program around, ordering it to do, well, whatever it does. Each program has a different set of menus, depending on what the program is for.

For example, if you're working with Media Player, you can use menus to order the program to play a sound file. After you finish playing around with Media Player, you consult the menus again, and, like when you ask the waiter for a check, you can tell Windows 95 to close down the program.

No matter what menu you're ordering from, just do the following to make that menu (and program) do exactly what you want it to do:

1. **Move the pointer until it's directly over the menu that you want to open.**

2. **Click once.**

   Whoa — a menu drops down outta nowhere and gives you tons of choices of stuff your program can do for you.

3. **Move the pointer down to the word that describes what you want the program to do.**

   For example, if you want to open a program, go to the Start menu and choose the program that you want to play with.

4. **Let go of the mouse button.**

   The program should do what you told it to do with your menu choice.

Here's your chance to see a menu in action. For our very next trick, we show
you how to open a sound file in Media Player. A sound file is the computer
equivalent of the sound track on your CD-ROM. And Media Player is the
computer equivalent of your CD player. If you haven't started Media Player,
click Start, glide over Programs, then Accessories, and click Media Player.

1. Click the File menu.

Ta da! The menu drops down so you can browse through it, as shown in
Figure 1-9.

Figure 1-9:
The File
menu
offers,
well, not
desserts,
but
commands
you can use
to boss
around
files.

2. Click Open.

You see a new window. It's the Open dialog box, as shown in Figure 1-10.

The sound file

Figure 1-10:
When you
first choose
Open,
Media
Player
shows you
a sound file
you can
play.

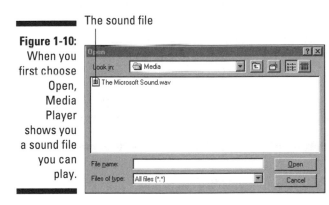

3. Click The Microsoft Sound.wav.

Yes, I know, that's a pretty techie name. But .wav just stands for wave — it's a name the techies take from sound waves, because the file has sounds in it. The Microsoft Sound file's full, ugly name shows up in the box called File Name, toward the bottom of the window. So now you've selected the file you want to open.

4. Click the <u>O</u>pen button.

Now you've loaded up your computer version of a track on a CD. Notice how the buttons came alive, as shown in Figure 1-11 — they're black now, meaning you can click them the way you press buttons on your CD player. (Before, without anything to play, the buttons were grayed out, meaning they didn't have anything useful to do.)

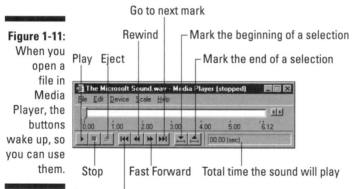

Figure 1-11: When you open a file in Media Player, the buttons wake up, so you can use them.

Go to next mark

Rewind — Mark the beginning of a selection

Play Eject — Mark the end of a selection

Stop Fast Forward Total time the sound will play

Go back to previous mark

5. Click the Play button (the right-pointing triangle, underneath the 0.00 second mark).

You hear the Microsoft Sound — the odd chimes that ring to show that Windows 95 is starting. Fantastic, huh? Well, maybe not much. But you can see how you can play sounds using the menus in Media Player.

And if you still don't believe how great menus can be, follow these steps and see how menus can help you make Media Player as loud or soft as you want it:

1. Choose <u>D</u>evice➪<u>V</u>olume Control. (Click <u>D</u>evice and then click <u>V</u>olume Control.)

You see a window like the one shown in Figure 1-12.

Figure 1-12:
The Main
Line Output
window
controls
volume.
Yours may
not look just
like this, but
it probably
works the
same way.

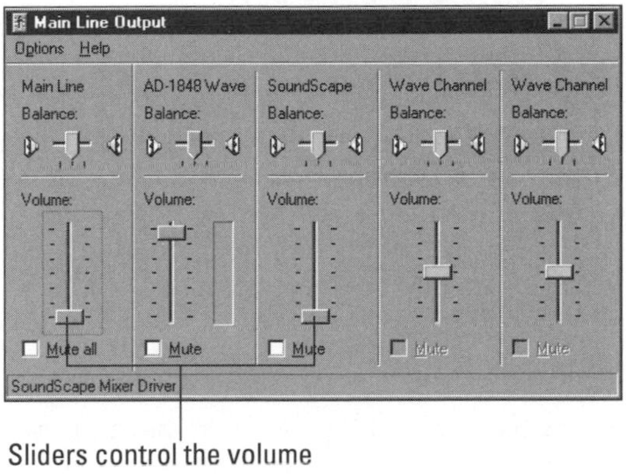

Sliders control the volume

2. **Drag the Volume sliders up and down to increase and decrease the volume. (It won't hurt your ears.)**

3. **Click the X to close the volume control window.**

Um, er . . . Did you make sure to turn your speakers on? They sure can't make much noise without power. (Duh.)

4. **Click the Play button again to hear the Microsoft Sound even louder (or softer).**

Psst. Want to show your parents something they may never have known was possible? Put a music CD into the computer's CD-ROM drive. Like your CD player, the computer has a special tray for the disk to go in, but on the computer, it slides out (you plop the CD in) and then it slides back in, like a drawer in your desk. Wonder where the CD-ROM drive is? Look for a panel about five inches wide on the front of your computer and a button right underneath that makes it slide out and in.

After you put the music CD into the drive and press the button to send the drive back into its cabinet, go to the Device menu in Media Player and choose CD Audio. After a moment the whole display changes, showing all the tracks or times of pieces. Click Play (the button with the triangle pointing to the right). The music comes out through the computer's speakers — and it will go on doing that even when you move on to do other stuff. The quality may not be as super-sensurround as your boombox, but still, getting a computer to play your favorite rap, hiphop, rock, or country song is pretty awesome, huh? (To find out what the other buttons do, just let your pointer hover over one for a second; a label comes up, telling you what the button does.)

Two-for-One: Having Several Programs Open at Once

You know those two-for-one sales down at the mall? You buy something you really, really want, and then, because it's on sale, you come home with two of them. Well, Windows lets you have two, three, even four programs open at once. For example, you can leave the music playing on Media Player and then go over to another program and write about it. All you need to do is use the menus you find in the Start menu; check out "On Your Mark, Get Set, Go!" earlier in this chapter to find out how to open a program.

For example, if you already have Media Player open, here's how to open Notepad, a program for writing: Click the Start button and then choose Programs⇨Accessories⇨Notepad. The Notepad opens, as shown in Figure 1-13.

Notice that the music is still playing. Media Player just goes on playing the CD until the end, unless you go back and click the Stop button. So you can work in another program with background music.

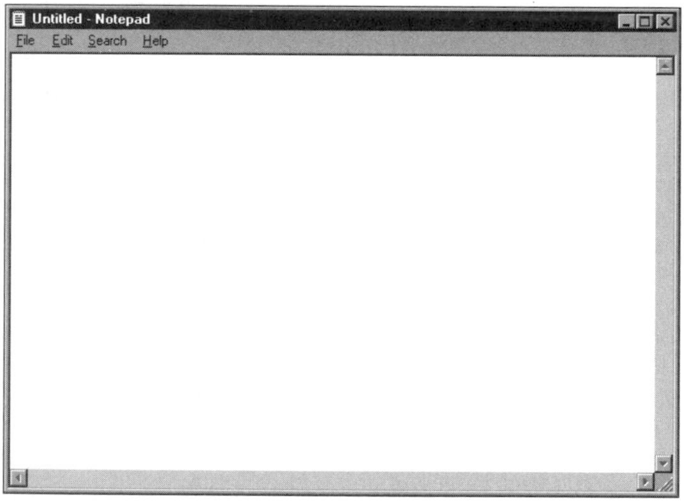

Figure 1-13: Notepad lets you take notes — but not much else.

Tapdancing on the Keys

On the computer, you write by pressing the letters on your keyboard. But what a lot of keys there are! Every keyboard is a little different, but most have a bunch of letters, numbers, and punctuation marks all arranged as on a typewriter. But then, over on the right, your keyboard may have a bunch of arrows (good for old-fashioned games) and a numeric keypad, which is like your parents' handheld calculator.

If you know how to type, type your name in Notepad (you open Notepad by clicking the Start button and then choosing Programs⇨Accessories⇨Notepad). If you don't know how to type, hunt and peck. Some tips about computer typing:

- ↙ To make capital letters, hold down the Shift key and type the letters.
- ↙ To make a space, press that big bar down at the bottom of the keyboard.
- ↙ To start a new line, press Enter.
- ↙ To back up over a typo, wiping it out, press Backspace (sometimes it looks like an arrow pointing to the left, just above the Enter key).
- ↙ For most numbers, use the ones above the letters. (To make the numeric keypad do numbers, you have to press the Num Lock key, which locks it into numbers.)
- ↙ To have the computer put the time and date in your work, choose Edit⇨Time/Date.

You see that row of keys at the top or side of your keyboard, all beginning with F? That stands for Function. And some programs use those keys like commands on a menu. Click a Function key, and it does something useful. In Notepad, for example, if you want to get the date and time inserted in your document, press F5.

Computer keyboards are pretty tough, but you can really mess them up if you spill soda on the keys. The sugar in the soda makes everything sticky, inside and out. Ditto for crumbs. Don't eat at the computer — that's the best rule. And we know this sounds like Mom, but if your fingers are all greasy from that third doughnut and the pizza, um, well, you'd better wash up before sitting down at the computer keyboard. The slime makes the keys yucky for the next person, but even worse, the goo leaks down into the guts of the keyboard and makes keys jam or stop working.

If you do spill something into the computer keyboard, turn the keyboard upside down as quickly as possible so nothing further can leak inside. Be sure to tell someone. Turn off the computer — see how to in "Stop: Turning Your Computer Off Without Breaking Anything" in this chapter — and then dry off the keyboard as thoroughly as you can . . . and keep it upside down.

Printing the Proof to Show Your Friends

Printing is simple — if your computer's printer is turned on. When you are using a program like Notepad, printing lets you get a copy of what you write on the computer. Printing lets you show your friends at school, or send a copy of your letter to your grandparents. Your printer is that gizmo near your computer, with all the paper stacked up. Many printers make black letters on white paper, but some can print in colors, although not quite as bright as those on the screen.

To print something, follow these steps:

1. **Turn on the printer, if it isn't already on. (Wait while it grinds and clanks and settles down.)**

   Show your child exactly how to turn on the printer, so little fingers don't accidentally press one of those other buttons and break its connection with the computer or something worse.

2. **In the program you've used to write or draw, choose File⇨Print.**

   For example, after you write something in Notepad, you would choose File⇨Print.

   In some programs you may be asked how many copies to print and other questions. The simplest thing to do, at least the first time, is to click the OK button and just get one copy, the regular way.

   After a moment, whatever you're working on gets printed.

3. **Take the sheet out of the printer (gently). Admire it. Show it to your parents, or send it to Grandpa and Grandma.**

Safe Not Sorry: Saving What You've Done

No, working on the computer is not like putting your money in a piggy bank or going to the bank with your earnings from a summer job.

Saving stores whatever you've been working on, with whatever name you give it. That's good, because the computer doesn't have a very good memory after you turn it off. In fact, nada. It forgets everything! And if someone trips over the power cable while you're working, well, forget it! Everything you've done could be out the window.

If you are writing something long, such as a letter to Santa or a class report, or if you are making a gigantic drawing of alien spaceships, you should save it every ten minutes so you won't lose much work if your clumsy friend turns the computer off by mistake, reaching for another CD. Ditto, if you get part way through the work, and have to stop for supper. Saving lets you bring the picture or letter back on-screen to work with some more on another day.

Here's how to save your work:

1. Choose File⇨Save.

You see the Save As dialog box, as shown in Figure 1-14.

Why is it called a dialog box? Well, this one lets Microsoft Windows 95 ask you what you want to call your fabulous document, and where you want to put it on the hard disk, deep inside your computer. So it's like, well, a conversation. You're having a *dialog* with the computer.

Windows 95 suggests a place to save your document here

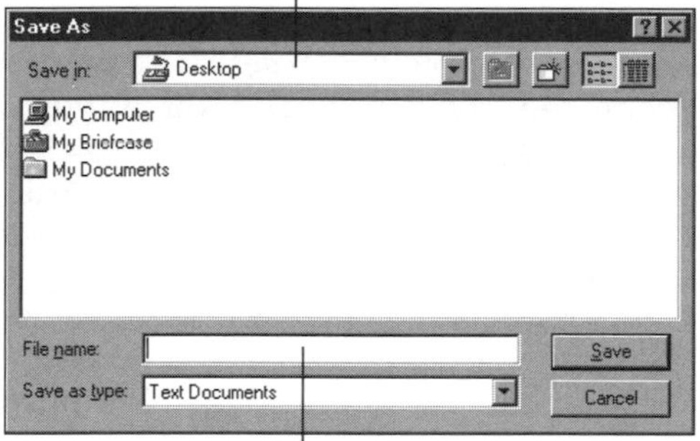

Figure 1-14:
The Save
As dialog
box lets
you name
and save
your work.

Save As
Save in: Desktop
My Computer
My Briefcase
My Documents
File name: Save
Save as type: Text Documents Cancel

Type the name of your document here

2. Type a name for your fantastic document, such as My Name.

The suggested title, Untitled, gets replaced with your name. If you happened to click inside Untitled, you may want to wipe it out by pressing the Backspace key to erase letters, and then type your name.

3. Click the Save button.

The program now takes everything you have worked on and gives it the name you just typed. It also saves what you did under that name on the hard disk inside your computer. Where exactly? Well, each program starts out suggesting you save the document to one place, but after someone has saved documents to another location, the program may suggest that location the next time.

But I've Got to Use the Computer Now!

How long have you been on the computer so far? Well, has anyone else wanted to use it during that time?

If your parents use the computer for their work, or for grownup games such as going on the World Wide Web to look up golf scores or recipes, you should sit down with them and work out a schedule. You want to know when you can use the computer. And they need to know that the computer will be free when they just have to use it. Making up a schedule helps avoid fights and hurt feelings.

You can use Notepad to write up the times when you are good to go on the computer. Post that list right over the computer so everyone else can see.

Worried that your kids may inadvertently wipe out the home budget or address book you've saved on the hard disk? Consider getting a program such as Edmark's KidDesk Family Edition, which sets up a control center for each child, as shown in Figure 1-15. You can specify which programs a child can use and make *your* folders and programs off limits. Each child gets a personal desk with a calendar, a clock, and icons of their favorite programs. Even pre-readers can get their programs going on their own without your having to interrupt what you are doing to help them go through the launch sequence. *Bonus:* If you have a microphone, kids can leave voice messages for other family members.

Figure 1-15:
KidDesk
Family
Edition
gives each
family
member a
personal
desk, so no
one messes
up anyone
else's work.

Stop: Turning Your Computer Off Without Breaking Anything

Your computer looks pretty simple, but behind the scenes, it's like a circus act, juggling many little pieces of programs and trying not to drop or lose track of anything. If you just pull the plug on the computer, it instantly forgets where it was, and the next time you start, the computer may look like Jim Carrey on a bad hair day. You could lose some of what you were working on, or wreck a program.

Here's the drill for shutdown. Learn it and do it, or take the hit for messing everything up:

1. **Save whatever you have been working on.**

2. **Exit each program by clicking the big X in the top-right corner of its window.**

   If you want to get your CD out of the CD-ROM drive, make sure that you have exited the Media Player program, and then press the button on the CD-ROM drive to open it. Take the disk out — and then press the button again to close the drawer.

3. **Choose Start⇨Shut Down.**

   Yes, use the Start button to stop. We know that it doesn't make too much sense, but that's the way you do it.

   After a moment, you see the Shut Down dialog box, as shown in Figure 1-16.

Figure 1-16:
You can shut down completely from this dialog box.

4. **Click Yes.**

   Open windows close on-screen, the hard disk spins and whirs, the printer hiccups, and you wonder if the computer will ever shut down. Finally, you get a message saying that it is okay to turn the computer off.

5. **Turn off the computer, screen, printer, and speakers.**

6. **Clean up all your stuff so the next person doesn't have to look at it.**

   Do you have to? No. But it's a friendly thing to do.

Chapter 2

Poking Around Your Desktop

• •

In This Chapter

▶ Exploring the taskbar

▶ Looking inside My Computer

▶ Throwing stuff into the Recycling Bin

▶ Working with shortcuts

• •

*T*he Windows 95 desktop is a lot like your backpack. Wait a sec! What do you have in your backpack? Here's what we found in a backpack lying around in our house:

- ✔ Box of gerbil food (slightly crushed)
- ✔ Dried out peanut butter candies
- ✔ Paperbound library book on the rain forest
- ✔ Spiral notebook, called Journal
- ✔ Two pencils
- ✔ Old baseball hat
- ✔ One mitten
- ✔ Loose change
- ✔ Sand

That backpack has tons of junk in it — stuff we use, stuff we used to use, and stuff that is in there just for the heck of it. What does all this have to do with Windows 95, you may ask? Well, we want you to think of your Windows 95 desktop as kind of like that backpack. Your desktop, which is what you see after you fire up Windows 95, is like a backpack that holds icons for a whole bunch o' junk on your computer. (See Chapter 1 if you need some tips on how to get Windows 95 up and running, or if you want some more info on icons.)

When the folks at Microsoft packed the Windows 95 desktop, they put in some items, which appear as icons, or pictures, on the desktop, as you can see in Figure 2-1.

Figure 2-1:
The
Windows 95
desktop.

Icons are shortcuts to programs or information. You may not have all of these icons, because your folks chose different options when they installed Windows or adjusted things afterward. But we bet you have some, if not all, of the following icons on your desktop:

- ✓ **My Computer:** How much does that weigh? Shows you what information is on your computer.

- ✓ **Inbox:** A post office box for electronic mail. Don't worry about this item: It's really meant for folks at an office who get electronic mail. (You can find out how to send and receive your own electronic mail in Chapter 10.)

- ✓ **Microsoft Network:** Sometimes, if your folks installed it. (If not, you may see an icon that offers to install it for you.) For the inside info on MSN, as it's called, please see Chapter 12.

- ✓ **Recycle Bin:** The trash. Where you put stuff you don't want to use any more.

- ✓ **Internet:** Now that's a lot! This is the way to connect to almost every phone system in the world, and the computers at the other end, over the Internet. Usually brings up a program called Internet Explorer that lets you cruise the Internet.

✔ **My Briefcase:** A thingy that holds files you want to use on your computer, and on your laptop computer, if you have one.

✔ **My Documents:** A place on the computer where you can store whatever work you do.

✔ **Taskbar:** At the bottom of the screen, a bar that contains the Start button and buttons for programs you have started.

How much does your backpack weigh? *The New York Times* interviewed four fifth graders and found their school backpacks averaged 15 pounds. Try yours on the scales in your bathroom. Do you measure up?

Even if your backpack outweighs a small elephant, you probably don't have the whole World Wide Web and the Internet in there, like Windows 95. There's a lot on the desktop, and in this chapter you get to poke around to find out what's there.

Playing Around with the Taskbar

Peekaboo. The taskbar — a strip of useful buttons starting with the Start button — comes and goes. Now you see it, now you don't:

✔ If you don't see the taskbar along the bottom of the screen, in the bottom quarter inch or so, move your pointer down there to bring it out from hiding.

✔ No luck? Try the left, right, or top of the screen. Someone may have dragged the taskbar there, before it went into hiding.

When the taskbar appears, it looks like Figure 2-2.

Figure 2-2:
The taskbar has three main areas: the Start button, the task list, and the notify area.

| 🏁 Start | 📄 HiJaak PRO | 📄 C:\~JP documents\id... | | 📺 🔊 8:27 PM |

Start button   Task list   Notify area

On the far left of the taskbar, you see the Start button. Then you see the task list just to the right of the taskbar, with space for buttons that represent programs you have open, but that you shrank temporarily, to get them out of the way. And finally, at the far right, you see an area where Windows 95 notifies you of vital information, such as what time it is and how to adjust the volume on your speakers.

Want to move the taskbar to the side or top of the screen? You can put that taskbar in its place by following these steps:

1. **Click anywhere in the taskbar where there isn't a button.**

2. **Keep pressing your mouse button down and drag that sucker to any edge of the screen, wherever you want it.**

3. **Let go of the mouse button.**

   The taskbar jumps to that location. Of course, because the taskbar may also slide out of sight there, you ought to tell everyone else in your family, or they'll have a hissy fit, and you'll hear them yelling, "Where's the Start button?!!"

A real Start-a-rama

The Start button is the biggest, brightest part of the taskbar, and it does the most for you. Yes, you use this button to start any program you put on your computer, but you can also use it to do a ton more (we talk about firing up a program using the Start button in Chapter 1). Controlling the Start button is like getting ahold of the remote: You're in charge.

But chill. Just let your fingers relax. When you first try the Start button, you may feel as if you have to hold the mouse button down all the time, as menu after menu splashes out in front of you. But all you really have to do is glide over a menu title, and it opens up. You don't have to hold down the mouse button as you go. Of course, if you like, you can click Programs and then click one of the items on the next menu, and so on, if you prefer.

So what exactly is that thingamajig that opens up when you hover? Those are menus and submenus and subsubmenus, and so on. Many of the menus have other stuff inside, such as groups of programs, tips on using the programs, even documents you may want to use, as well as, finally, some real programs.

Just to the right of every menu is a right-pointing triangle, showing that it contains something; the contents show up when you hover over it, as shown in Figure 2-3.

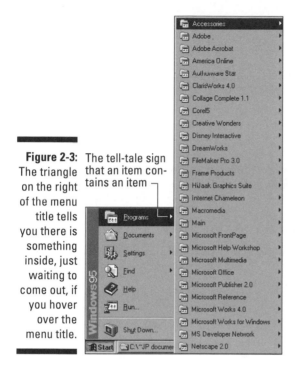

Figure 2-3: The tell-tale sign that an item contains an item
The triangle on the right of the menu title tells you there is something inside, just waiting to come out, if you hover over the menu title.

It's not the X-Files — it's Documents

You can also open a document with the Start button. Document-shmockument. A document could be a book report, a list of clothes you want to buy, or a full-length novel on why you don't like square dancing. In the Windows world, the word document can mean anything you've made on the computer, including a report, a picture, or a list. To open a document, do this:

1. Click Start and slide over the item called Documents.

In a moment, you see a list of documents you've recently created.

2. Click one of these document names.

Windows 95 opens whatever you clicked in whatever program you used to create it.

Setting things up

Have you ever seen all the dials and buttons and levers in the cockpit of an airplane? Well, Windows 95 has at least that many controls. You can adjust some of those controls by using the Settings option on the Start menu.

When you glide over Settings, you see the following options rise before your very eyes:

- ✔ **Control Panel:** This folder is packed with so much cool stuff that we had to devote almost an entire chapter to it — turn to Chapter 4 to discover all the cool stuff you can do with this groovy Control Panel.

- ✔ **Printers:** You only use this when your folks buy a new printer and they need to set it up.

- ✔ **Taskbar:** You can customize your taskbar to within an inch of its life using this setting.

Here's how to adjust some of the settings available under the taskbar setting, including making the icons in the Start menu larger and smaller and hiding the taskbar:

1. **Click Start, slide up to Settings, and then click Taskbar.**

    You see the Taskbar Properties dialog box, as shown in Figure 2-4. You can make changes to the taskbar and the Start menu here.

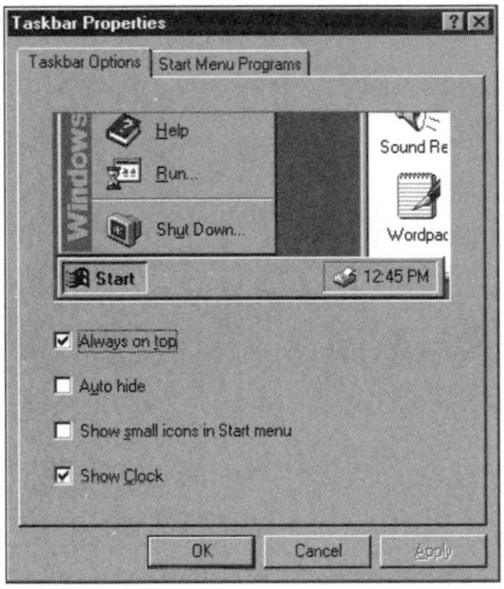

Figure 2-4:
Here's where you adjust the taskbar and Start menu.

2. **Keep your eye on the sample picture at the top of the dialog box and click the white box next to Show small icons in Start menu.**

    The icons shrink at your command. Kind of the reverse of Open Sesame. Feel like Mr. Big now?

3. **If you want the taskbar to slip down out of sight when you're not using it in order to make more room on the desktop, click the Auto hide check box.**

If you already see a check mark in the check box, don't do anything, because clicking would remove the check mark. Of course, if you would like the taskbar to stay on-screen all the time, make sure the little white box is empty.

Removing a check mark by clicking it is known as deselecting the option. Aren't you glad you know that?

4. **Click OK to make these changes.**

Show your folks the changes you've made. You don't want to surprise them, do you? Make sure these little adjustments are okay with everybody who uses the computer. For example, the little icons may be too hard for Grandma to see easily. Maybe you could show her how to set them back to large.

Help! I've fallen and I can't reach the remote!

Never fear. In Windows 95, it's not Spiderman or Batman who saves you. It's a nerdish guy called Help. Help is right there on the Start menu. Don't be shy about asking. Sometimes — not always, but sometimes — you get exactly the info you need.

Help has step-by-step instructions and tips, so it's a little like having an older sister who can sit next to you and tell you where to go and how to operate.

Here's how to ask for help when you need it:

1. **Click Start and then click <u>H</u>elp.**

   In a moment you see a dialog box with three tabs on it, as shown in Figure 2-5. The first tab shows the Help topics as if they made up a table of contents in a book. The second tab shows a long list of topics you may want to know about — that list is called the Index. The third tab, called Find, displays a list of every word in the Help documents, so you can choose one to read more about the topic.

2. **If you don't see the Index, as shown in Figure 2-5, click the Index tab.**

3. **In the text box at the top of the window (the one that invites you to type the first few letters of the word you're looking for), type a word that is related to what you want to know about.**

   For example, if you wanted some help figuring out something to do with the taskbar, you would just type **taskbar**.

   As you type, notice how the list under where you are typing slides up to that word.

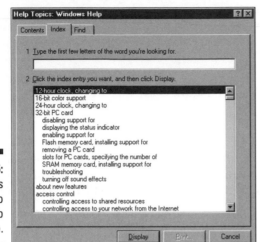

Figure 2-5:
Help tells
you how to
get a job
done.

4. **When you see the topic most related to the subject you want help on, click that topic.**

   For example, if you typed taskbar in Step 3, and you wanted information about making your taskbar get outta town, you would click Hiding in the list of topics.

   After a moment, a screen pops up with all kinds of helpful information about the topic you were looking for.

   If you want to look for more information about your topic, or you want to start a whole new search on a different topic, go back to the original Help window by clicking the Help Topics button at the top of the window that you have been reading.

5. **In the Windows Help window, click Help Topics and then click the Contents tab to see the same material arranged as a set of books, as shown in Figure 2-6.**

6. **Double-click the book next to the topic that is the most closely related to what you want to know.**

   For example, if you wanted to read about how to hide the taskbar, you would click How To.

7. **Keep on double-clicking through the topics until you find the information that you want to read about.**

   For example, if you clicked How To in Step 6, then you would continue searching for information on hiding the taskbar by double-clicking the book called Change Windows Settings, and then the book called Change Taskbar settings. Look what's there! Double-click the topic called Hiding or Displaying the Taskbar.

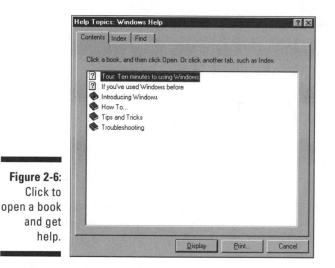

Figure 2-6:
Click to
open a book
and get
help.

You read Help with one eye, and work on the screen with the other. So it helps to have the Help window stay on top of your work while you read it. To do this, click Options, slide down to Keep Help on Top, and choose On Top. A check mark shows up next to On Top, and from now on, the Help window stays on top of every other window — until you close the Help window by clicking the button with the big X in the upper right-hand corner.

8. **To put away Help, click the Close button (that's the X in the top-right corner of the Help window).**

Run for your life

This command is like one of those pictures your parents have that shows dinosaur times. It's an antique. See, back when your parents went to school, you had to type everything in, to make the computer do anything. If you like typing, you will love this command. Instead of just using the Start menu to start a program, you type in what disk drive the program is on, and where the program is on that disk, and then, well, not the name of the program, exactly, but some weird eight-letter abbreviation, followed by the extension .exe. Doesn't that sound like fun? No human being in their right mind should have to use this command. *Hint:* If you have someone at school you really dislike, suggest they use the Run command. Of course, the next day, when they come back to school, it'll be you who has to do the running — away from them.

Shut up about Shut Down, will ya?

This is a great command, because it puts the computer to bed without wrecking anything. When you finish using the computer, don't just switch it off, or yank the plug. You could really mess up the computer that way. Instead, you should do what the geeks call "an orderly shutdown."

Basically, you just choose this command on the Start menu and click OK. Then the computer hums and whirs and thinks and after a few minutes you see a message on the screen saying it is safe to turn the power off. For more details, see Chapter 1.

Honey, I shrank the program

Now you can take any window you have open on the desktop and shrink it down to a little button on the taskbar. That way, when you want to open it again, you just click the button. No more rambling through the Start menu.

Shrinking comes in handy when you have several programs going at once and you get a headache and say, "I wish I could look at just one, for a little while, without closing the others down."

Want to try this? Just follow these steps to make a window disappear into a button on the taskbar:

1. **Start any program.**

   For example, you could start the Accessory called Notepad by clicking Start⇨Programs⇨Accessories⇨Notepad.

   In a moment, the program window opens. But imagine you just thought of something else you want to do first.

2. **In the top-right corner of the program window, click the first of the three buttons — the one with the line at the bottom, as shown in Figure 2-7. (This button is called the Minimize button.)**

Figure 2-7:
The buttons in the top-right corner let you shrink, enlarge, or close the window.

Click the Minimize button to shrink the window

The whole window disappears, zooming down into the taskbar, where you see a new button, with the name of the program, or the window. (Can't see the taskbar? Slide your pointer down to the edge of the screen, at the bottom, and the taskbar should rise to the surface, like a dinosaur coming out of the swamps.)

Want to bring your program back to life?

3. **To reopen the program window, click the program's button down on your taskbar.**

Bingo! You have your program window open again. That whole area of the taskbar can hold dozens of programs shrunk up into little buttons. (It's not a good idea to open more than three or four programs at once, though, because they get a-w-f-u-l-l-y sssssllllllloooooowwwww.)

Getting the right corner

Windows 95 manages to pack quite a bit of stuff into that little right-hand corner of the taskbar. You usually see some, if not all, of the following items:

- ✔ **The time of day:** Use this to make sure that you don't get so wrapped up in Windows 95 that you forget to catch your favorite show.

- ✔ **A speaker icon:** If you have a sound card and speakers, you may see a little icon of a speaker.

- ✔ **Other little icons:** If your folks have installed some programs called *system utilities* (they are useful for controlling Windows 95, and your computer, as a system), well, then you see those icons, too.

All in that little corner over on the right. Of course, the only one that is really interesting is the volume control. Here's how to turn up the volume if you have this control on your machine:

1. **Click the icon of the loudspeaker, over on the right of your taskbar.**

A little window appears with a slider, like the sliding controls on your CD player.

2. **Drag the rectangle up toward the word Volume.**

3. **Click elsewhere, to put away the Volume Control.**

Now when you get a message boing from the system, you'll hear it. Ditto, your CD, if you are playing it the way we talk about in Chapter 1. Hey, why not put another CD in the drive? Better check that volume.

This little box over on the right of the taskbar is called the Notify Area because it, well, notifies you of what time it is. Silly, isn't it? But for nerds like you, there is one other use you can make of the area. If you start a printing job and then decide you want to stop it in the middle, click the Printer icon (it only shows up when you are printing), and you see a list of documents you have just sent to the printer. Click the one you want to stop then choose Document⇨Cancel Printing. You'll save paper.

Hey, It's My Computer!

Blockhead: Who's taller? Mr. Taller, or his baby?

Smarty: The baby, because he's a little Taller.

Groan. But if you look inside your computer, it seems like it keeps getting bigger, and taller, and wider, and soon it is so crammed with stuff you can't figure out where it all goes. Thank goodness that stuff is all just a bunch of little electronic signals. It wouldn't fit, otherwise.

See that icon at the top of your desktop called My Computer? That's the way you can look inside your computer to see what programs and documents you have stored on the hard disk, and on any disks you've slid into the floppy drive, or the CD-ROM drive.

1. Double-click the My Computer icon.

You see a window like that shown in Figure 2-8, with icons representing your disks, plus folders for dealing with Windows itself, your printer, and your network (if you are tied to another computer or linked to the Internet).

Figure 2-8:
The My Computer window lets you look at the contents of your disk drives.

2. Double-click the icon for your C drive — the hard disk inside your computer.

You see a bunch of folders, arranged more or less in alphabetical order, as shown in Figure 2-9. (Your window may not have the toolbar with the scissors, and so on, but don't worry, yours will work just fine.)

```
C:\                                                    _ □ ✕
File  Edit  View  Help
 (C:)                        ▼  🗁 ✂ 🗐 🗐  ↶ ✕ 🗐  🗗 ☰☰
Name              Size │ Type             Modified            ▲
📁 ~corel.t               File Folder       10/13/95 5:41 PM
📁 ~JP documents          File Folder       8/8/96 2:22 PM
📁 Acroread              File Folder       6/21/96 3:47 PM
📁 Anykey               File Folder       5/5/95 8:52 AM
📁 aol30                File Folder       8/19/97 9:05 PM
📁 Aol30a               File Folder       6/25/96 7:56 PM
📁 aol30B               File Folder       9/25/97 11:21 AM
📁 Ati                  File Folder       7/12/95 9:49 PM
📁 Backup               File Folder       5/5/95 8:54 AM
📁 Bindery              File Folder       6/2/97 4:54 PM
📁 Cdmedia              File Folder       5/5/95 8:58 AM
📁 Collwin              File Folder       10/2/97 4:08 PM    ▼
182 object(s)          32.2MB
```

3. **Look for the Win95 folder. If you can't see it right away, then, in the lower-right corner of the window, point to the down-pointing arrow; click the arrow, and continue to press the mouse button to *scroll* down to the Win95 folder.**

Pressing this down arrow is called scrolling because it is a little like something that Romans and Greeks did with their scrolls. Imagine a long, long sheet of paper all rolled up on a stick, and now imagine that you are unrolling it.

4. **Double-click the Win95 folder.**

You see even more icons, names, folders, and whatnot.

5. **Scroll down to the very bottom, in the W's.**

6. **Find a document called Winhlp32.hlp and double-click it.**

In a moment you see the Help for Windows in Figure 2-10.

```
Help Topics: Windows Help                              ? ✕
 Contents  │ Index │ Find │
   1  Type the first few letters of the word you're looking for.
      [                                                    ]
   2  Click the index entry you want, and then click Display.
   ┌──────────────────────────────────────────────────┐▲
   │ alternate mouse button                            │
   │    using to get Help information                  │
   │    using to print Help information                │
   │ annotating a Help topic                          │
   │ arranging open windows                           │
   │ bookmarks, adding to Help topics                 │
   │ button help                                      │
   │ character size, changing                         │
   │ colors                                           │
   │    Help window colors, changing                  │
   │ command option boxes, using                      │
   │ comments, adding to Help topics                  │
   │ Contents tab in Help, using                      │
   │ context-sensitive Help                           │
   │ controls, getting Help on                        │
   │ copying                                          │
   │    information from a Help topic                 │▼
   └──────────────────────────────────────────────────┘
              [ Display ]   [ Print... ]   [ Cancel ]
```

It's a long way down, but you can locate anything you have on the computer in the same way.

Windows 95 lets you to take different views of the same stuff, too.

7. In the Win95 window, choose View⇨List to see the items in an alphabetical list, such as that shown in Figure 2-11.

But maybe you want to see how big an item is, or what kind of thing it is, or when it was last worked on.

8. Choose View⇨Details.

Now you can see more information about each item, as shown in Figure 2-12.

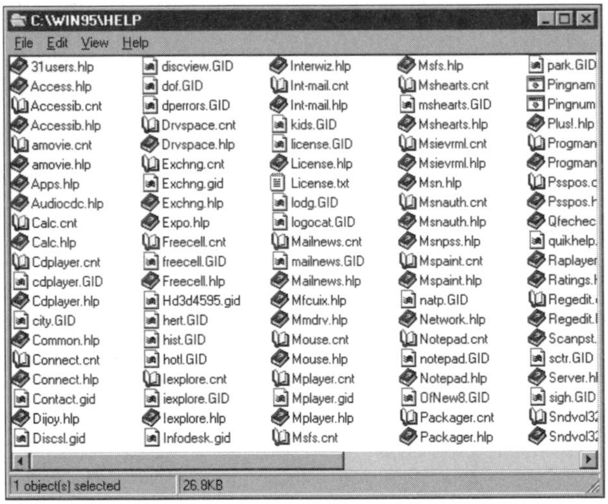

Figure 2-11: The List View lets you to look through more items at a glance.

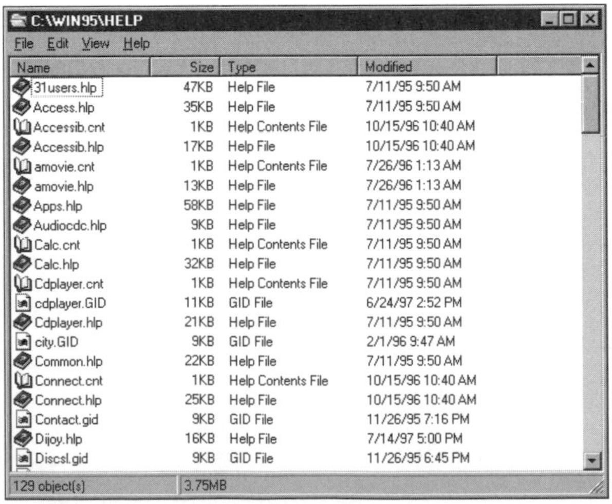

Figure 2-12: In this view, you see the details that nerds like.

The window shown in Figure 2-12 lets you get up close and personal with the following items:

- **Name:** Well, duh, it's the name of the file or folder.

- **Size:** How big it is, in computer measurements. All you have to know is that a KB or kilobyte is not very big, and a MB or megabyte is pretty big.

- **Type:** What kind of file it is. Sometimes this is an abbreviation for a program, sometimes it is an abbreviation for some standard format, or maybe it just says "File Folder."

- **Modified:** Actually useful, this is the last day and time you tinkered with the file. Helpful, if you have a few files with similar names and want to know which is the latest.

What the heck are these KB, or kilobytes? Well, kilo means a thousand, in European talk. And a byte is 8 bits. Bits? Is that like a little bite of something? No, a bit is like one light bulb on a theater marquee. It is either on or off. It represents a 0 or a 1, in computerese. So a byte is eight light bulbs, which is just enough 0's and 1's to stand for a single letter of the alphabet in the ancient code that most computers use. So one kilobyte, or K, pronounced *kay,* or a thousand bytes, is really about a thousand letters or numbers. (Actually, it is 1012 bytes, which is close.) Not a lot of information there. Now if you put together a million bytes, you end up with a megabyte (pronounced *meg*). A billion bytes, and you have a gigabyte (pronounced *gig*). Don't ask what comes next.

Want to list every item by date? You may, if you can't remember the filename, but remember it was the latest version you worked on. Just choose <u>V</u>iew➪Arrange by➪Date.

Don't Talk Trash. It's a Recycle Bin

Sometimes you finish a soda, and you can't find a trash can for miles. On Windows, though, you can always find a place to throw stuff away. What kind of stuff? Maybe you wrote a paper for school, and you never want to look at it again, ever. Maybe you drew a picture for a birthday card, and you don't need it anymore. Whatever — you can throw it away, so it doesn't clutter up your computer anymore.

See the wastebasket with the three arrows in a circle (those three arrows in a circle stand for recycling)? You can toss stuff in here, and no one will yell at you for littering. (Unless that was your Dad's expense report.)

Don't touch anyone else's work. And even with your own, make sure you really aren't ever going to use it again, before you actually throw something away.

To show you how to throw stuff away, we want you to make a file we know you don't need, then show you how to get rid of it.

Making up a silly example to throw away

1. **Choose Start⇨Programs⇨Accessories⇨Notepad.**

   The Notepad window pops up.

2. **Type something silly.**

3. **Choose File⇨Save.**

   You see the Save As dialog box, which may suggest putting your document on the desktop for safekeeping, as shown in Figure 2-13.

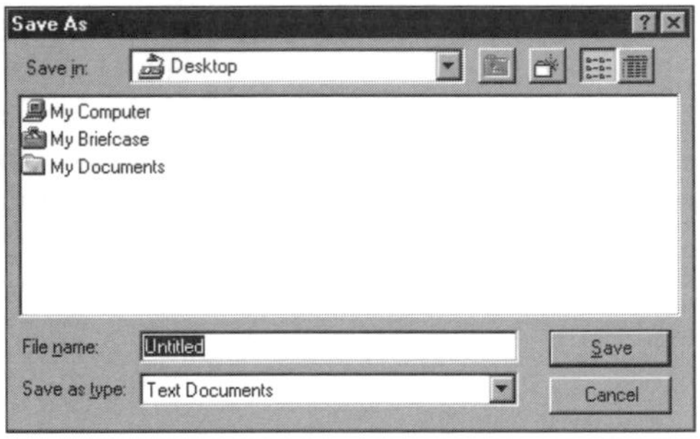

Figure 2-13:
Notepad
usually
suggests
saving the
document
to the
desktop.

If you don't see Desktop in the Save In text box at the top, click the icon of the folder with the up arrow to go up, up, up until you come out on the desktop, with Desktop in the text box.

4. **In the File Name box, type a name for your test document.**

   For example, you may want to call it Silly.

5. **Click the Save button.**

   The little note is now saved on the desktop.

If you see a few extra characters tacked on the end of the name, as in Silly.txt, don't worry. The .txt just means it is a file made up of text, without any fancy formatting.

6. **Click the Minimize button on every window that's open to clear them away so you can see the desktop underneath. (The Minimize button is the button with the line in it, at the top-right corner of a window.)**

Throwing stuff away (and getting it back)

Just follow these steps to put whatever you want to get rid of in the Recycle Bin:

1. **Click the icon for the file you want to get rid of, and, still holding down the mouse button, drag that file over on top of the Recycle Bin.**

   The Recycle Bin looks like a wastebasket, but it has the three arrows chasing each other in a circle, meaning that the contents can be recycled.

   If you get a message asking whether you really want to delete the file, click OK.

   In a moment, the file is absorbed. You have thrown it away. But it may not be gone for good. What if you made a mistake, and you remember that you really need that file?

2. **Double-click the icon for the Recycle Bin.**

   You see the contents of the Recycle Bin, with the file you threw away still there as shown in Figure 2-14.

Figure 2-14:
The Recycle Bin secretly holds onto stuff you throw away, in case you change your mind.

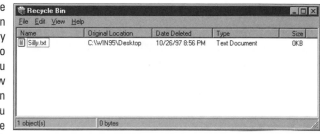

If the file came from a floppy disk, Windows asks if you want to delete the file, and if you say OK, Windows erases it from the disk, but does not store it in the Recycle Bin. How come? Well, who knows? But probably the programmers at Microsoft did this because they knew they couldn't easily put the file back on the floppy disk if you took the disk out of the disk drive.

When you drag a file from your hard disk to the Recycle Bin, it is not actually moved, just relabeled on your hard disk; it is only really erased from the hard disk when you choose to empty the Recycle Bin.

3. **If you want to rescue the file, drag it out of the Recycle Bin, onto the Desktop.**

   Okay. So now you really want to get rid of this document. You take two steps.

4. **Drag the file back into the Recycle Bin.**

5. **With the right button on your mouse, click the Recycle Bin.**

   In a moment, a menu appears, as shown in Figure 2-15.

6. **Click Empty Recycle Bin.**

   You are asked if you really want to delete the items in the Recycle Bin. You do.

Figure 2-15:
Right-clicking an object brings up a menu like this.

<u>O</u>pen
E<u>x</u>plore
Norton UnErase
Empty Recycle <u>B</u>in
Empty Norton Protected Files
<u>P</u>aste
Create <u>S</u>hortcut
P<u>r</u>operties

7. **Click Yes.**

   Now everything you put in the Recycle Bin is really gone for good. So you see the Recycle Bin can recycle, if you get desperate, and need to get your trash back. But once you empty it, hey, forget it — those files are history.

Short (cut) and Sweet

So you just love some particular program, window, or file, and you want it right up there on the Desktop so you can get to it without having to go through all those menus from Start. The solution: You make a shortcut.

A shortcut puts a picture of the program, window, or file on the desktop. To open the program, window, or file, you double-click the icon. Here's how to set up a shortcut:

1. **Choose Start⇨Find⇨Files and Folders.**

   You see a dialog box that helps you find a program, a document, a folder, or whatever, as shown in Figure 2-16.

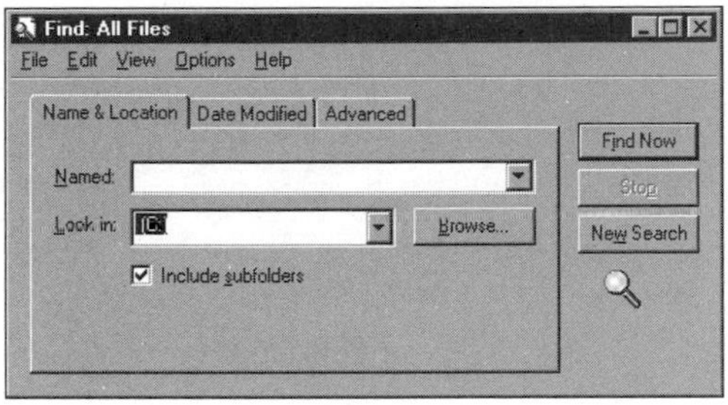

Figure 2-16:
The Find
dialog helps
you locate
files when
you have no
idea where
they might
be.

Find: All Files

File Edit View Options Help

Name & Location | Date Modified | Advanced

Named:

Look in: [C]

☑ Include subfolders

Find Now
Stop
New Search

2. In the Named box, type the name of the program or file you want to make a shortcut for.

For example, if you were looking for Notepad, that's what you would type.

3. Click Find Now.

An extra part of the window opens up, and Windows shows you a bunch of files that have the word you typed in them. For example, if you had typed Notepad, you would see a list like the one in Figure 2-17.

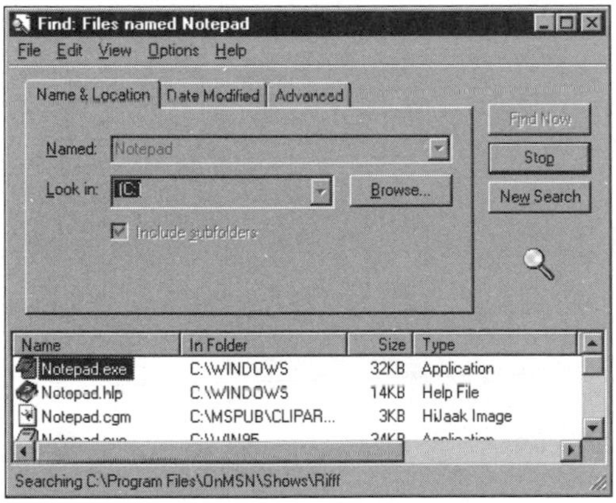

Find: Files named Notepad

File Edit View Options Help

Name & Location | Date Modified | Advanced

Named: Notepad

Look in: [C]

☑ Include subfolders

Find Now
Stop
New Search

Name	In Folder	Size	Type
Notepad.exe	C:\WINDOWS	32KB	Application
Notepad.hlp	C:\WINDOWS	14KB	Help File
Notepad.cgm	C:\MSPUB\CLIPAR...	3KB	HiJaak Image
Notepad.cpm	C:\WIN95	34KB	Application

Searching C:\Program Files\OnMSN\Shows\Riiff

Figure 2-17:
Windows
lists files
that have
the word
you typed
in their
names.

4. Drag the program or file out onto the Desktop.

(Click it, and without lifting your finger off the mouse button, move the pointer out into the Desktop, in effect dragging the program out.)

A new icon appears. If you were making a shortcut to Notepad, you would see an icon called Notepad.exe. That's the shortcut.

5. Click the Close button on the Find dialog box to put it away.

Now, whenever you want to open the program, window, or file, all you have to do is double-click the shortcut.

Chapter 3
Taking Apart a Window

● ●

In This Chapter

▶ Looking around a typical window

▶ Using buttons

▶ Widening the borders

▶ Exploring the bars around the windows

▶ Responding to the program in its dialog box

▶ Making one window active

▶ Moving a window

▶ Finding a missing window

▶ Arranging a lot of windows

● ●

Do you like to wash windows? No? Well, forget it. On your screen, you never have to wash the electronic windows — unless you put your finger on the screen after eating peanut butter.

On the computer, windows do a lot more than open and close and let you look through them to see if the pizza guy is coming with a pepperoni special. Sure, these windows let you look at whatever you are working on — Notepad, the Media Player, or any other programs inside their own windows. But electronic windows do a lot more than just show stuff, because they have more pieces than your windows at home.

Imagine these windows on your screen are made out of some weird kind of Lego® blocks or a set of those plastic tubes and boxes. Each piece makes the window do something different. The trick is to find out what each little part does. When you find out what each piece of the electronic window does, you can make the window jump like an inline skater taking a curb.

Every Button in Your Window Is Hot

You know all those buttons on the control pad for your video games? Well, the bits and pieces of a computer window are like those buttons. They let you make the window change — zap — like a Transformer turning from a car into some megamonster.

The good news about windows: All windows are set up the same way. Basically.

The semi-good news: Depending on what program you're using, the windows may offer a few extra pieces.

Take a look at the basic setup that all windows have — without the peanut-butter-and-jelly schmeers, of course. To get things rolling choose Start➪Programs➪Accessories➪WordPad. (If you don't have WordPad, try Notepad, its little brother.) In a moment, a window opens, with the program inside, as shown in Figure 3-1.

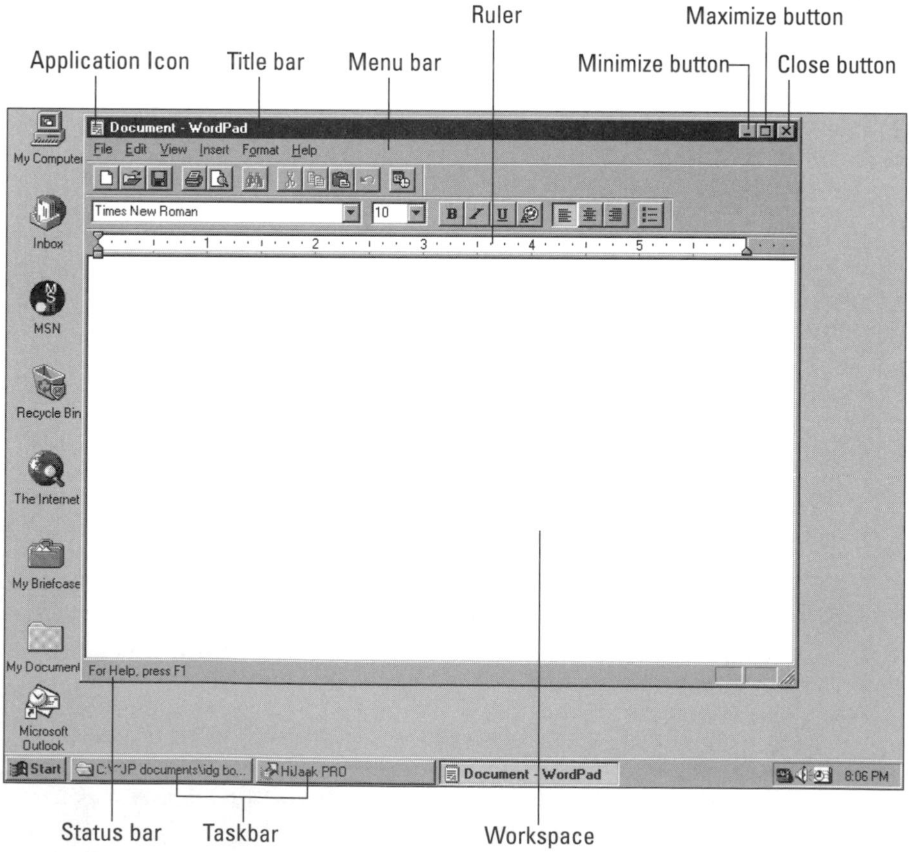

Figure 3-1: The pieces of an average window in Windows 95.

NERD ALERT

Where did they come up with that name, Windows?

Have you ever wondered why Microsoft came up with the name Windows for its operating systems, as in Windows 3.1 and Windows 95? The name makes sense because Windows places each document or program in its own separate window surrounded by a frame on the screen. Result: You may end up with half a dozen or more windows all open on the screen as you work, sort of like in the logo.

The original idea goes back to the Xerox Palo Alto Research Center, where inventors were trying to come up with a computer that would show pictures, not just letters and numbers; after that they came up with that, they realized they needed frames around the pictures to control them. Apple Computer got the idea for frames from Xerox PARC and made the Macintosh; Microsoft got the idea from Apple Computer and made Windows.

Button, button, who's got the button?

Do you put body glitter in your belly button? Do you put buttons all around your baseball cap?

Buttons are all over the place on the windows in Windows 95. But they're not like buttons on a shirt, or on your belly, or even on your hat. They're more like the buttons on a car radio or a remote control — they're square and some have pictures on them to show you what they'll do. These buttons are hot because they help you do all kinds of things with your programs.

You probably already know how to use buttons. Can you point? Can you click the mouse button? Good, 'cause using buttons is as easy as pointing with the mouse and clicking.

You know how the little arrow on the screen moves whenever you move your mouse around on your desk? Well, you've probably also figured out that by pointing at something on the screen and clicking the left mouse button, you can make something happen. Ta da! Pointing and clicking works the same way with the little square buttons you see around the edges of each window on-screen.

Got a magnifying glass? No? Well, lean close to the screen, and look at the button under the File menu, as shown in Figure 3-2. (If you don't see this button, choose View⇨Toolbar to bring up a row of buttons. If you don't have WordPad, try launching the Calculator from the Accessories list, or just look at the Start button.)

New button

Figure 3-2:
The New
button,
bigger than
life.

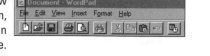

If you look carefully, you notice that each button has shining white lines along the top and left side, as if light were coming from the top-left corner of your screen. And each button seems to have a tiny shadow on its right side and bottom edge. The effect is 3-D.

In some programs, you may find buttons that just look like pictures until you hover over them with your pointer. At that moment, the 3-D button rises up, begging you to click.

Each button stands for a command you can issue to the computer, telling it what to do. Clicking buttons, then, is a way of bossing the computer around. (You may prefer to use the drop-down menus instead of buttons. That's fine, because everything that you can do with a button can also be done by using a command in some menu; you just have to find the right menu item. Turn to Chapter 1 if you need some help working with menus.) The buttons are handy to use when you're in a rush.

Making a button do what you say

Ready to experience the thrill of making a button respond to your whims? Just follow these steps:

1. **Open your favorite program and move the mouse so that it's hovering over a button.**

   For example, you can open WordPad by choosing Start⇨Programs⇨ Accessories⇨WordPad. Then you can use your mouse to point to the color palette to make whatever you type appear in color. Or you can point to the New button (it looks like a sheet of paper and is under the File menu). You use the New button to create a new document where you can jot down what's on your mind.

   When you are moving your pointer toward a button, make sure that you get the very tip of the arrow on top of the button, as shown in Figure 3-3. That's the part that makes the button say ouch! Watch to see a label appear, indicating you have entered the button's space, and it's ready for you to click.

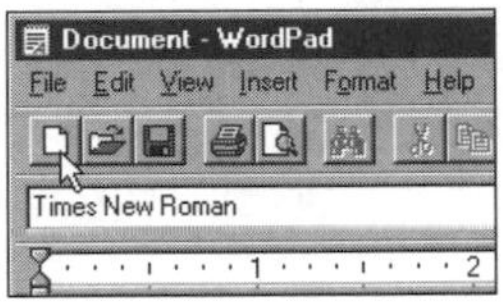

Figure 3-3:
Get the tip
of the arrow
over the
button
before you
click.

2. Click the button.

Clicking the button tells the program to do whatever the button is intended to do. For example, if you're in WordPad, and you have your mouse pointer over the New button, clicking the New button makes the New dialog box appear. It wants to know if the new document should be in a format that Word can read. Go head and click the OK button. You see a new sheet of paper to write on, or at least a white space on your screen.

But when do I use the other mouse button?

Oh, you noticed? Yes, your mouse has two buttons. (Or maybe three, in rare cases.) Most of the time you have to use the one on the left. Whenever you hear someone saying "Click," you can figure that they mean, "Click the left mouse button."

Beginners can go for years using only the left mouse button. That's a good idea. Don't urge the right mouse button on anyone who may already feel a bit overwhelmed. But if you have a leftie in the house, and the standard mouse arrangement seems difficult, choose Start⇨Settings⇨Control Panel, and double click Mouse. Then on the Button tab, choose the Left-handed setup. Basically, you are flipping the buttons. Now the right button will be the main one to use, and the left button will be for extra menus and a few other minor chores.

Do you like exploring, just to find out what's there? The right mouse button is for you. Curious? Point to almost any object, and right-click. That is, click with the right mouse button. Sometimes, as shown in Figure 3-4, you see a menu drop down, offering options that you never even thought of (or a repeat of many of the options on the regular menus). For example, if you hover in the middle of the open space on your screen, away from all windows and right-click, you see a menu appear offering ways you can change the way the screen looks.

Figure 3-4:
Right-clicking may bring up a special menu.

How many clicks is enough?

Zap, zap, zap! BOOM! Eeek! Kaboom! When you're busy shooting down alien spacecraft in your favorite video game, you keep clicking the gun button like crazy.

With most on-screen buttons, one click is enough. You click the button, and it does its thing.

But if you click something other than a button, such as the icon for a program or the name of a document, and you find you are waiting, and waiting, and nothing is happening, you can always try a double-click: that is, two clicks in rapid succession. That may get the computer's attention.

Double-clicking is like zooming into hyperspace: It doubles your speed. For example, if you see a list of documents and you want to open one, you usually click the name or icon of a document to select it; click the File menu to see the items on that menu; and then click Open — and after a few moments the document opens. Or you can just double-click the name or icon of the document to open it right away. Off the hook!

If you double-click a thingamajig and it is actually a button that expects a single-click, you may accidentally turn it on, and then turn it off. Always try a single-click first.

We recommend that beginners click once and wait to see if anything happens. If nothing takes place, they can try double-clicking.

Magic buttons! Make a window big! No, make it small! Make it go away!

Do clothes just magically pile up on your bed? Maybe you couldn't figure out what to wear and you kept tossing outfits on top of outfits. Or you took off a baby T-shirt and, well, just threw it somewhere. When your mom opens your door, she screams, "How can you find anything in this mess?"

We know: You don't care.

But when the same mess happens on-screen, you'll care. That's because there isn't as much space on the screen as on your floor, and bed, and chair.

After you have been playing on the computer for a while, you may end up with a lot of windows open on the screen, and they can easily blot out whatever you want to see. Or you can't see enough of what you are working on, because its window just isn't big enough. Time to shrink some windows and make others bigger.

Look up! In the top-right corner of your window you see three key buttons that let you change the size of your window in an instant (as shown in Figure 3-5).

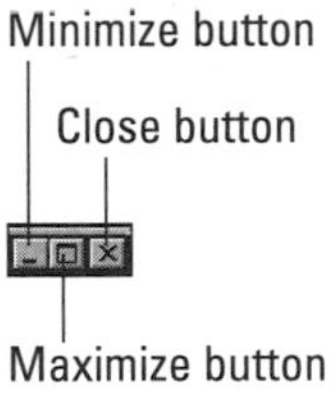

Figure 3-5:
Use these
buttons to
shrink a
window,
make it
bigger, or
close it.

Minimize button

Close button

Maximize button

Getting down with the Minimize button

Want to fold up a window that you aren't using right now, but you think you may use again soon? You can put that window on a shelf. You shrink the window down to a button on the taskbar to get it out of the way. To do this magic trick, you use the first of the three buttons located in the top-right corner of any Windows 95 window — the Minimize button. It's called that because it makes the window into the absolute minimum, its smallest size.

Sometimes you have two programs up on the screen, each in its own window. You work for a while in one program, and then you want to go over to the other window to work in the other program. To make room for that program, you'd like to shrink your current window, but you don't want to exit the program. The Minimize button, shown in the margin, reduces the entire window to a little button. Why bother? After minimizing, you can restore the window quickly, rather than having to go through the delays involved in starting the program again and then reopening the document you were working on.

Minimizing a window doesn't get rid of your work or exit the program you're working in. Minimizing just turns the window into a button containing the name of the program or the name of the window.

Where does the window go? If you minimize the window for a program, it goes down on the taskbar. If you minimize a document within a progam, it goes to the bottom of the workspace in the program window.

Whenever you want to look at that window again, click the button it became when you clicked the Minimize button. If the button representing the window has a Restore button (it looks like two documents on top of one another), click that. Immediately, the window jumps back onto your screen, at the same size it was before.

Pumping things up with the Maximize button

Take it to the max! The best, the most, the greatest! The biggest on Earth!

Well, not quite that big. But you can make your window expand to take up as much space as it can get on your screen — the maximum possible. You click the Maximize button to do this trick. That's the middle of those three buttons at the top-right corner of your window. The button looks like a sheet of paper, with a big black line at the top.

After you click the Maximize button, the window explodes, taking up every square inch of space, out to the edges of the screen, even covering up the taskbar at the bottom.

Don't feel confident of hitting the correct little button to maximize the window? Then double-click anywhere else in the title bar. That'll expand your window the same way.

Maximizing a document or program on your screen makes using the computer easier for young children. Their attention is not diverted by dangling bits of other windows or other icons.

While you work on a document, it may appear in its own window inside the program's work area, which is just part of the program's window. After you enlarge the program window, you may want to go ahead and enlarge the document window, as well, so you can see more of what you're working on. After you click the document's Maximize button, the document takes up more room. The three buttons that were at the top-right of the document window now move up just underneath the buttons that control the program window, and the Maximize button changes to a picture of two documents, one in front of the other. It's now called the Restore button, which you can read more about in the following section.

Giving a window a chance at a come back: The Restore button

You know how, on TV, when someone drinks the magic potion and suddenly gets bigger than a house, he wants to come back down to normal size? Well, your windows feel that way, too.

When you click the Maximize button, the button itself changes. It turns into the Restore button, which shows two documents, one on top of the other. That's so you can change the window back to normal.

The Restore button puts a program window back to the way it was before you clicked the Maximize button.

If you have maximized or minimized a document inside the work area of a program, the Restore button shows up, letting you bring the document back into view, at the same size it was before.

X marks the spot: The Close button

Tired? Want to go out roller-blading? This button's for you. It's the X.

Not *X-Files*, or X-rated, just X. X is the Close button. It's the right-most button in the top-right corner of the title bar. It closes the window you're looking at and shuts down the program, too, if it's a program window. When you click the Close button, the window is put away and does not appear on your taskbar, or anywhere else for that matter. It's gone. It's history.

Even though the Maximize, Minimize, Restore, and Close buttons are conveniences to the computer user, they can cause great fear if clicked in error. Imagine how you would feel if you spent an hour drawing a masterpiece and then by mistake clicked the Minimize button, thinking all is lost. One way around surprises and disappointments is to practice together for awhile:

1. **Choose Start➪Programs➪Accessories➪Wordpad.**

2. **Type your name, the name of your pet, or the name of your team in the workspace that appears.**

3. **Click the Maximize button for the program window.**

   Talk about what just happened. The window took over the screen!

4. **Click the Restore button (the one that looks like two documents, one on top of the other).**

5. **Type whatever you want in the window.**

6. **Click the program window's Minimize button.**

   Talk about where the window went and how it got shrunk onto a button down there on the taskbar.

7. **Click the button to bring the program window back.**

   Repeat Steps 2 through 6 until you all feel comfortable using these buttons. (And as long as you aren't doing any real work, clicking the Close button — the big X — won't risk losing anything valuable. You just have to start the program again.)

The silliest button ever

Look up in the top-left corner of a program's window and you see a logo for the program — an image or emblem for the product. Secretly, this little picture acts as a very odd kind of button.

Want to exit a program fast? Double-click this button. (Of course, you could just click the X, or Close button, once to get the same effect.) But Microsoft seems to have kept this button here for people who are coming from an earlier version of Windows, where you could put away a window by clicking in this corner. Microsoft never throws away anything; they just pile new stuff on top of the old.

If you like choosing items from a menu, you can use this button to get a drop-down menu offering to minimize, maximize, or close the

window. This whole approach means you have to take two clicks (or one click, a glide, and a release) to accomplish what a simple click would do with the Minimize, Maximize, or Close buttons. If there were a Department of Silly Buttons, this one would surely belong there, particularly when you realize that double-clicking the button has the same effect as choosing the Close command on its own drop-down menu.

The menu also lets you move the window by using the arrow keys, which is a little like using a knife to eat jello, and resize the window in a way that rarely works well. (Using the mouse is much easier, as we show you in "Making a Window Dance," later in this chapter.)

Staying Inside the Border

We love those commercials that show a guy staggering through the desert to get to the border. He doesn't make it. Instead, he gets to a fast food joint.

Windows 95 has borders, too. In fact, every window has a border all the way around, or almost all the way, depending on how you look at it. Mostly the border is that thin strip marking the window off from the background, as shown in Figure 3-6; the border seems to rise up from the background, catching the light on the left, or top, and casting a shadow on the right and below. Sometimes, though, pieces of the window lie on top of the border, and all you see is the edge. (If you want to make the border bigger, read on.)

Small kids find it much easier to work with a large border around the window. They may just be getting used to the hand-eye coordination required to use the mouse. One way to make this task easier for them is to increase the size of the window border, to give them more room to zoom and mouse around. Follow these steps to make things easier for smaller fingers:

1. Choose Start⇨Settings⇨Control Panel.

The Control Panel window appears.

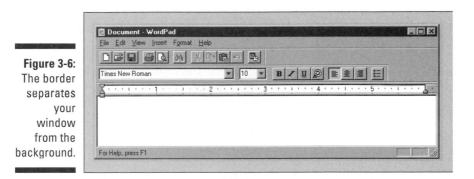

Figure 3-6:
The border
separates
your
window
from the
background.

2. **Double-click the Display icon.**

   (The borders are part of the overall display.)

3. **Click the Appearance tab.**

4. **Press the down arrow in the Item list box.**

   A list of items appears. The one you want, the Active Window Border, may be up out of sight, so you have to press the up triangle in the scroll bar on the right to bring that item into view.

5. **Scroll up and click Active Window Border.**

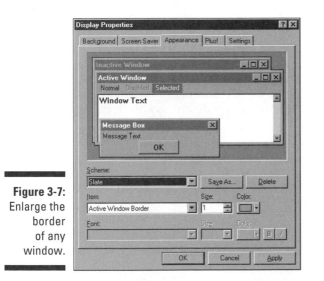

Figure 3-7:
Enlarge the
border
of any
window.

6. **Press the up arrow in the Size (shown in Figure 3-7) text box until the number 20 appears.**

   That'll make the border plenty big enough.

7. **Click OK.**

Working with the Bars in Your Windows

Some folks put bars on their windows to keep burglars out. But that's not what Microsoft had in mind when it invented bars for its windows. And the Microsofties weren't thinking about the kind of bars where Homer Simpson gets drunk. (They're so straight at Microsoft that they don't think of things like that. They think about work.)

If your house has a garage, it may have a work space or workbench with shelves for tools and manuals and materials like nails and screws and those little gizmos you use to hang pictures. In Windows 95, the windows come with shelves like those, full of tools, buttons, and gizmos. But Microsoft calls these shelves *bars*.

At first, a window bar just looks like a row of words or pictures, but after you get a closer look, you see that each bar has its own purpose, telling you a particular kind of information about your work, or offering a particular set of tools. Here's a set of bars you can get into without a fake ID.

The title bar: Why you care

Duh. The title bar tells you the window's name. Like, what you're looking at. If you are looking at a program, the title bar tells you the program name. If you are looking at a document, you get its title. (Of course, if you have just started a new document, its title is, well, Untitled.)

The title bar is the top horizontal bar extending across the width of the window. It starts on the left with the program logo (secretly, the silliest button in Windows 95), includes the window name, and ends on the right with the Minimize, Maximize, and Close buttons, as shown in Figure 3-8.

Figure 3-8:
The title bar tells you the name of the window.

Title bar

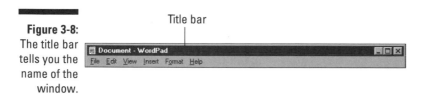

The title bar for the window you are working in is highlighted, that is, a brighter color than the title bar of any other window. You can always tell which window is active, because it's on top, and its title bar is vibrant, compared to the dead look of the others.

You may think that you don't need a title bar. After all, you wouldn't forget the program you're working on, would you? Well, maybe not when you have only one program open, but as you get more familiar with Windows 95, you may work and play with more than one program open at the same time and have many documents open in their own windows, as we describe in "Two-for-One: Having Several Programs Open at Once," in Chapter 1. So one window gets partially hidden behind others. Spotting the title bar helps you zip to the window you want.

The menu bar: A salad bar for commands

Serve yourself! Like a buffet restaurant, the menu bar lets you pick — whatever. It's that row of words just below the title bar, like that shown in Figure 3-9. Each word names a different menu — kind of like soups, salads, pasta, main courses, desserts, and drinks on the menu at your favorite restaurant. Only here in Windows 95, each program's menu offers, well, just a list of commands you can issue to your computer. Not as tasty as restaurant menus, then. Boo! Hiss! But these menus really let you get cooking on your own computer stuff.

Menu bar

Figure 3-9:
The menu
bar shows
groups of
commands.

Document - WordPad

File Edit View Insert Format Help

Different programs have different menus, but they all work the same way. For the full story on ordering something from a menu, see "Ordering Fast from the Menus" in Chapter 1.

Sometimes even your rave fast food restaurant is out of your favorite combo meal. That happens on computer menus, too. Some items may be grayed out. They just aren't available right now, because the program doesn't think they apply to what you are doing.

If you realize that you want some other menu, glide your pointer over to another menu title. That menu drops down instead. Tired of menu reading? Just click somewhere else in the window, indicating that you are no longer interested in issuing a command.

Beginners like to click to open the menu, read for a while, and then click a command. But you can go faster, if you want: Click the menu title, slide down to the command you want, and then when it is highlighted, release the mouse button.

Is Grandma still a little nervous about all this menu stuff? To get your grandparents familiar with all the selections on the menu bar without a lot of clicking, select one title such as File and click once. The drop down list of commands emerges. Bring the pointer back up to the menu bar and hover over each title. Each menu now drops down — without any further clicking. Now let Grandma hover and slither all over the menu, exploring. When you're both finished exploring the menu bar, just click once in a blank space in the menu bar, or anywhere there is no button.

If you notice that you are using the same menu item over and over and would like a faster way to issue the command, see if there are some keys listed on the right of the menu, next to the command; the idea is that you can press that key, or those two keys at once, instead of laboriously opening the menu. They're called shortcut keys, and you can read more about them in "Tapdancing on the Keys" in Chapter 1.

Toolbars and their many buttons

Ugh. Grunt. Groan. Getting ready for school can take forever, particularly if you have to look good. And who doesn't? So in your bathroom you probably have a shelf with toothpastes, hairsprays, deodorants, cold pills, and about a thousand other bottles and tubes and boxes, right? These are your tools for the day. Just finding the right hairbrush or gel takes five minutes.

In your program window, you have *toolbars* that act like your bathroom shelf. But here the tools are buttons with pictures or letters on them (to show you what the tool does). The buttons on the toolbar help you go faster than you can through a menu. With the button, you don't have to hem and haw and guess which menu to open, much less pick the right command, because the button is the command, right there in the open, just waiting for you to click. With one tap on the mouse button, you tell the computer what to do. Now if you could just get your hair to stay put with one flick of the brush!

You've studied all the dials on the dashboard of your jet fighter when you are attacking oil wells or just landing at a new airport with your flight simulator. At first, you have no idea what the heck those controls all do, but gradually you figure them out. Same deal with the buttons on your toolbar.

They look cool, and impressive, and really small, but how can you know what those pictures mean? Well, as a kid, you just click and find out. But parents, and particularly grandparents, are a lot more cautious. Here's how you can show them what the buttons mean — before pushing one.

1. **Open your favorite program.**

   Pick a program — any program. If you can't make up your mind, you can always try good old WordPad by choosing Start⇨Programs⇨ Accessories⇨WordPad.

2. Look at the toolbar buttons on top.

Each button has a picture of some sort on it. Talk together to try to figure out what each one means.

3. Now grab the mouse and slowly wave the pointer across the toolbar.

Neat! A little label drops down when you hover over a toolbar button. The word or phrase tells you what that button can do for you, as shown in Figure 3-10.

Figure 3-10:
Tips drop
out of
nowhere to
tell what a
button
does.

Don't know what the words or phrases mean? You can do any of the following to find out what they're trying to tell you:

• Check the glossary at the back of this book — in the glossary we spell out many nerdy sounding words so that you can understand them and get on with your life.

• Look in Help by choosing Topics or Contents and Index from the Help menu and then clicking the Index tab and typing in the phrase. (For details about using Help in Windows 95, turn to Chapter 2.)

• Just click the button and see what comes up! (*Remember:* This approach is tough for grownups to try; it goes against their training.)

The ruler of the known universe

No, this electronic ruler's more like the one you have to keep in your desk at school, as you can see in Figure 3-11. Not every program has a ruler, because you don't always need to measure from side to side or top to bottom.

With the computer ruler, at the top of your document, you can tell how wide your report is, or how tall (some rulers go down the left side of the window).

In word-processing programs, you can also use gizmos on the ruler to set margins, indents, and tabs. Try dragging the up arrow and down arrow on the WordPad ruler, to see where your first line and second line start.

Figure 3-11:
The ruler
lets you see
how far
you've
typed, or
how big
your
drawing is.

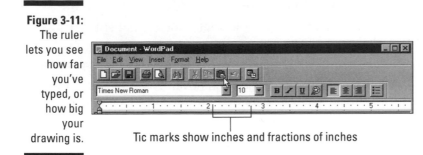

Tic marks show inches and fractions of inches

The status bar (if you're totally, like, lost)

If you have had your name announced in assembly or over the PA system by the principal, maybe for best attendance, no tardies, or good grades, then you have gotten a lot of status for a little while.

But in a window, the status bar is a lot less glamorous. It just tells you the status of your work. It lives at the bottom of your window, as shown in Figure 3-12. You could say that in Windows 95 the status bar has a lowly status.

Figure 3-12:
The status
bar.

For Help, press F1

The status bar tells you information that only nerds really care about, such as what page you are on, what kind of special features you have turned on, and what's going on. For example, if you turn on the Numbers Lock key (Num Lock) to use the numeric keyboard, you may see a little box in the status bar saying NUM. (Each program has its own kind of status bar.)

Hear ye! Hear ye! The scroll bars

You know how in those old knights-on-horseback movies, the town crier or the court snob or whatever he is unrolls a big piece of paper and reads to the crowd? He is unrolling a *scroll* of paper. Well, when we gave up writing with quill pens, you probably thought we were through with paper that comes in big rolls, where you have to unroll it to read it. No way.

On the computer, you can only see part of what you've written or drawn. There just isn't room on the screen to show it all. So how do you see the rest? You scroll up and down to see the rest, using a gizmo on the side of your window called the *scroll bar*. It's as if there were a big roll of paper behind the screen; you have to roll up to see one page and down to see another. For the people who invented windows, that was, well, scrolling.

One scroll bar frames the right-hand side of your document window, making a vertical scroll bar, as shown in Figure 3-13. Another scroll bar may show up along the bottom so you can move left and right. The up and down or left and right arrows, the little box inside the bar (sometimes called an *elevator*), and the bar itself all help you move quickly around the document you're working on.

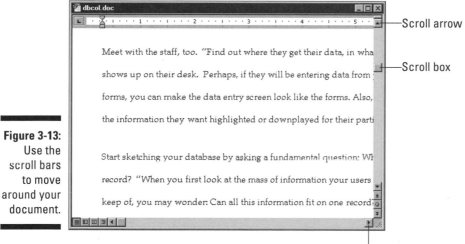

Scroll arrow

Scroll box

Scroll arrow

Figure 3-13:
Use the scroll bars to move around your document.

If you have a very short document, your program may not bother to put up any scroll bars, on the theory that you don't need them. Later, after you have typed for a while, scroll bars appear, so you can move back and forth.

To skim the good part of your book report by using your scroll bar, follow these steps:

1. Move the pointer until it is over one of the scroll arrows.

To see the text that's hidden below the screen, point to the down arrow at the bottom of the scroll bar. To see what lies above the screen, point to the up arrow.

Get the idea? The arrows point to the part of the document they will show if clicked.

2. Click once.

If you clicked a vertical scroll arrow, the text moves one line up or down. If you clicked a horizontal scroll arrow, the text moves one tab space (about half an inch) to the left or right.

To move through one screen's worth at a time, like, if you're too impatient to go line by line, follow these steps:

1. **Move the pointer until it is in the gray area between the scroll box and one of the scroll arrows.**

2. **To scroll back one screen's worth, click in the space between the scroll box and the Scroll Up arrow. To go forward a screen, click once in the space between the scroll box and the Scroll Down arrow.**

To go quickly through several screens, lean on the scroll arrow for a while.

The little elevator — the scroll box — changes size to indicate how much of the document you can now see in the window. If you have a very short document, the elevator swells up like a mosquito at a picnic, taking up most of the room in the scroll bar. But if you have a 50-page report on the presidents of the United States, your elevator will be this tiny little rectangle, indicating that what you see in the window is just a small fraction of the whole document.

To move around much faster, click the scroll box and drag it up or down. You skip through many pages at once, going backwards if you scroll up and going forwards if you scroll down.

In some programs such as Word, the scroll bar offers even more ways to zip around your document. For instance, in Word, you can set special arrows to take you to the next or previous footnote, graphic, table, and so on. Keep your eye out for extra buttons in the scroll bars; these make you into a power user, because they increase your efficiency.

Chatting with Your Program Using Dialog Boxes

Blockhead: What did one wall say to the other wall?

Smarty: "Meet you at the corner."

Sometimes you have to talk to your computer. How? No amount of shouting helps. You have to type stuff and click choices in a special kind of window called a *dialog box*.

When a program needs extra info from you so it can carry out some command you've just given, you see a dialog box. A dialog box lets you have a heart-to-heart with the program—you know, a sharing and caring dialog.

Basically, the dialog box asks you questions about what exactly you want the program to do, and you answer. Like, "What do you want me to call this document?" And you type the answer. Or the dialog box offers you choices and lets you pick.

When a program has more questions or options than fit in the dialog box, the programmers put groups of questions or options on different *tabs*. These are like the dividers in your school notebook. To see another group of questions or options in a dialog box, you click its tab.

Text boxes: Where you get to type the text in the dialog box

U-Name-It. Or U-Type-It. Text boxes are usually highlighted with the program's standard suggestion when the dialog box appears, as shown in Figure 3-14. But you can get rid of that and write your own stuff in.

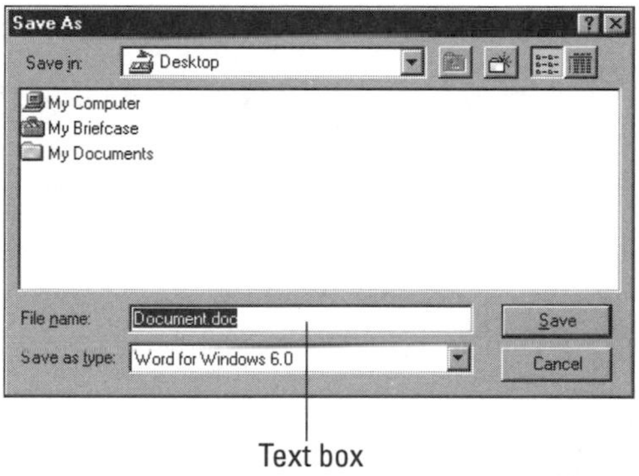

Figure 3-14:
Use the text box to type in information.

Save As

Save in: Desktop

My Computer
My Briefcase
My Documents

File name: Document.doc   Save

Save as type: Word for Windows 6.0   Cancel

Text box

Accept what the text box says or type something else, such as the name of the file, when you are saving a document. If you want to change the text in a text box, just follow these handy-dandy steps:

1. Double-click the word or phrase in the text box.

Now the information in the text box is highlighted. Highlighting means that the text is selected and whatever you type next will replace the text that's there now.

> If the text in the box is already highlighted, you don't have to select it by double-clicking.

2. Type the new text.

List boxes — regular size

David Letterman makes his living making up top ten lists. We can't count that high. So here are our hot three, and not.

Hot:

✔ Soccer

✔ Ghost stories

✔ Chocolate chip cookies

Not:

✔ Carrots

✔ Tight jeans

✔ Chains

Lists let you know what's in and what's out. In Windows, a *list box,* like the one you see in Figure 3-15, offers you a chance to choose one item from a list. And because you don't have to type anything, you can't mess up with a typo or something like that.

List box

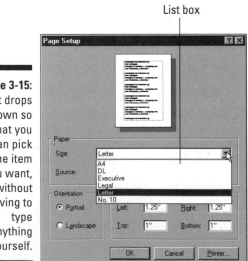

Figure 3-15:
A list drops down so that you can pick the item you want, without having to type anything yourself.

To select an item from a list box:

1. **Place your pointer on the appropriate item in the list box.**

   If you don't see the item you want, use the scroll bar on the side to zip on down.

2. **Click that item.**

   It is now highlighted.

3. **Click OK.**

Drop-down list boxes

Some lists take up even more room than the box has to offer. So the program puts a little arrow next to the box, meaning: "Click me to see a really big list drop down."

Drop-down list boxes contain more information than regular list boxes so you have to scroll through them to see all of their offerings. It's like you're still on vacation and you stop in for lunch at one of those diners that has a menu the size of the Empire State Building and your younger brother asks you, "What's on the menu?" Fortunately, using a drop-down list box takes a lot less time to answer:

1. **Click the arrow to the right of the drop-down list box.**

   A list of options appears.

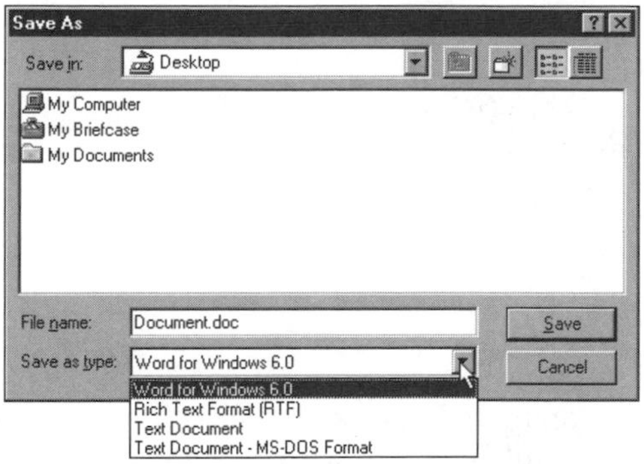

Figure 3-16: The drop-down list box offers lots of options.

2. **Scroll using the scroll bar on the right until you find the item you're looking for.**

3. **Click the item you want.**

4. **Click OK.**

Using the arrows alongside the boxes can be very tricky the first few times, especially for little hands. Kids tend to alternate between having a heavy hand on the mouse and being very timid with the clicking — just where is that pointer supposed to go anyway? If the pointer is not placed in the correct spot, nothing happens, which leads to frustration. Explain to your kids that it's the very tip of the arrow on the pointer that needs to be on the button, and have them practice a bit by using drop-down lists from any dialog box.

Check boxes

These are easiest of the bunch of dialog box controls. You see a bunch of choices, each with a little white box next to it, similar to the one shown in Figure 3-17. Simply click the box next to the item you want. A check mark in the box appears. Click OK and you're on your way.

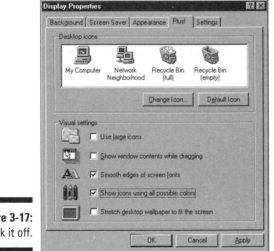

Figure 3-17:
Check it off.

Command buttons

Who's in charge here? You are. In dialog boxes, the command buttons come with their names right on the buttons. You know right off what they do. The most common command buttons are OK, Cancel, and Help!

When you have filled in every box, clicked every option, and are ready to have the program carry out your instructions, click OK.

When you have made a complete mess out of the options and want to forget everything, click Cancel. The program ignores whatever choices you made, throwing them away.

Want to see what the effect of all these options will be? Click Apply. The choices you have made are applied to whatever thing you selected just before issuing the command that led to this dialog box.

Need help fast? Click the Help button or the question mark. A window appears with a list of topics and an index you can skim through to find the information you need.

Making a Window Dance

Blockhead: If a bunch of cattle is a herd, what is a bunch of windows?

Smarty: Windows 95.

That's the way your screen looks when you get going with Windows 95: windows, windows everywhere.

In this section, we show you some neat (formerly top secret) tricks that you can do with a whole window — or a whole herd of windows. So saddle up and tell those windows, "Giddyap, you little doggies!"

Making a window stand up and beg

You can probably remember when you were on a long car trip staring out the window wishing something would happen. Like the window itself would stand up and dance. Well, in Windows 95 the windows aren't quite that athletic, but you can make one active, even when all the others are just sitting around on the screen.

When you make a window get up and boogie, well, at least, get active, its title bar lights up, changing from some dull color like gray to a real color, like blue. (Just which color, you get to decide.) The window jumps to the front, blotting out any other windows nearby. And after it's active, you can actually do something with the contents — like write a letter or finish a drawing.

Only one window is active at a time. All the others lie around, looking kinda dull, waiting for you to wake them up, as in Figure 3-18.

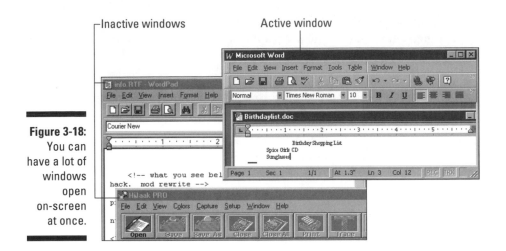

Inactive windows   Active window

Figure 3-18:
You can
have a lot of
windows
open
on-screen
at once.

Here's how to make a window active: Click any part of the window. Yes, that's it. The window's title bar changes color, and the whole window jumps to the front, ready to rock and roll.

If you can't even see the window, you may have to shrink or close other windows. To shrink a window so it becomes a button on the taskbar, click its Minimize button (the one that looks like a line at the bottom of a square, way up in the top-right of a window). To close an interfering window, click the X or Close button in the same area.

Changing a window's stripes

No, it isn't your fault! Telling which window is active — and which ones are inactive — isn't easy because of the standard settings for stuff like the color of the title bars. Microsoft likes to call all these settings the "default" settings because they take effect if you don't suggest something better. Of course, a lot of people feel guilty when they hear that they are using default settings. So here's how to change things, to make inactive windows look really different from active windows:

1. **Choose Start⇨Settings⇨Control Panel.**

   You see a collection of little programs that let you control Windows all arranged in this window (shown in Figure 3-19) as if it were some kind of panel on your spacecraft's dashboard.

Figure 3-19:
The Control
Panels let
you keep
Windows 95
under
control.

2. Double-click the Display icon.

The Display Properties dialog box appears, giving you a lot of ways to change the look of your screen, including the windows. In fact, there are so many choices that this dialog box is divided into sections with tabs, just like your school notebook.

3. Click the Appearance tab.

A simulated screen with several windows open appears in the work space, as shown in Figure 3-20. This will be your example — look here to see how the changes you make will look on your screen.

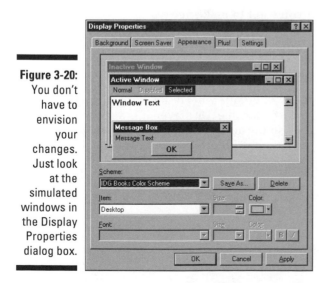

Figure 3-20:
You don't
have to
envision
your
changes.
Just look
at the
simulated
windows in
the Display
Properties
dialog box.

4. Click the arrow next to the Item list box.

This list shows elements that you can tweak.

5. Select Inactive Title Bar.

This tells the dialog box that you want to make a change to the way the inactive title bar looks.

6. Press the arrow in the Color list box to see the colors.

7. Select red by clicking the red box.

In the sample, your inactive title bar instantly changes from gray to red. And just in case you have any doubts about it, the words Inactive Window appear on the title bar.

Of course, if you don't like red, you can choose some other color in the box of colors. If you don't like any of the changes you have made, click Cancel to put away the dialog box and ignore everything you've done.

8. If you get a set of colors you like, click Apply to see them applied to your screen, and if they look good, click OK. (If not, click Cancel.)

Notice how easy it is to tell the inactive windows from the active one!

Switching windows

Sometimes you just can't make up your mind, and you keep wanting to go back and forth between two windows. Or maybe you have a game in one window, and you are making notes of secret codes in another window. When you have more than one window open at a time, you'll probably want to go back and forth.

1. Click the window that you want to make active.

The window you've just been working in drops behind and becomes inactive.

2. When you're ready to switch back, click the other window.

Can't find the other window? Perhaps you shrank it by mistake. Look on the taskbar for a button with its name. Or maybe it is smaller than the window that's now active, so the active window is blocking your view. In that case, shrink your current window by using the Minimize button to find the other one.

Moving a window around

Hey, get picky! Sometimes you just don't like where Windows 95 places a window. Maybe it's covering up another window you want to get to, or it's too far over to one side, or part of it seems to have slid off the edge, so you can't reach part of the window. No problem. Here's how to move that window:

1. **Place the pointer inside an empty area on the title bar, as shown in Figure 3-21.**

Figure 3-21:
Aim for a blank area on the title bar.

| 📄 Document - WordPad · | ▬ □ ✕ |
| File Edit View Insert Format Help | |

2. **Hold down the mouse button and, keeping that mouse button pressed down, move the pointer, pulling the window to a new spot.**

    Notice that the window keeps moving as long as you keep dragging.

Try grabbing the title bar, and then whirling the window around, if you want to get dizzy fast. Neat, huh?

Make sure that you place the pointer on the title bar itself and not on top of any of the icons on the right or left side. You don't want anything accidentally disappearing, scrolling, blowing up, or shrinking on you.

Changing a window's size or shape

Moving is one thing, but maybe you want the window to be a different size or shape! Here are several ways to change the window's size and shape.

  ✔ Drag the size grip — the slanting lines down in the lower-right corner of the window, as shown in Figure 3-22.

Figure 3-22:
Grab and
resize the
window.

✔ Point to the border, and when the pointer turns into a two-headed arrow, drag the border in or out.

✔ Point to any corner of the window, and when the pointer turns into a two-headed arrow, drag the corner diagonally, outward or inward.

Something weird happened? Or nothing at all? Go back and make sure that at the moment you press the mouse button your pointer is really the two-headed arrow. It easily slips back into being the regular arrow, and all that does is select some other window, the desktop, or worse.

Setting up two windows next to each other

Most of the time you just want to look at one window at a time. That's why when you open a program or a document, Windows 95 figures you'll want to look at a pretty good-sized window and opens it right on top of whatever window you were just looking at. Thoughtful, huh? But what happens when you *want* to look at two windows open at the same time?

Maybe you want to look at your notes while you write a report. Or you have a list of all the kids on your Little League team and you're typing a different note to each kid, giving out the "volunteer" assignments for the season. You may want to have the team roster open so you can look at those names as you create the assignments.

1. **Open the two windows that you want to look at.**

2. **Move the active window to the right side of your screen.**

   (If you forgot how to move a window, look at the section, "Moving a window around," earlier in this chapter.)

3. **Resize the window so that it only takes up half the screen.**

4. **Click in the inactive window to make it active.**

5. **Drag that window to the left side of the screen, and resize it so that you can see your other window, over on the right.**

   If you have a document within one of the program windows, you can resize it the same way.

   Now you can look at both windows, side by side, as shown in Figure 3-23.

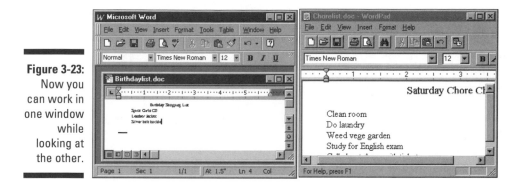

Figure 3-23: Now you can work in one window while looking at the other.

Finding a missing window

A lost window can cause panic in the best of us. Sometimes while you are busy in the kitchen making a cup of hot chocolate, someone else gets busy "practicing" how to use the mouse. You come back, all smiles with your freshly made cup of cocoa, look at your screen, and yell, "Where'd all my work go?"

Well, think of that lost window as a being a piece of paper that's been whisked off your desk by a breeze. It's around someplace. But where did it go?

✔ A good first try is to see if the missing window is on your taskbar, shrunk into a button. But remember, you'll only find the missing window's button on your taskbar if you or someone else minimized the window.

✔ Let's take the scientific approach: Look carefully on your desktop. Is there a little corner of the title bar or window border visible beneath all the other windows? If so, just click it to make the window reappear.

But what if it's really lost? If you've searched everywhere and you still can't find that missing window. Look carefully at the edges of your screen. See a strip or small rectangle that doesn't belong there? If you do, take the following steps:

1. **Click any part of that little shape.**

2. **Hold down the Alt key and press the spacebar at the same time.**

   Notice a little menu pops up, as shown in Figure 3-24.

Figure 3-24:
Finding this little pop-up menu can be a life-saver when your window is lost.

3. **Select Move.**

   A four-headed arrow appears that activates the arrow keys on your keyboard.

4. **Click the arrow keys until enough of the window is in a more workable position on your desktop.**

Laying out windows

So now you have windows on top of windows on top of windows. Looks like the clothes on your bed, right? Here's how to get Windows 95 to straighten all those windows so they look neat, and you don't have to do any laundry or dusting.

Making a splash

You can make your windows look like a waterfall. Well, sort of. The first way to tidy up your desktop is to put one window a little in front of and below the next, one after another, in a kind of waterfall or cascade. Cascading leaves each window's title bar (and not much else) exposed so you can easily get to it.

1. **Right-click with your mouse on a blank space on the taskbar.**

   Remember: Right-clicking just means clicking the mouse's right button. When you do, a little pop-up menu appears, as shown in Figure 3-25.

2. **Click Cascade to make the waterfall of windows, as shown in Figure 3-26.**

Figure 3-25:
This pop-up
menu gives
you a
choice in
displaying
your open
windows.

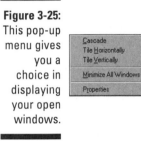

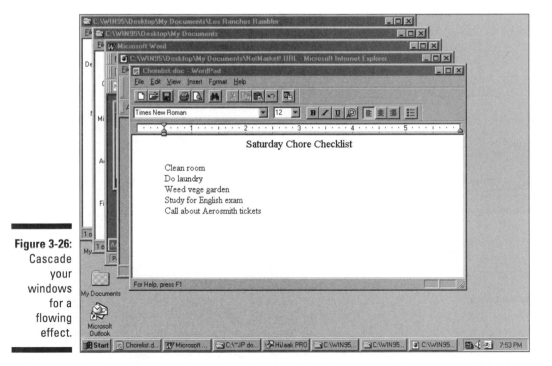

Figure 3-26:
Cascade
your
windows
for a
flowing
effect.

Laying out windows like tiles on the bathroom floor

Think of those rows of ceramic tile in your bathroom. Now imagine if every single one of those were an open window on your screen and you sort of have the idea of tiling. Tiling is useful when you want to look back and forth, comparing several documents.

Windows 95 can scrunch all the open windows so you can see them squooshed up and they end up taller than they are wide, but still a lot smaller than before, stacked next to each other. This is called vertical tiling. Or you can have Windows 95 make them wider than they are tall, and stack them up next to each other, which is called horizontal tiling.

1. **Right-click with your mouse on any blank space on the taskbar.**

   A little pop-up menu appears.

2. **Click Tile Horizontally or Tile Vertically.**

   Depending on which option you click, your windows will appear tiled vertically, as shown in Figure 3-27 or horizontally, as shown in Figure 3-28.

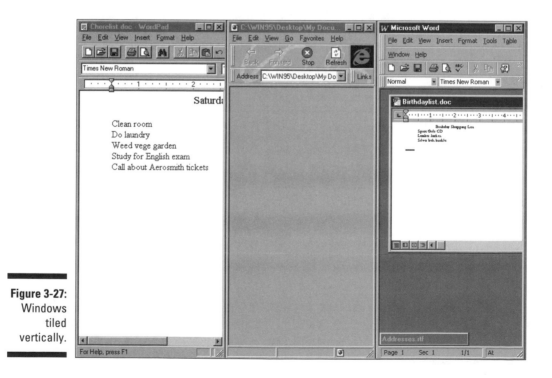

Figure 3-27: Windows tiled vertically.

If you don't like the cascading or tiling effect of your windows, just right-click a blank space in the taskbar and choose Undo Tile from the pop-up menu.

You can only cascade or tile open windows. Minimized or closed windows don't appear.

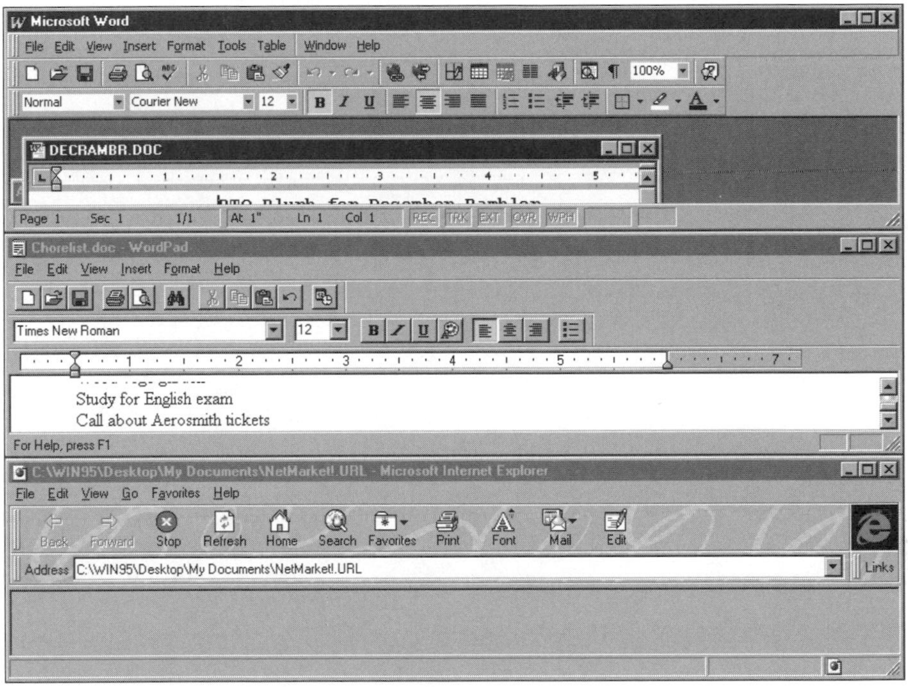

Figure 3-28:
Windows
tiled
horizontally.

Chapter 4

Playing with the Look and Feel

● ●

In This Chapter

▶ Changing the way the screen looks

▶ Having fun with fonts

▶ Mousing around

▶ Changing the feel of the keyboard

▶ Turning up the volume

● ●

"I just caught a frog down at the lake," says the biology teach. "We'll look it over and then dissect it."

He unwraps the package. Inside is a peanut butter and jelly sandwich.

"Oh my goodness," he says. "I distinctly remember eating my lunch."

*B*arf! Yuck! Or as your mom says, "I tell you and tell you — you should look very carefully at what you put in your mouth."

But sometimes you don't listen to Mom. You're one of a kind. You have your own favorite T-shirt, you know just what you like to order when you go out for fast food, and you comb your hair a certain way. You have your own look.

When it comes to your computer, you also have the chance to express your own taste. You can change all kinds of things about the way your computer looks and acts, making it *your* computer — different than any other computer on the planet.

In this chapter, we show you how to play with lots of stuff on your computer — changing the colors and pictures on the screen, fooling with the way your mouse works, turning up the volume, adding and subtracting software, and making Windows 95 easier for folks with special needs to use — all aspects of what Microsoft calls the Windows *interface*. (It's you face to face with the computer.) The interface is the part of the software you see on the screen, and act on.

Why You Should Care about the Control Panel

Do you put flashy new book-covers on at the beginning of school so that you don't have to look at the same covers all year? You can, like, change the way the screen looks the same way. No, you don't wrap paper around the monitor. You twist knobs and press buttons in a part of your computer called the *Control Panel,* changing the settings that control the way your computer looks and acts.

When you're looking at the screen right after you start the computer, you may see everything just the way Microsoft set it up at the factory — unless your parents have already messed around with the interface. But basically, you see the following items:

- ✔ **Icons:** For example, you see an icon called My Computer.

- ✔ **Background:** Microsoft likes to call this the *desktop,* as if your desk had tipped up vertically, against the wall. Go figure.

- ✔ **The taskbar, with the Start button:** You may not see the taskbar if someone has gone and hidden it from you, which we tell you how to undo in Chapter 3.

The Control Panel lets you change all these things — and a lot more aspects of the interface, such as the colors, pictures, mouse behavior, and volume.

Unveiling the Control Panel

To start tinkering with all the things you can change with the Control Panel, just choose Start⇨Settings⇨Control Panel. A window opens with more than two dozen icons, as shown in Figure 4-1. Each icon lets you control some part of Windows 95.

Aaaggh! What are all these things in the Control Panel window? Chill: You don't need most of them! (You get to leave most of them for your parents.) We'll just look at the icons you really want to use in Table 4-1. P.S. You may have more icons in your window, too, depending on what your family has installed on the computer, but don't freak; you probably don't need to mess with those. (Ask your parents.)

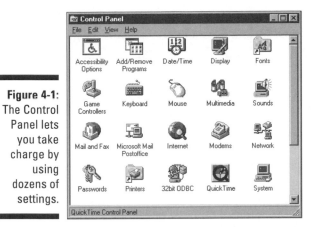

Figure 4-1:
The Control Panel lets you take charge by using dozens of settings.

Table 4-1	Icons to Know and Love
This Icon	*Does This*
Accessibility Options	Lets you adjust the screen, keyboard, and mouse for people with special needs.
Date/Time	Lets you change the date and time on your computer so that it can act like a calendar and clock.
Display	Lets you change the way the screen looks.
Fonts	Lets you add or subtract fonts — so you can make your writing stand out.
Game Controllers	Lets you hang a joystick on your computer and adjust the joystick.
Keyboard	Lets you tinker with the way the keyboard works.

(continued)

Table 4-1 *(continued)*

This Icon	Does This
Mouse	Lets you adjust the way the mouse and its pointer work.
Multimedia	Lets you adjust sound and video.
Sounds	Lets you pick and choose what sounds Windows 95 will play, such as when you get an error message.

Some of the areas of the Control Panel should be off limits to anyone who's not responsible. You may want to claim exclusive rights to click the following icons:

✔ **Add/Remove Programs:** Helps you install new software, and — even better — when you're tired of some software, helps you get rid of it. Always start here to remove a program, because the program comes with many little files that get placed in tiny crevices throughout your hard disk, and you can never find them all without help.

✔ **Internet:** Lets you set up your connection with the Internet Service Provider, the company that actually plugs you into the World Wide Web.

✔ **Mail:** Controls electronic mail.

✔ **Microsoft Mail Postoffice:** You don't need this because it is for office folks.

✔ **Modems:** Lets you install and set up a modem so that you can dial out over the phone lines to connect with other computers or the Internet.

✔ **Network Neighborhood:** Again, an office issue, unless you have decided to network together all your personal computers.

✔ **Passwords:** Lets you assign a password to each person so that she sees only the interface she likes when she signs on.

✔ **Printers:** Helps you set up and control a printer.

✔ **System:** Even you may want to keep hands off the System settings unless you have a good friend who is a Windows 95 programmer and who can help you recover if you make a mistake.

Get Back! Repapering Your Computer's Back Wall

You see it all the time, behind everything — it's the background, duh. But you can make your background a lot more interesting than your aunt's living room wallpaper. Here's how to change the pattern that shows up behind all your windows and icons:

1. **Close any windows you may have open so that you can see the effect of your changes right away.**

2. **Choose Start⇨Settings⇨Control Panel.**

   You see the Control Panel, which contains the Display icon.

3. **Double-click the Display icon.**

   You see a picture of your screen in the middle of the Display Properties dialog box, shown in Figure 4-2. The Display Properties dialog box is your command center for changing many things that you see on your screen, including how fun or boring your desktop looks.

   If you aren't on the Background tab, please click that now.

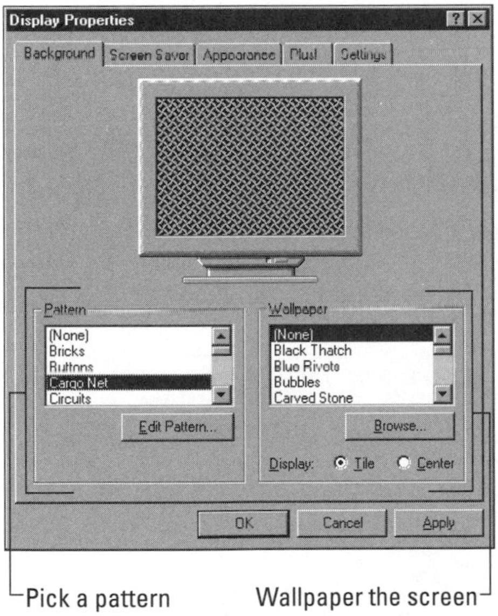

Figure 4-2:
The Display
Properties
dialog box
controls the
look of your
screen.

Pick a pattern   Wallpaper the screen

Underneath the miniature version of your screen, you see two lists. The first list shows patterns — crosshatchings, line drawings, little dots, and blobs that can fill the whole background. The second list has pictures, more like the kind of wallpaper you see in old houses, or hotels. You can now pick a pattern for the background or cover the background with wallpaper. (You can't combine a pattern with a wallpaper, though.)

4. **Under the list of Wallpapers, click the radio button next to the word Tile.**

   This fixes things so that you can see the wallpaper all over the mini-screen, like the ceramic tiles on a bathroom wall.

5. **To find the wallpaper that you want, scroll through the options in the Wallpaper list. Click the name of the wallpaper that you want to try and then click the Apply button.**

   In a flash, the screen behind the dialog box fills up with the wallpaper that you want to look at.

   You can see that you have to apply a wallpaper in order to tell what it will really look like. (The little screen in the dialog box gives you only a vague idea of what the wallpaper will look like.) So always choose Apply to try out a wallpaper before making your final decision and clicking OK.

6. **To make room so that you can try out some patterns, choose the Wallpaper called None. Then click a pattern from the list on the left and click the Apply button.**

   The pattern goes on the background of the screen now. Here are a few patterns to try: Buttons, Cargo Net, and Daisies. Want to make someone think the computer is broken? Try Dizzy.

   Notice that the pattern looks the same on the screen as it does inside the little screen in the dialog box. A pattern doesn't change scale the way a wallpaper does. So you may not need to click Apply to see what some patterns will look like.

7. **When you have settled on a pattern or wallpaper you like, click OK.**

If you still don't like any of the possibilities, you can make your own, as we describe in the next section.

Creating Your Own Background

At first, the wallpapers that come with Windows 95 are fun, but after a while, you'll probably want something different. The neat thing is that you can make your own background and show it on-screen. The screen really puts a spotlight on your art.

1. **Choose Start⇨Programs⇨Accessories⇨Paint.**

2. **Make up a painting.**

   For tips on how to paint, see Chapter 7.

3. **Choose File⇨Save and give the picture a name.**

   It's probably best to make the name eight characters or less. Otherwise, some parts of Windows and some programs may get confused, or Windows may wipe out the middle part to shrink the length to eight. Make a note of the place where Paint saves the picture.

4. **Close or minimize Paint.**

5. **Open the Display Properties dialog box.**

   If the dialog box is not open, choose Start⇨Settings⇨Control Panel, double-click the Display icon, and then click the Background tab.

6. **In the Display Properties dialog box, click the Browse button.**

   You see the File Open dialog box that helps you locate the picture you just saved. For tips on finding a file, please see Chapter 6.

7. **In the File Open dialog box, locate your painting and click OK.**

8. **When you return to the Display Properties box, click Apply.**

   Your personal wallpaper fills the screen! Now yell, very loudly, "Hey, come take a look at this!"

Choosing a ready-made color scheme

Are you into black clothes? Camo? Then you may want to darken the screen. Of course, if you like bright and cheerful colors, you may like to try on a different set of colors, like a new T-shirt. Here's how:

1. **Choose Start⇨Settings⇨Control Panel.**

2. **Double-click the Display icon.**

   The Display Properties dialog box appears.

3. **In the Display Properties dialog box, click the Appearance tab.**

   Too much! You see a window with too many bars inside, showing a sample color scheme, as shown in Figure 4-3. No, the colors aren't plotting against you. Windows just calls some combination of colors a *color scheme,* and you pick one you like to make a wallpaper or pattern more to your liking.

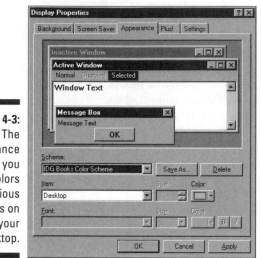

Figure 4-3:
The
Appearance
tab lets you
pick colors
for various
gizmos on
your
desktop.

4. Pick a color scheme from the drop-down list called Scheme.

If you have trouble reading small type or if you have a grandparent who has trouble reading it, try one of the schemes labeled Large, or even Extra Large. These schemes enlarge the lines and type and everything so that they are gigantic — at the same time as changing the colors way over to can't-miss-'em bright.

5. To see what the color scheme looks like when applied to a real dialog box (like the one you are looking at), click Apply.

Other people in your family may not like the color scheme you pick out. Most people, for example, think High Contrast Black is really, really, really ugly. Ditto for High Contrast White: It looks as if you're staring right into the sun without your shades. So if you find a scheme you like, hey, ask folks to take a look before you impose it on them.

6. Click OK.

The computer waits a moment and then changes to the color scheme you chose.

Making up your own color scheme: Way cool

Want to stand out from the crowd? You can modify any of the color schemes to make a new one of your own. Just follow these steps:

1. **Pick the color scheme closest to what you like.**

   Check out "Choosing a ready-made color scheme" in this chapter if you need some help picking out a color scheme.

2. **In the Item box of the Appearance tab, pick some part of the interface, such as the bar that shows a window is active, or the bar that shows a window is not active, and then, on the right, click a new color or a new size for it, and then click Apply.**

3. **When you have made all your changes, click Save As, give your scheme a name, and click OK.**

   From now on, your combination of colors will be on the list of choices in the Scheme list, so you can always get it back, even if you go on to try other schemes. Neat, huh?

Making Everything Bigger or Smaller

Zoom! You can make everything on-screen get bigger or smaller. If someone in your family has trouble seeing small stuff, you may want to make all the windows — and their titles and everything — bigger. But if you want to make everything look like ants, you can do that, too. Here's how:

1. **Choose Start⇨Settings⇨Control Panel.**

2. **Double-click the Display icon.**

   The Display Properties dialog box appears.

3. **In the Display Properties dialog box, click the Settings tab.**

   You see a tiny monitor, showing a picture of the Control Panel, as shown in Figure 4-4.

   In the area under the picture of the monitor, you see three controls:

   - **Color palette:** The first box lets you pick the number of colors you want Windows 95 to use to display anything, from photos to icons.

   - **Desktop area:** The second box lets you set the *screen resolution* so that windows look big and fuzzy, or small and sharp.

   - **Font size:** The third box lets you enlarge the size of the letters that Windows uses to label icons.

4. **Watch the picture of the Control Panel inside the monitor, at the top of the dialog box, while you go to the Desktop Area bar and drag the arrow left or right.**

   You see the miniature image of the Control Panel get bigger or smaller depending on which way you slide the arrow.

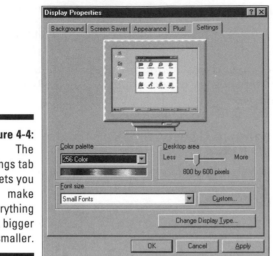

Figure 4-4:
The
Settings tab
lets you
make
everything
look bigger
or smaller.

5. Click the Apply button.

You're told to wait a moment. The screen goes black, and then it comes back with the area you picked. A message appears telling you that you wanted to resize your desktop, and then asks whether you like the effect enough to keep it.

6. If you like the way things look, click Yes. If not, click No.

If you click No, Windows 95 confirms that you have gone back to your original settings or, as it says, restored your original desktop size. Of course, it has never changed: The screen is still just as big as it was. But this dialog box really lets you set the amount you want to see — whether close up, with only a little in view, or far out, with lots you can see, but all tiny.

7. Click OK.

Squinting? Helping Someone with Special Visual Needs

You can make the text on icons, titles, and menus look larger, so that anyone who has eye problems or a visual handicap can see the words better. Or maybe you just like text that jumps off the screen.

If you'd like the text labels for icons and other items to be larger, make sure that you have closed every other program and saved your work, because you are going to need to shut down and restart to see the change. Then follow these steps:

1. **Choose Start⇨Settings⇨Control Panel.**

2. **Double-click the Display icon.**

   The Display Properties dialog box appears.

3. **Click the Settings tab.**

   If the Font Size box is grayed out, drag the slider under Desktop Area to the right, or switch the color palette from 16 to at least 256 colors by selecting from the drop-down list.

4. **In the Font Size box, choose Large Fonts from the drop-down list and click OK.**

   Windows 95 asks whether it's okay to restart the computer, because that is the only way you can see the results of your choice.

5. **Click OK.**

   The computer shuts down and restarts. When it comes back to life, your text looks bigger.

Thinking about playing with the color palette? Well, that may not be as easy as it seems. Your computer can probably show photos that look just as good as Nick at Nite, or, you know, old movies on TV. You can make pictures look more realistic if you use the Settings tab to tell the computer to use more colors — for example, millions of colors. But the problem is that pouring all that paint on the screen takes a lot of computing effort and slows everything down. It also demands a fancy version of the electronics that send information to the screen — known as a *video card*. Your computer may not offer all the colors that Microsoft imagined, so don't be disappointed if you get a message telling you that, sorry, you can't go that high. In general, you do fine at 256 colors.

Helping out the visually impaired

It's no fun having to put your nose to the screen in order to make out what it says. In this chapter, we mention a few ways you can use the Display icon within the Control Panel to make life easier for folks who need more than glasses. For information about assistive technology (software and hardware) for people with visual disabilities, visit the Arkenstone site on the World Wide Web, at www.arkenstone.org.

If someone in your family has a hearing disability and may miss any signals coming from the computer via sounds, double-click the Accessibility icon in the Control Panel, click the Sound tab, and set up the computer to give visual warnings at the same time as the usual sound alerts and, if you want, to provide text explanations as well.

Save That Screen!

No, your screen is okay. It doesn't really need saving. But screen savers are fun anyway. See, in the old days, if you left the same text on the screen for a day or so, it burned into the screen, and ever after, whenever you looked in that area, you could see a kind of ghost image of that text. Very distracting. So people developed this trick: Whenever the screen had been motionless for a certain amount of time, the system would switch to some other image, something moving, so no one part would get burned into the screen.

As a result, we now have screen savers you can buy that show flying toasters, silly sheep, jumping fish, and so on. Microsoft gives you a few screen savers with Windows 95 (the standard one shows window after window flying out of the dark), and your folks may have installed some more. Here's how to switch screen savers:

1. **Choose Start⇨Settings⇨Control Panel.**

2. **Double-click the Display icon.**

   The Display Properties dialog box appears.

3. **In the Display Properties dialog box, click the Screen Saver tab.**

   You see the Screen Saver tab, shown in Figure 4-5.

4. **In the Screen Saver box, click the title of a screen saver and then click the Preview button.**

   The screen goes black for a second, and then it shows the screen saver you picked.

5. **After you have finished marveling at the screen saver, stop the preview by clicking anywhere on-screen.**

   If that doesn't work, press the Esc key to escape.

6. **If you like the screen saver, use the arrows next to the Wait box to tell the computer how long to wait before starting the screen saver.**

   The waiting period is the time Windows 95 must wait to make sure that you don't type anything, use the mouse for anything, or disturb the screen in any way. If you don't do anything for that length of time, Windows 95 decides that it is okay to run the screen saver.

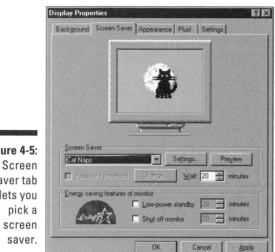

Figure 4-5:
The Screen
Saver tab
lets you
pick a
screen
saver.

If you want to try another screen saver, select it and preview it. Keep going until you get just the one you want waving at you from the screen when you walk by.

7. Click OK.

From now on, after whatever wait you specified, the screen saver starts up on your computer, and plays and plays and plays until you come in and move the mouse or tap the spacebar on your keyboard.

People differ widely about how long you should leave a computer on. One fact: Turning a computer on puts more of a strain on its innards than just leaving it on. So a lot of folks leave a computer on all day, which doesn't eat up a lot of electricity. The screen, though, deserves a rest if you're not going to be looking at it for a few hours. Most screens sold in the last year or so go to sleep if unused for several hours; you may see that the power light is on, but the screen has gone blank. That's okay. Click or move your mouse to bring the screen back to life. If you have an older screen, consider turning it off after use, even if you leave the computer itself on.

Font-for-All

You know how your handwriting is different from everyone else's? Well, you could say that you have your own font. On the computer, having a lot of fonts makes your words jump up and dance, so you may want to check out the way different fonts make your work look.

A *font* is a set of letters, numbers, and punctuation marks that all look alike. If you are doing a report or drawing and want it to look really awesome, try out some different fonts in your program. If you want to know, in advance, what a font looks like, you can use the Control Panel. Here's how:

1. Choose Start⇨Settings⇨Control Panel.

2. Double-click the Fonts icon.

You see a set of icons for all the fonts that you can use on your computer — those shown in Figure 4-6, for example.

Font Name	Filename	Size	Modified
Abadi MT Condensed	ABAC.TTF	64K	4/6/96 12:00 AM
Abadi MT Condensed Extra Bold	ABAEXBC.TTF	60K	5/1/96 12:00 AM
Abadi MT Condensed Light	ABALC.TTF	65K	5/1/96 12:00 AM
Alcott	Alcott__.ttf	51K	2/13/96 3:31 PM
Alcott Bold	Alcob___.ttf	44K	2/22/96 12:30 PM
Alcott BoldItalic	Alcobi__.ttf	43K	2/22/96 2:04 PM
Alcott Italic	Alcoi___.ttf	43K	2/13/96 3:28 PM
Algerian	ALGER.TTF	68K	5/1/96 12:00 AM
American Uncial	AMERIUNC.TTF	45K	5/1/96 12:00 AM
Animals 1	animals1.ttf	86K	4/23/94 12:00 AM
Animals 2	animals2.ttf	30K	4/23/94 12:00 AM
Antique	Antique_.ttf	169K	5/6/96 3:53 PM
Arial	ARIAL.TTF	64K	7/11/95 9:50 AM
Arial Black	Ariblk.ttf	102K	10/15/96 10:40 AM
Arial Bold	ARIALBD.TTF	66K	7/11/95 9:50 AM
Arial Bold Italic	ARIALBI.TTF	73K	7/11/95 9:50 AM
Arial Italic	ARIALI.TTF	62K	7/11/95 9:50 AM
Arial MT Black	ariblk.TTF	102K	10/15/96 10:40 AM
Arial MT Condensed Light	ARCL.TTF	77K	6/11/92 9:32 AM
Arial Narrow	arnar.ttf	122K	11/17/96 12:00 AM

C:\WIN95\FONTS

File Edit View Help

1 font(s) selected

Figure 4-6: Each font has its own name.

Icons that carry the label TT, for True Type, look good on-screen and on paper, no matter how big you make them. Fonts that carry the label A may look a little jagged if you make them too large.

So what is this TrueType stuff? Well, it's a step forward. In the old days, you built a font by creating a bitmap for each letter — a grid, like graph paper, with some boxes filled in and others not filled in. Each box was a computer switch, or bit, that was turned on or off. But that meant the slanting lines and curves ended up looking crude and jagged, like a staircase. Enter TrueType, where every letter is built mathematically in a bunch of formulas that describe the angle and width of every little line needed to build up every letter. TrueType fonts take whatever dots you have and draw with them so that you end up with much cleaner characters. You get a smooth line on the screen (where you may have 96 dots per inch, say) or on paper (where you may have 300 dots per inch). TrueType fonts, then, are scaleable. You get one description of the font and then multiply it by the size, changing its scale mathematically.

You don't have to have one file for 12 point, another file for 18 point, and so on. Two advantages, then: A single font takes up much less room on your hard disk and because the math doesn't care what size dots you use on-screen or on paper, the edges and curves always look smooth.

3. **Double-click a font's little icon to see what it looks like.**

   You see a window like that shown in Figure 4-7.

Information about the font

Alphabet, numbers, and punctuation

Figure 4-7:
The Font window shows you how the whole alphabet looks in that font.

Different sizes

4. **Make sure that your printer is turned on and then click the Print button in the Font window.**

   The Print dialog box appears.

5. **Click OK.**

   You get a printout on paper so that you can see how the font will look in your report on famous TV monsters.

   If you like the way the font looks, you can choose it from the list of fonts available in the various programs that you use. Often you'll find a menu option called Fonts under the Format menu, and in some cases, you'll see a drop-down list of fonts. Now you know which one to pick.

It's fun to print out half a dozen fonts and compare them in the big sizes (60 and 72 points). Take one letter and look at the way different fonts draw it. Are there little extras at the end of the line? Does the stroke change width as it goes up or around? How high is the bump in the *h?*

Never, never, never delete a font unless you are the one who put it on the computer. If you happen to delete a font needed by Windows 95, you may end up with no menus, no window titles, no nothing. Be particularly careful of any font with a label in red (these are often used on-screen) and any font whose name begins with MS, the sacred initials of Microsoft itself. A good general rule: Don't delete any fonts. Then you know you're safe.

Mousing Around

Smartypants: The early bird gets the worm.

You: But the second mouse gets the cheese.

Oooh! You can hope your computer mouse doesn't get caught in a mouse-trap. But sometimes when you move it, you may feel that the pointer on the screen moves a little slow or too fast. Or when you click the mouse button twice quickly, the mouse doesn't seem to get the point. Here's how to adjust the mouse so that it says "Cheese!":

1. Choose Start⇨Settings⇨Control Panel.

2. Double-click the Mouse icon.

You see the Mouse Properties dialog box, as shown in Figure 4-8.

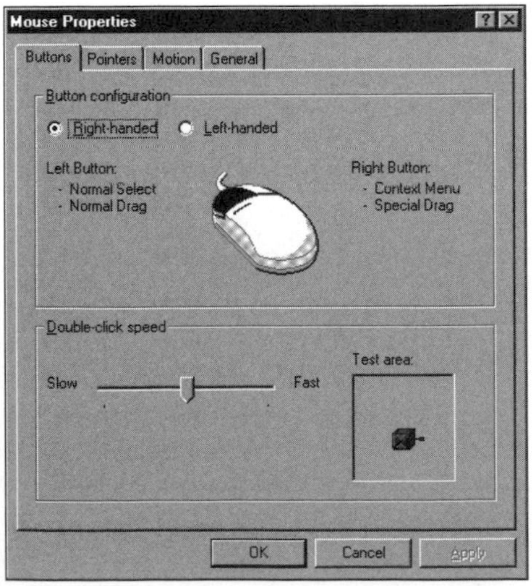

Figure 4-8:
The Mouse Properties dialog box lets you adjust the way the mouse and its pointer work together.

Mouse Properties				? X

Buttons | Pointers | Motion | General

Button configuration

◉ Right-handed ◯ Left-handed

Left Button:
- Normal Select
- Normal Drag

Right Button:
- Context Menu
- Special Drag

Double-click speed

Slow ——————— Fast

Test area:

OK | Cancel | Apply

3. **Click the Buttons tab, and at the bottom of the Buttons tab, drag the slider bar to adjust the Double-click speed.**

   Try double-clicking in the Test Area, to see if you like the results. You want the mouse to be able to keep up with you if you are very fast, or mellow out if you are, say, a little slow.

4. **If you sometimes feel that the pointer isn't moving as fast as the mouse, or vice versa, click the Motion tab, drag the slider bar to Fast or Slow, and then click Apply.**

   Feel like you've gone into hyperspace at 10Gs? Well, drag that bar back. Most people like the bar near the middle — not too fast, not too slow.

5. **Want to freak out the next person who uses the computer, or cause a headache? On the Motion tab, click Show Pointer Trails and drag the slider over to Long so that a set of ghost-like pointers trails behind the real one.**

   Okay, turn it off. The only reason Microsoft put this feature in is that on laptop computers the screens are often so bad that you can't tell where your pointer is. The trail helps users spot their pointer. And, yes, if you leave it on too long, you can make people dizzy.

Making the Keyboard Easy for Heavy Fingers

Little fingers tend to lean on the keys, and, then, brrrrappp! That letter gets typed on the screen about a dozen times. If this happens to a beginner, or a family member who has special needs, here's how to adjust the keyboard to avoid "sticky keys."

You can use the Control Panel to tell the keyboard, "Hey, wait a minute before you start repeating a letter over and over and over — when I am just leaning on a key."

1. **Choose Start⇨Settings⇨Control Panel.**

2. **In the Control Panel, double-click the Keyboard icon.**

   You see the Keyboard Properties dialog box, as shown in Figure 4-9.

3. **On the Speed tab, in the Character Repeat area, drag the Repeat Delay slider to Long to tell the keyboard, "Wait longer before you start repeating the letter."**

4. **In the Repeat Rate control, move the slider to the Slow side so that even if the keyboard thinks it ought to start repeating the letter, you won't get a whole lot of letters all at once.**

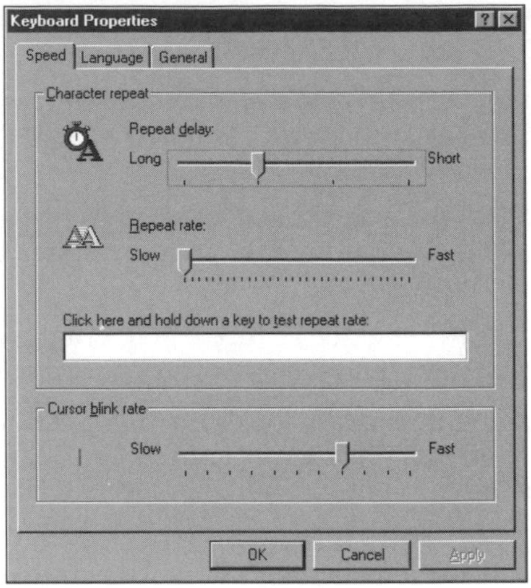

Figure 4-9:
The
Keyboard
Properties
dialog box
lets you
adjust the
way the
keyboard
responds.

5. Try out your new settings by typing in the text box and then holding down one key for a while.

6. If you like this pace, click OK.

If your child has special needs that go beyond slowing up the repeat, double-click the Accessibility icon in the Control Panel dialog box, and use the Keyboard tab to make keystroke combinations easier (Shift + a letter, for example), to tell Windows to ignore accidental or unintended repeated keystrokes, and to have sounds go off whenever someone happens to press the keys that lock the keyboard into all capitals. Click the Mouse tab to use the arrow keys on the numeric keypad instead of the mouse.

More keyboard help on the Web

You may want to use the World Wide Web to check out assistive technology. Intellitools, for example, manufactures a special keyboard and a talking word processor, described at www.intellitools.com. Edmark features a Touch Window and other items in their Special Needs section, via www.edmark.com.

For kids who need a *switch program*, that is, a tool that lets a child communicate via a toggle switch, visit R. J. Cooper at www.rjcooper.com or Don Johnston, Inc. at www.donjohnston.com.

For neutral advice, see the Alliance for Technology Access at www.ataccess.org, Augmentative Communication Consultants at www.acciinc.com., or the Center for Applied Special Technology at www.cast.org.

Making Your Computer Louder

You probably think of your ghetto-blaster as your main sound machine. But your computer can play for you, too — even though it probably doesn't have the volume or depth of your boombox.

Pumping up the volume

Have you ever heard your computer make any sound? If so, you have a *sound card*. Alas, without a sound card, you can't play music or hear games yell at you. Here's how to find out whether you have the right gear, and then how to adjust the volume for sounds of all kinds and music from your CDs.

1. **Choose Start⇨Settings⇨Control Panel.**

2. **In the Control Panel, double-click the Multimedia icon.**

   You see the Multimedia Properties dialog box, as shown in Figure 4-10, which keeps track of all the hardware and software that let you play music, have a character speak, or show video with sound effects.

Lets you make and edit music

Controls sound   Lets you play music from your CD-ROM drive

Controls video   Shows all hardware and software for multimedia

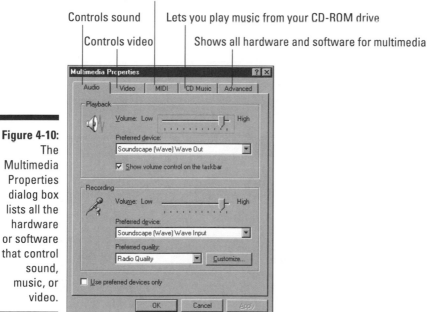

Figure 4-10:
The
Multimedia
Properties
dialog box
lists all the
hardware
or software
that control
sound,
music, or
video.

3. **On the Audio tab, make sure that something or other is showing in the Preferred Device box in the Playback section and then adjust the slider to the volume you like. If there is no preferred device, you probably don't have a sound card installed; it's time to ask your folks what gives.**

4. **Click the check box beside Show Volume Control on the Taskbar so that you can adjust the volume directly from there from now on.**

5. **Click the CD Music tab and adjust the slider to the volume you like.**

6. **Click OK.**

Sounding off

Your computer can play a sound every time it does something big, such as closing a program or starting Windows. Windows 95 calls those exciting things "events."

You can tell Windows 95 which noise to make during which event — and the results can sure surprise the other folks in your family when the computer blurts out something unexpected.

1. **Choose Start⇨Settings⇨Control Panel.**

2. **In the Control Panel, double-click the Sounds icon.**

   You see the Sounds Properties dialog box, as shown in Figure 4-11.

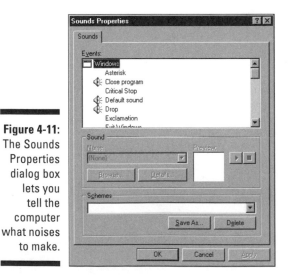

Figure 4-11:
The Sounds
Properties
dialog box
lets you
tell the
computer
what noises
to make.

3. **Scroll through the list of events and select an event that has a loud-speaker next to it, such as Close Program or Exit Windows.**

4. **Click the Preview button to hear the sound you selected.**

   If you don't hear anything, turn up the volume. Look on your taskbar, on the right, to see whether you have a loud speaker; press that, and then slide the volume control bar up. If you don't have such an icon, see "Pumping up the volume" in this chapter.

5. **Click OK.**

   The sound will now be played whenever the computer performs that activity.

   You may want more sound files to play with. The names of sound files end in .wav. To discover other sounds on your computer, choose Start⇨Find, type ***.wav** in the text box, and then click Find Now. You see what folder the sounds are in. Then you can go back to the Sounds Properties dialog box and steer to those locations to attach one of those .wav files to another event. You can also find a ton of free sounds on the Web. Go to the sites of bands you like, and you can download all kinds of noises, including some music.

Part II

Working and Playing with Windows 95

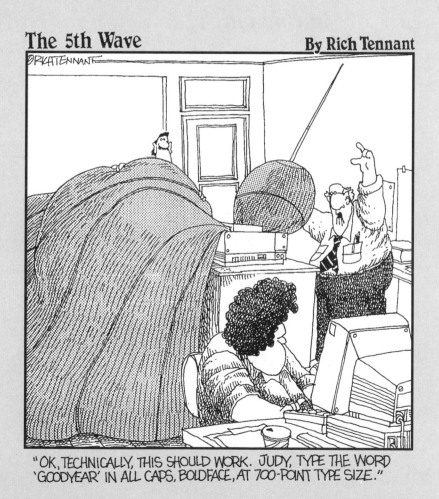

The 5th Wave — By Rich Tennant

"OK, TECHNICALLY, THIS SHOULD WORK. JUDY, TYPE THE WORD 'GOODYEAR' IN ALL CAPS, BOLDFACE, AT 700-POINT TYPE SIZE."

In this part . . .

Wanna have some fun? Then this part's for you. You find games to play when you need a break, music to listen to when the computer's beeps and boops get boring, and video to watch when someone else is hogging the TV. Wanna have some *more* fun? Check out the list of family activities. And just in case you think this part is all about fun, we add some "gotta know" info about cutting, pasting, and copying, plus a rundown of the mini programs, such as WordPad, Calculator, and Paint that are attached to Windows 95.

Chapter 5

Cutting, Copying, and Pasting

- -

In This Chapter

▶ Highlighting text

▶ Obliteration

▶ Snap! What the electronic clipboard does for you

▶ Cutting text and pasting it somewhere else

▶ Revealing the Clipboard

▶ Copying and pasting

▶ Leaving Scraps on the desktop

▶ Undo! Having regrets

▶ OLE! Updating what you're pasting

▶ Collecting clip art

- -

*I*f you have a report to do for school, or you just want to make a list of a thousand reasons your band is the best, it's time to get down to the nitty gritty of typing something (more commonly known in the computer biz as, "entering text"); one of the things that sets the computer apart from a typewriter is its fabulous ability to make corrections and changes. No more clumpy white stuff to paint over your typos. You still cut and paste when you edit a book report or a letter, but you use your fingers instead of scissors and glue.

First You Select It, Then You Make a Change

The way you make a change on the computer, whether you're drawing something or writing, usually involves two steps: First you select the thing you want to change, and then you make the change. In this section, we show you how to select some text, and then some art, as examples.

Selecting some text

1. **Start WordPad by choosing Start⇨Programs⇨Accessories⇨WordPad.**

2. **Type something, like your name and address.**

3. **Click and hold the mouse button down, just to one side of the material you want to select.**

4. **Without letting the mouse button up, drag the pointer through the material you want to change.**

   The passage is highlighted, as shown in Figure 5-1. That special look means that text is now selected. So you can now do something special to that passage, like make it bigger or turn it red.

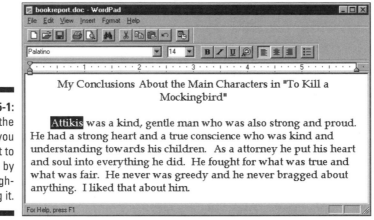

Figure 5-1: Select the text you want to change by highlighting it.

Here's a faster way to select a word. Place your cursor anywhere over the text you want to select and double-click. The word is highlighted and ready for you to type in a change.

If you select the text by using either of these methods, make sure that you don't click after highlighting the text, unless you want to wipe it out. If you do click, your word will disappear. If you decide you want to unselect the highlighted text, just click anywhere else in the document and the highlighting disappears telling you that the text is no longer selected.

Selecting a patch of a painting

If you do much computer-painting, you may want to know how to select a chunk of your picture.

1. **Start Paint by choosing Start➪Programs➪Accessories➪Paint.**

2. **Make a big painting.**

3. **On the Tools tool palette, click the dotted rectangle.**

4. **Move over the drawing and then click and hold down the mouse button at one corner of an imaginary rectangle you are about to select.**

5. **Drag the pointer diagonally to surround an area with a dotted rectangle and then release the mouse button.**

    The edges of the rectangle vibrate.

6. **To see what you can do with the part of the picture you have selected, try dragging it up and down.**

Off with the Old, On with the New

If you've ever typed on an electric typewriter, you know what a pain it is to make changes on a paper page. Personal computers now make editing a snap. The basics are the same if you're using WordPad, which comes with Windows 95 as one of the accessories, as described in Chapter 7, or if you're typing with a high-powered word-processing program like WordPerfect.

Did you know that the techie-sounding word *text* comes from a Latin word, *texere,* meaning to weave? Eventually, the word came to mean "woven material" which morphed into meaning "literary composition," eventually arriving at our 20th century doorstep as *text.*

Wipe out! Deleting text forever

Okay, so maybe the image of a surf board jutting up and over the foam of a gigantic wave is a little too drastic here. But if you permanently delete something by accident, you may feel a little like that surfer twirling under the wave gasping for air.

The more things change . . .

The basics of word processing haven't really changed a whole lot since the early days of the first personal computers, back in the early 1980s. Oh, there are many more bells and whistles now (it takes several dozen floppy disks just to install the most popular word-processing program, Microsoft Word), but most folks just don't need all that stuff. Most of us just want the convenience of writing something and have the ability to change our minds and easily make the adjustments on the page. WordPad may be plenty for ordinary work.

Deleting an entire line

Just in case you *want* to delete some stuff on the page forever, there are a few simple ways to do it. In the case of a book report, say you decide to get rid of the line, *My Conclusions About the Main Characters*.

TIP

1. **Highlight the line that you want to remove.**

   When highlighting a whole line, you can use one of the two methods mentioned in the section above, or you can place your cursor anywhere in that line and quickly click three times.

2. **Press the Delete key.**

   The entire line is gone forever.

Getting rid of a few letters

If you want to erase just a few letters, it's easier just to place the cursor to the right of the letters you want to get rid of and press the Backspace key until those letters are gone. Deleting in this way is also permanent.

The Electronic Holding Area

When you are in art class and make a collage poster, you have to first round up all those magazines. Then you have to carefully cut out all the pictures or words you like and put them in a box to keep them safe. When you are finished cutting, you pick out the ones from the box that you think are absolutely fabulous. Finally, you get out the glue and stick on the pieces in just the right spots. That's a huge job. Fortunately cutting, copying, and pasting on the computer is a lot easier (and faster!), although the concept is the same. But instead of putting stuff in a box, you put it on an electronic clipboard.

Think of the electronic clipboard (affectionately called just the Clipboard) as the place inside the computer where you throw the images you want to cut, or any text that you're not sure what to do with. Maybe you're thinking of using that sentence, paragraph, page, or graphic someplace else in your document either right away or sometime in the future. While you are making up your mind, you place that section in the Clipboard for safe keeping.

Move over!

You have to save anything you want to move (like a word, phrase, or picture) into the Clipboard before you can paste it to some other place. We use WordPad here for this, but the directions we give you work in any program you're using.

1. **Highlight text that you want to move to someplace else.**

2. **Choose Edit⇨Cut.**

   Notice that the text has disappeared. But don't worry, it's really only skeedaddled over to the Clipboard, which stays hidden.

   The Toolbars on most applications have a little Cut button, as shown in Figure 5-2, that you can press, which replaces the step of pulling down the Edit menu and selecting Cut.

Figure 5-2:
The Cut ✂
button.

3. **Place the cursor just before the spot where you want the text to appear.**

4. **Choose Edit⇨Paste.**

   The text you cut out before now appears in the new spot.

You can also cut and paste from one document to another. You need to add a step but the basics are the same. Just follow these steps:

1. **Highlight text that you want to move to the other document.**

2. **Choose Edit⇨Cut.**

3. **Choose File⇨Open.**

4. **Select the name of the document you want to paste information into, as seen in Figure 5-3.**

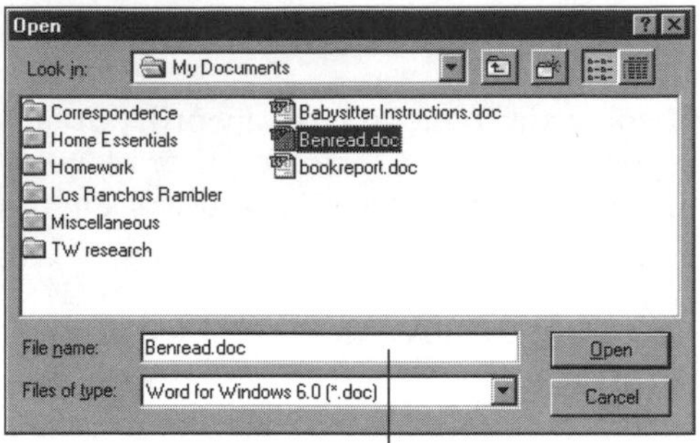

Open

| Look in: | 🖫 My Documents | ▼ | 🔁 | 🗐 | 🔡 | 🔢 |

📁 Correspondence   📝 Babysitter Instructions.doc
📁 Home Essentials   📝 Benread.doc
📁 Homework   📝 bookreport.doc
📁 Los Ranchos Rambler
📁 Miscellaneous
📁 TW research

File name: | Benread.doc | Open
Files of type: | Word for Windows 6.0 (*.doc) | Cancel

Figure 5-3:
You can cut and paste between documents.

The file you select appears in this box

5. Click Open.

The new document appears.

6. Place the cursor just before the spot where you want the text to appear.

7. Choose Edit⇨Paste.

The text you cut appears in the new spot. Pretty neat, huh?

Most word-processing programs have a Paste button also, as shown in Figure 5-4. (If you're not sure what a button in a Toolbar represents, just hover over it with the cursor and the name of the button appears in a little balloon.)

Figure 5-4:
The Paste button.

Cutting and pasting is really very easy, but because it involves cutting, sometimes it's a little scary to try. Some people are so timid about trying to cut and paste that to avoid it they always use the delete or backspace key, turning their computer into a typewriter, which is okay, but hey! we never heard of a typewriter that cost as much as your computer. So give cutting a try with your whole family. (Ever notice how it's more fun to watch someone else make mistakes?) Doing an activity together will take a lot of the fear out of it and may even provoke some giggles.

1. **Pick a relative or friend who lives far away that everyone in your family likes.**

2. **Have each person type a letter to that person by using WordPad.**

   If some of the kids in your family are too young to do this, have them dictate a letter to you.

3. **Open a new document and type in Dear Whoever You're Sending the Letter To.**

4. **Open Dad's (or anyone else's) letter and re-size it on your screen so you can look at both documents at the same time.**

   You can read all about resizing windows in Chapter 3.

5. **Copy Dad's whole letter.**

6. **Paste the letter into a new document.**

7. **Close Dad's letter.**

8. **Open some else's letter and resize it on your screen so you can again look at both documents at the same time, as shown in Figure 5-5.**

9. **Select the portions of the letter that you want to add to the New document.**

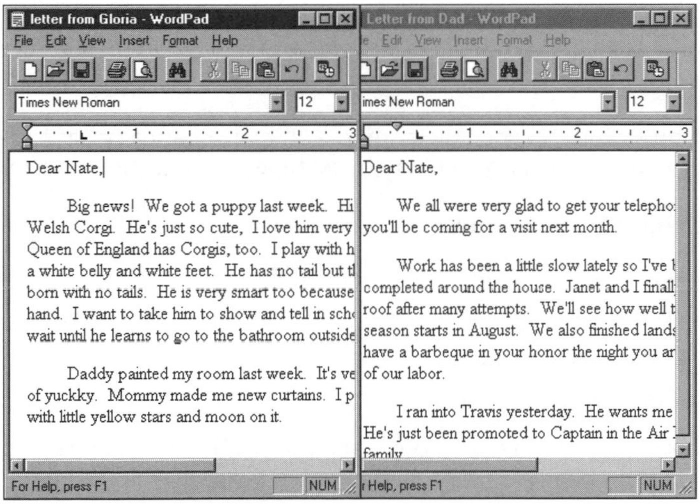

Figure 5-5: Write a letter to someone from the whole family.

10. **Close the original letter.**

11. **Continue Steps 3 through 10 for each member of the family.**

12. **After you have everything pasted into the letter, do whatever editing want.**

    You have created a letter from the whole family.

The Clipboard does a little more than store your text and pictures until you are ready to paste them to another document. It also serves as a kind of Rosetta Stone, meaning it translates from one application to another. So if you cut something from, say, Microsoft Works, you can paste it into your WordPad file without doing anything other than cutting and pasting.

Checking what's on the Clipboard

The contents of the Clipboard can get rather large, like if you put a big picture with a lot of colors in there. You may want to check what's in there before pasting something from it to another document so you don't accidentally pour a rainbow of colors into a letter when you didn't mean to. Or, you may just want to see what's there just for the heck of it. That's where the Clipboard Viewer comes in. It lets you check out just what's being stored on the Clipboard. Of course, if you just cut or copied something, that is what is supposed to be on the Clipboard, because the Clipboard only holds one thing at a time. But sometimes your fingers slip, and you aren't sure whether you really copied something or not: time for the Clipboard Viewer.

For some strange reason, Microsoft doesn't automatically have the Clipboard Viewer ready to go, so you have to install it yourself the first time you use it.

1. **Choose Start➪Settings➪Control Panel.**

2. **Click the Add/Remove Programs icon.**

    The Add/Remove Programs Properties dialog box appears.

3. **Click the Windows Setup tab.**

4. **Double-click Accessories.**

    The Accessories dialog box appears, as shown in Figure 5-6.

5. **Click the check box next to Clipboard Viewer so a check appears there.**

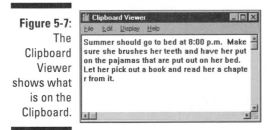

Figure 5-6:
You only
have to
install the
Clipboard
Viewer
once.

6. **Click OK.**

7. **Click Apply.**

You may now be asked to insert your Windows 95 setup disks; if asked, do that now, and follow on-screen directions.

Now you can check out what's on the Clipboard at any time by following these steps:

1. **Choose Start⇨Programs⇨Accessories.**

2. **Click Clipboard Viewer.**

You see the current contents of the Clipboard, as shown in Figure 5-7.

Figure 5-7:
The
Clipboard
Viewer
shows what
is on the
Clipboard.

Clipboard Viewer

File Edit Display Help

Summer should go to bed at 8:00 p.m. Make
sure she brushes her teeth and have her put
on the pajamas that are put out on her bed.
Let her pick out a book and read her a chapte
r from it.

When you are discovering how to cut, copy, and paste, it may be helpful if you keep the Clipboard Viewer open on your screen so you can instantly check what's being stored on it.

Sometimes you want to take a chunk out of what you are working on, but you think, "Hey, I may use this some other time." You can save it as a different document. If you'd like to save what's on the Clipboard in a new document, instead of pasting it somewhere else in this document, choose Save As from the Clipboard Viewer's File menu. Type in where you want to save it to.

So you realize, "This stuff on the Clipboard — well, it's not what I want there. How can I get rid of it?" If you'd like to delete what's on the Clipboard, follow these steps:

1. **Select the Clipboard by clicking anywhere in the Clipboard's window.**

2. **Press the Delete key.**

   A dialog box appears, as shown in Figure 5-8, asking you to make the final decision.

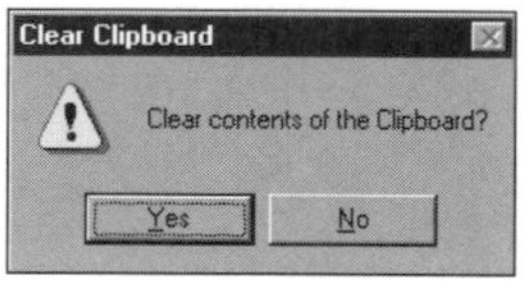

Figure 5-8:
Save
precious
memory
on your
computer
by deleting
the
contents
of the
Clipboard.

3. **Click Yes.**

   Poof! Everything on the Clipboard is deleted.

Double up! Copying and Pasting

You've seen the commercials with twins who say they get double the pleasure because they are, like, copies of each other. Well, you may want to have the same text in one place and another, and the best way to do that is to make a copy of the first text and then paste it in the other spot. Copying is great if you just want to say the same thing over and over and over and over and over????????? You may want to copy your great slogan from a letter, and put it into a school report, copying it from one document to another. You may even want to put a copy of the same slogan into your picture for the school fair; that's copying from one program to another, because you begin in a word-processing program like WordPad and end up in a picture program like Paint.

1. **Highlight the text that you want to copy to someplace else.**

2. **Choose Edit⇨Copy.**

    You can also click the Copy button, as shown in Figure 5-9.

    This is a very unsatisfying step because when you complete it nothing visually happens. The text you copied is still there and you don't see it being magically lifted off onto the Clipboard. But relax, it's made that great journey to the Clipboard.

    The Toolbars on many applications have a little button that you can press, which replaces the step of pulling down the Edit menu and selecting Copy.

3. **Open the document you want to paste the text into.**

    In most programs, you open a document by choosing File⇨Open and clicking the name of the file you're looking for.

4. **Choose Edit⇨Paste.**

    The text you copied from the other document appears in the new one.

We show you how to copy and paste from one document into another, or from a document in one program to a document in another program. This technique works just as well when you want to copy and paste within the same document.

Figure 5-9:
Look for this double Clipboard button to copy in a jiffy.

Little Scraps — No Mess!

When you cut or copy something to the Clipboard it replaces what you previously stored there. That helps the Clipboard from getting too large and taking up gobs of memory, but what if you need a place to store a cut or copied sentence from here and a paragraph from there until you're ready to paste them into the appropriate document? That's when Scraps comes in. Now we're not talking about the little morsels that you feed to your dog.

Scraps enables you to move text out of one document and onto your desktop for temporary storage. When you pull some text onto the desktop, a little Scrap Icon appears with the highlighted text in it. The icon stays on your desktop until you put it into some other place. You can make as many scraps as you like until you are ready to use them.

We bet you can't wait to see how a Scrap works. Wait no longer:

1. **Highlight the text that you want to copy to another place.**

2. **Point to the highlighted text and, keeping the mouse button pushed down, drag the highlighted text onto a blank spot on your desktop.**

3. **Let go of the mouse button.**

   Notice that a little Scrap Icon appears just like the one in Figure 5-10.

Figure 5-10:
Scraps stores little bits of text until you're ready to use them.

4. **To cut something out of your document, select it, click the Cut icon, then move out over the Desktop, right-click on the Desktop, and then choose Paste from the menu that appears.**

   If you forget what's in all those Scrap Icons, click the icon once and a brief description of the scrap is displayed below the icon.

5. **To put the scraps into a document, start a new document.**

   Or open an existing document that you want to paste the information in the Scrap to.

6. **Select the Scraps icon that has the information you want to put into the new document, drag it into the window of the new document, and then release the mouse button.**

Do this with as many pieces of scrap as you need to until your document looks the way you like.

If you have some Scraps that you decide not to use, just drag them into the Recycle Bin to get them out of the way.

Make a Big-Time Mistake? Don't Panic!

Everybody makes mistakes. But ever notice how you just get more flustered when you make mistakes on the computer? Why? Who knows. Maybe it's the high-tech thing, or maybe it's just that you're not real familiar with your computer yet. However, the computer is more forgiving than most people realize. It has an easy mechanism for dealing with the dreaded word, mistake.

The first thing to remember when you make a mistake, whether it be in typing, formatting (such as changing fonts or underlining), or completing a task such as copying and pasting, is to DO NOTHING. That's right, do absolutely nothing. Take your hands off the keyboard. Take a deep breath, if you must. If you don't do anything after you make the mistake, then Windows 95 lets you undo what ever you just did (such as cutting, pasting, deleting, or typing a word).

As soon as you realize that you've made a mistake that you want to undo, just choose the Undo icon, which looks like a bent arrow, or choose Edit⇨ Undo, as shown in Figure 5-11. Yes, it's that simple. The very last thing you did on your computer is now officially undone.

Figure 5-11:
No big deal.
The Undo
command
lets you
change
your mind.

If you feel uncomfortable pulling down a menu when you've just made a mistake, hold down the Ctrl key and press Z to undo instead. Also, if you have made a series of errors, use the drop-down menu next to the Undo icon to select one, two, or more errors to be undone.

Many applications have numerous ways to undo a command. Check the application's manual to find out what creative ways the programmers have come up with to fix a mistake.

Now that we've told you about all the wonderful ways you can undo your mistakes, we must tell you that in certain circumstances the Undo command won't work. Luckily, these circumstances are very rare. For example, after you delete data from the Clipboard, you can't use the Undo command to put it back. Similarly, if you go to the Recycle Bin, right click, and choose Empty Recycle Bin, you can't get those items back without special software such as First Aid or Norton Utilities (and a lot of luck).

Now it's time to have some real fun. Call everyone in the house because this is something everybody can do. Even the smallest fingers in your family can handle this activity (unless, of course, they tend to drool all over the keyboard).

This activity is called Mistakes-R-Us. You're going to accidentally, on purpose, make lots of mistakes and then fix them. By the time this activity is over, you won't have any qualms left about how and when to use the Undo command.

1. **Open WordPad by choosing Start➪Programs➪Accessories and clicking WordPad.**

2. **Type in anything you want.**

   Well, almost anything if the whole family is there.

3. **Choose Edit➪Undo.**

   Notice whatever you typed just went up in a cloud of smoke.

4. **Do this a lot.**

5. **Now type something in and highlight part of it.**

6. **Choose Edit➪Cut.**

   The highlighted text vanishes from the screen.

7. **Choose Edit➪Undo.**

   It comes back.

8. **Let your imagination run wild and do all sorts of things, stopping occasionally to undo a few of your actions.**

   Now don't hog the computer. Let everyone try it.

If deleting text is a little dull, try this instead.

1. **Open Paint by choosing Start⇨Programs⇨Accessories and clicking Paint.**

2. **Click the Airbrush, which looks like a spray can.**

3. **Select blue and spray on the blank screen.**

4. **Select red and spray on another part of the screen.**

5. **Choose Edit⇨Undo.**

    You see a menu as shown in Figure 5-12.

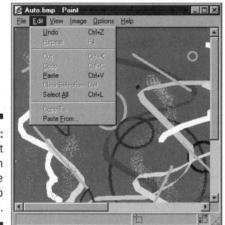

Figure 5-12:
Using Paint is a fun way to use the Undo command.

Notice that only the last action is undone.

6. **Continue Steps 1 through 5, using the Paintbrush this time.**

Adding Chips, Clips, and Other Art

Clip art is little drawings or pictures that have been predrawn and are ready for you to paste into your documents. Clip art is great when you are writing a notice to the team, a newsletter for the school paper, or a report for the teacher.

Many programs already have some clip art available for you to use, and your folks can buy programs that contain loads of clip art. Usually the clip art is sorted by type. So, you'll find animals, banners, shapes, school supplies, parties, and many other categories of clip art. Ask your parents where to find the clip art you already have before whining for more.

How do you use clip art?

Placing clip art into your document is easy. Just open the program containing the clip art and copy the art that you like. The clip art is then stored on the Clipboard waiting for you to paste it into the new document. (This process is like the copying we describe in "Double up! Coyping and Pasting" earlier in this chapter.)

Not all programs let you paste clip art into them. If you hear a buzz or a nasty beep when you try and paste the clip art, you know that the receiving program doesn't like clip art and refuses to make friends with it.

Almost all of the newer programs accept clip art. But, if you're not sure whether the application you are using supports clip art, do a test before you spend too much time working on a document by copying the particular clip art and pasting it into the receiving application. If it works, fine, if not, you may want to use a different program.

What you can and can't use clip art for

There are some copyright rules associated with clip art. Because we are not lawyers, we won't get into the wheres and wherefores, but as a general rule: You can use clip art for anything that you don't make money from or distribute to the world. If you want to use it for your own personal school report or a letter to Grandma, fine, but for the school newspaper or a Web site, where you are publishing it to the world, you should get permission from the manufacturer.

Many word processing programs already come with clip art that you can use. But there are also some wonderful collections from PhotoDisc, Master Series, MasterClips, and Corel. A great catalog for clip art collections is the Publisher's Toolbox (1-800-390-0461).

Chapter 6

Messing Around with Documents, Folders, and Floppies

In This Chapter

▶ Exploring the territory
▶ Creating a folder to put your documents in
▶ Selecting more than one file or folder
▶ Getting rid of something
▶ Copying floppies

*O*ne of the greatest things about your computer is that it keeps all your work, and all your electronic tools like programs and accessories, in one place. Gone are the days of looking for a little piece of paper in your desk with some absolutely must-have info on it or trying to read a crumpled up page that you discover in your pant's pocket. All your work is here, on your computer — clean, crisp, and ready to reread, reuse, or reprint. But because your computer has to hold so much, it acts like one of those file cabinets you see in offices. Each hard disk or floppy disk or CD-ROM disc is like a drawer. Inside the drawer are tons of folders, and inside those folders are documents.

In this chapter, you discover how to find a document, set up a folder to put it in, grab a whole bunch of documents to move or copy, and, finally, how to get rid of a document you don't need anymore — plus how to move some documents off your hard disk onto floppy disks to take to school or save on a shelf, just in case the computer goes kaflooey kaboing.

Getting Up Close and Personal with Windows Explorer

If you used to have Windows 3.1 and loved the old File Manager or you're a budding techno whiz, you probably want to use the Windows Explorer as seen in Figure 6-1, because it gives you lots of information, maybe even more than what you need, all in one spot.

To start Windows Explorer, choose Start⇨Programs⇨Windows Explorer.

In a moment, you see a window like that shown in Figure 6-1, with two panes, one on the left for disks (and a few other items that act as if they were disks) and the folders on those disks, and on the right, the contents of whatever you choose on the left.

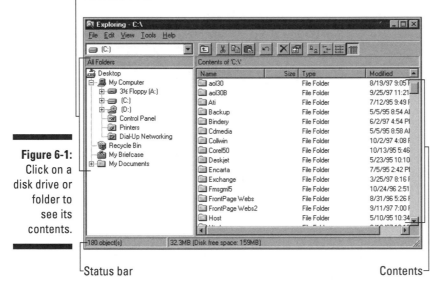

All Folders list

Figure 6-1:
Click on a disk drive or folder to see its contents.

Status bar   Contents

In the left-hand side, slide the scroll box up to the top to see what is at the very top level of your computer.

Oddly, your desktop is at the highest level, and then, within that is your computer, and then, within that, various disk drives, and a few other thingamajigs. You see the following items within the Desktop:

- Your floppy disk drive, called A
- Your hard disk, usually called C

- ✔ Perhaps a CD-ROM drive, too, if you scroll far enough down
- ✔ The Control Panel, with icons letting you adjust the look and feel of Windows 95
- ✔ Printers, to add or control printers
- ✔ Dial-Up Networking, to let you dial out to the Internet
- ✔ Recycle Bin, the temporary holding spot for trash
- ✔ My Briefcase, for files that get shuttled between a laptop and this computer
- ✔ My Documents, a convenient folder in which you can place your work

You can see that as you move from left to right, you're going down into the depths, from your computer to one disk on the computer and within that disk to various folders and within those to individual documents.

When you want to open a disk drive or folder to see its contents, click the plus sign next to the folder. The contents appear on the right side of the pane on the left.

To see the contents of an item that has no plus or minus next to it, click it. The contents of that item appear in the pane over on the right.

If you would like the material on the right to show up in large icons, small icons, or text, choose those options from the View menu.

To close a disk drive or folder so you no longer have its contents open, click the minus sign next to it (over on the left-hand pane).

To put away the Windows Explorer, click its Close button (the big X at the top-right corner of the window).

Taking a Quick Look at My Computer

My Computer uses icons to tell you what you've got, and you can see it all in one glance as you can see in Figure 6-2.

To open My Computer, double-click its icon on your screen. You see icons representing your disk drives, plus your Control Panel, the controls for your printers, and the tools you use if you have to dial out to make a connection with the Internet.

Deciding between My Computer and Windows Explorer

In My Computer, you may think, at first, that someone at Microsoft forgot to show you the desktop and three other folders that appear in Windows Explorer — the Recycle Bin, My Briefcase, and My Documents. So if you really want to see absolutely everything in one place, use the Windows Explorer. But wait a moment. . . . My Computer is an icon on the desktop, as is the Recycle Bin, My Briefcase, and My Documents. So if you like to explore those by using icons, you're okay to go: Just double-click the icons on the Desktop. Like we said, two different approaches to the same information.

Figure 6-2:
With My Computer, you can see what's on your computer in a jiffy.

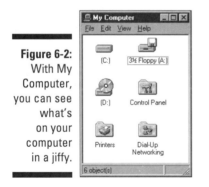

To see the contents of an item in the My Computer window, double-click the item. You see a new window appear, showing the contents of that item.

To see the contents of one of the folders that appear in the new window, double-click the folder. You see yet another window. (And another window and another, and this process can go on and on until you have literally dozens of windows all over the screen.) This scattering of windows is what My Computer is famous for. Some people love it, because they can easily have one folder's window open, another folder open, and drag a document from one to the other. Other folks hate My Computer because it just litters the screen with windows.

NERD ALERT

Unless you upgraded from Windows 3.1, don't even look over here

One of the biggest differences between Windows 3.1 and Windows 95 is the addition of My Computer and the Windows Explorer and the dumping of the File Manager into cyber oblivion. If you never owned Windows 3.1, you couldn't care less. But if you upgraded to Windows 95 you should know that everything you did from the File Manager you can now do (and more) from My Computer and the

Windows Explorer. Which one you use depends on you.

If you're an ex-Windows 3.1 user, you may also be wondering where the Directories went. Last seen they were abducted by aliens. But don't worry, so as not to create a Black Hole or anything, Microsoft replaced them with the mellower sounding Folders.

Finding a Document in a Haystack

Nobody hides documents in a haystack anymore. But finding a document on your computer can be just as tough as finding a needle in a haystack, when you forget where you put the document. Microsoft understands the problem, and lets you start off right by finding the document:

1. **Choose Start⇨Find⇨Files or Folders.**

   You see the Find All Files dialog box, as shown in Figure 6-3.

2. **If you know the full name of the document, type that in the Named text box. If you know only part of the name, type an asterisk for the parts you don't know.**

   For example, if you know the file had Frog in the title, but you aren't sure what came before or after that, you would type ***Frog***.

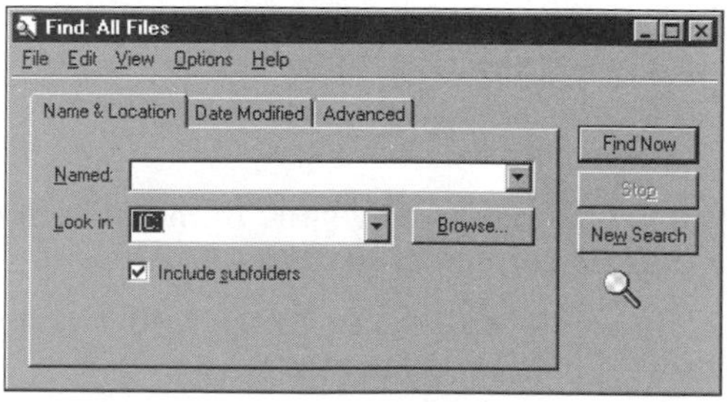

Figure 6-3:
The Find All Files can help you locate almost anything.

Find: All Files

File   Edit   View   Options   Help

Name & Location | Date Modified | Advanced

Named: [   ]

Look in: [C:] ▼   Browse...

☑ Include subfolders

Find Now
Stop
New Search

3. **If you have an idea where the document may be, make sure that shows up in the Look In text box so Windows doesn't waste your time looking in other locations.**

To select another drive, click the down arrow next to Look In and select a drive. To browse through a drive, click Browse and in the window, operate as you would in Windows Explorer by clicking a plus sign to open a folder or drive, selecting the folder you want searched, and clicking OK.

4. **Click Find Now.**

Windows now shows you any documents it finds in that location with that name. You may see one, several, or none.

5. **If you see the document you are after, and want to read it or work on it, double-click it to open it.**

If you don't find the file where you expected, go up a level and let Windows take a broader look. If that doesn't work, you may want to try the Modified Date tab if you can recall about when you last worked on the document, or the Advanced tab, if you recall the file type, the size, or even a single word you used within the file.

It's My Folder

A folder is just a type of container where you can put one or more documents — or even another folder or two, if you get really wild and crazy. As you start creating documents, like letters to your friends, flyers for your neighbors, or reports for school or work, you may want a folder to hold all of this stuff.

Here's how to create a folder to hold your work:

1. **Choose Start⇨Programs⇨Windows Explorer, and select the location in which you want to place your new folder.**

Here are some possible places you can stick that new folder:

- My Documents, down at the bottom, is a location a lot of programs suggest that you save your work in, so you may want to create a folder there.

- If you want your new folder to be visible from My Computer as well as Windows Explorer, select the hard disk, usually called C.

- Within any location, you can select a folder into which you want to slip your new folder when it is created.

Getting the scoop on file names

How long can a folder name be? Well, how many angels can dance on the head of a pin? Previous versions of Windows took a real verbal beating from users because you had to give files and folders yucky short names, using only eight characters, plus a three-character extension. So people had to give a letter to Mom a filename such as MomLtr02.doc, and put it in a folder with a wonderful name like LtrsHome. Later, no one could remember what the heck these abbreviations meant. With Windows 95, Microsoft told the world with great fanfare that you could now give your files any old name up to 255 characters as long as the name didn't contain the symbols, < > \ ? " : or *. Well, we won't get into all of the other "unofficial" exceptions except to say that if you are using a program that wasn't specifically created for Windows 95, like an older version of Microsoft Word, your file and folder names still can't be more than eight characters long.

2. Choose <u>F</u>ile➪<u>N</u>ew➪<u>F</u>older.

The folder appears with the temporary name of New Folder, as shown in Figure 6-4.

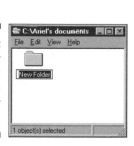

Figure 6-4:
Your newly created folder is waiting for a name.

3. Type in the name you want to give to that folder and then click elsewhere.

You now have a new, empty folder all named and ready to go.

Make a mistake naming that new folder? Click the folder name to select it. Choose <u>F</u>ile➪Rena<u>m</u>e. Type in the corrected name. Don't you wish changing your own name was that simple?

Protecting Your Files and Your Setup

If you don't want anyone messing around with your stuff, it's a good idea to have each person in your family create his own folder where he can store all his stuff and then declare that folder off limits.

If you live in a house with a lot of individualists, you may want to seriously consider giving each computer user his or her own password. This way each of you has your own wallpaper, Start Menu, and, depending on the programs you use, your own private documents that no one else can open. This way, kids don't have to look at the borrrrrring backgrounds that adults like, and adults don't get headaches looking at theirs. But also, you can write your diary in a program like Word and save the file with your password so no one but you can open it. Just like in all those movies where the spy has to guess a password in about five seconds to keep the world from blowing up. Here's how to set up passwords:

1. **Choose Start⇨Settings⇨Control Panel.**

2. **Double-click the Passwords icon.**

   The Passwords Properties dialog box appears.

3. **Check the "Users can customize their preferences and settings" option.**

   That makes the User Profile Settings active.

4. **To make sure that each person gets her own desktop and Start menu, check the two boxes in the User Profile Settings, as shown in Figure 6-5.**

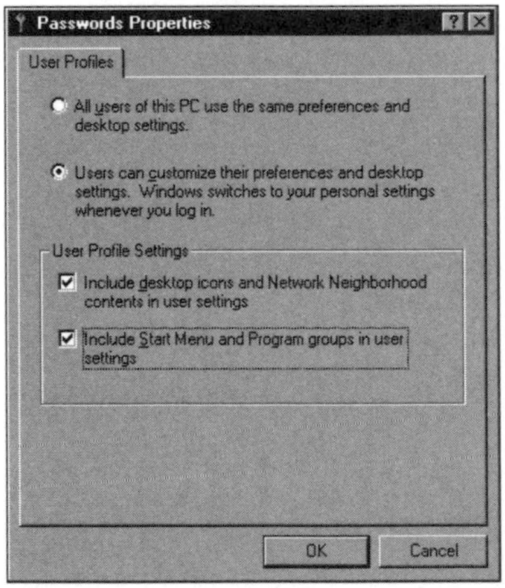

Figure 6-5:
You need to
set up a
user profile
before
giving out
passwords.

5. **Click OK.**

   Windows 95 asks if you want to restart your computer.

6. **Click Yes.**

   Now, you're ready to assign passwords. When your computer finishes restarting, the Welcome to Windows dialog box appears.

7. **Type your name in the User name field.**

8. **Type your password in the Password field.**

You actually don't have to type in a password to set a user profile if you don't want to. But if you do type a password, please write it down in a super-secret place so even if you forget it, you can still find it and use the computer again.

9. **Click OK.**

The Set Windows Password dialog box appears.

10. **Enter the password again in the Confirm new password text box.**

11. **Click OK.**

The Network dialog box appears.

12. **Click Yes to save your settings.**

Now customize to your heart's content. Windows memorizes the settings you have chosen and displays the desktop and Start menu you have chosen the next time you sign in with your name and password.

13. **Repeat all of this for each family member.**

Setting up user profiles and passwords for each family member is great, but one downside is that starting your computer will take longer. And everybody has to have some way to keep the password in a safe place, in case they forget.

Not every program lets you password-protect a file as you save it, but many do. For example, WordPad does not offer this option, but Word does. In the Save dialog box, click Options, and at the bottom of the page, under File Sharing options, type in your password; then go ahead saving the file. Afterwards, anyone who tries to open the file will be asked for a password. Unless you gave your password to everyone else, no one can open the file but you — that is, if you can remember your own password.

I Want Them All! Selecting a Bunch of Documents or Folders

Say you have more than one document or folder you want to open, move, copy, print, or chuck into the Recycle Bin. You can handle your files or folders one at a time, or you can round them up as a group and move, copy, or chuck them all at once.

But as with most things on Windows 95, you have several ways to accomplish your great roundup of documents or folders. Here are three ways to lasso a herd of documents and folders.

Why so many choices when we have so little time?

Question: Why does Windows 95 often have so many different ways to do the same thing?

Answer: Because, before Windows 95 there was Windows 3.1. And before Windows 3.1 there were earlier versions of Windows, and underneath those, various versions of the infamous disk-operating system called DOS. Each new version of Windows and DOS added

a new and sometimes faster way to do something, like selecting a bunch of folders. But so as not to offend the users of the older operating system, Microsoft kept in the old ways also. This is a great plus for the original consumer but a pain in the neck for newcomers, who can't decide which way is best.

Surrounding a bunch

This way works fine if you have a bunch of icons in a rough rectangle, and you want to select them all. In that situation, this method works quick as a mouse.

1. **Move your pointer to a space in the window near the corner of the group of icons representing the documents or folders.**

2. **Press the left mouse button down and drag diagonally over all the icons for the documents and folders, to form a box around them, as shown in Figure 6-6.**

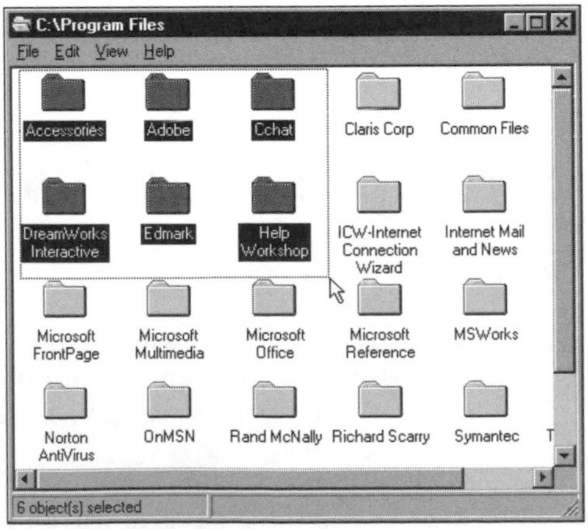

Figure 6-6:
Grab a bunch of folders (or files) at once.

Drag diagonally, and as you drag you see a rectangle appear, surrounding the icons for the documents or folders. (If you have used the selection rectangle in Paint, as described in Chapter 7, you will find this action easy and familiar.)

3. Release the mouse button.

Notice that the box disappears but the stuff you put the box around is highlighted. You have now selected all those documents or folders.

You can now issue commands that affect all the selected documents or folders. For example, on the File menu you can choose to open them all, print them all, or delete them all. From the Edit menu, you can ask Windows to make a copy of each file.

You can get the same effect by clicking the icon of a document or folder in one corner of the group, and then clicking the icon at the opposite corner — suddenly every icon in that imaginary rectangle gets highlighted.

Click and grab a bunch

Use this method when the icons or filenames for your documents or folders are all lined up in sequence in a straight column inside a window. (But make sure that you want every item in that column, because you can't leave anything out if it appears in the middle this way. For that kind of pickiness, see the next method.)

1. **Click the first (or top-most) icon or filename for a document or folder, and then hold down the Shift key.**

2. **Click the last file or folder that you want in the group, as shown in Figure 6-7.**

Figure 6-7:
Pick a set of
icons or
filenames
when they
appear
in a line.

Selecting All

Use this method when you want to select all the files in an open folder. Choose Edit⇨Select All. Notice all the files in that folder are now highlighted.

If you think this is fast, how about closing that folder and just selecting *its* icon?

Select the wrong document or folder? Just click anywhere outside the selection and the items are automatically deselected. That is, everything goes back to the way it was before you started messing with selecting a bunch at once.

Moving a Document or a Folder

Moving documents and folders to other locations is a lot like copying files (see Chapter 5 for the details on copying). Once again, we have the long way and the short way. Only this time, there's even a short-short way.

Slow: The traditional and ugh! long way

Some people like this method because you use the menu commands, and the pace is deliberate. No rushing here! Just follow these steps:

1. **Select the file or folder you want to move.**

2. **Choose Edit⇨Cut.**

3. **Select the folder to which you want to move your original document or folder into.**

4. **Choose Edit⇨Paste.**

Faster: Drag, drop, and forget it

You can use the ever easy and quick drag-and-drop method for moving documents or folders. (This method is easiest in My Computer.)

1. **Double-click My Computer, and open the folder that contains the document or folder you want to move.**

2. **Open the folder you want to hold the item you are going to move.**

   You now have two windows open, as shown in Figure 6-8.

3. **Drag the document or folder to its new location and release the mouse button.**

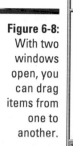

Figure 6-8:
With two
windows
open, you
can drag
items from
one to
another.

Not sure if you're moving or copying that file using drag and drop? To copy, you have to hold down the Ctrl key and then select the item and drag it over. To move, you just drag the item. Another way to tell is if you see the little square with a plus sign in it next to the document or folder you're dragging, go back and start again. That little square with the plus sign tells you that you're copying, *not* moving.

Fastest: One-handed drag and drop

Here's another way to move stuff around that's even easier on the memory cells:

1. **Point to the document or folder you want to move and then click the right mouse button.**

2. **Drag the file or folder to the place you want to move it to.**

3. **Release the right mouse button.**

   A shortcut menu pops up as seen in Figure 6-9.

4. **Select Move Here.**

Done!

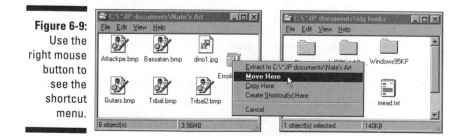

Figure 6-9:
Use the
right mouse
button to
see the
shortcut
menu.

Renaming a File or Folder

One minute you love the name you gave a file or folder, but in a few weeks you hate it. No prob. You're not married to that name. In fact, changing the name of a file or folder is a snap. Highlight the file and then pick whichever method turns you on:

> ✔ **Press the F2 key.**
>
> ✔ **Choose File⇨Rename.**
>
> ✔ **Click the filename (or the label underneath the icon) once.**

No matter which method you pick, you see a little box around the document or folder name letting you know you can type in the new name. Name away. After you have typed the new name, click elsewhere for the name to really take. Do this before you close the window — if you close the window while still editing the name, the name goes back to whatever it was before.

Trash It

If you begin to see folders in folders in your nightmares, and documents come flying at you in your dreams, perhaps it's time to do a little house-cleaning by getting rid of documents and programs you don't need anymore. That's where the funny looking Recycle Bin comes in. Throwing stuff in here when you don't need it anymore helps speed up your computer, too.

Microsoft calls this bin the Recycle Bin because in most cases where the document, folder, or program exists on your hard disk, you can recover the item if you change your mind. Not always. Not if the item starts on a floppy disk. But in most cases you can.

The first step in your housecleaning is to identify the documents and folders you don't need anymore. Look carefully at your Programs folder, too. See if there aren't any games or other applications that you installed but after awhile you just got bored with them. (But please check with your folks before dumping any software!) These are all candidates for the Recycle Bin. After you decide which items you want to dump, just follow these steps to get that junk on up and outta there:

1. **In either My Computer or Windows Explorer, select the document, folder, or program you want to throw out.**

2. **Choose File⇨Delete which brings up the Confirm File Delete dialog box shown in Figure 6-10.**

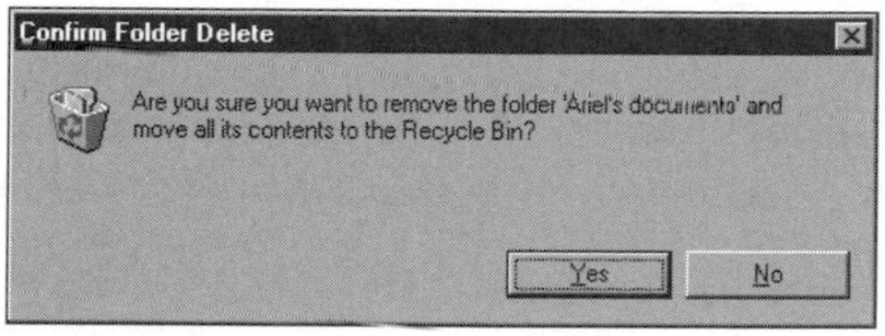

Figure 6-10:
This dialog
box makes
sure that
you really,
really want
to get rid of
that file.

Confirm Folder Delete ☒

Are you sure you want to remove the folder 'Ariel's documents' and move all its contents to the Recycle Bin?

Yes   No

3. Click Yes to delete the file, folder, or program.

The item drops into the Recycle Bin.

Just as you can either vacuum or sweep a floor to get rid of the dust, you have another way to toss files into the Recycle Bin. This method is definitely the vacuum one.

1. Select the document, folder, or program you want to toss.

2. Drag and drop it into the Recycle Bin.

The Recycle Bin does not have an unlimited memory. So if you go trash happy, keep in mind that it only holds a small amount. After this, the Recycle Bin automatically deletes the oldest files. When you want to permanently zap the files in the Recycle Bin from your computer forever, right-click the Recycle Bin to bring up a little pop-up menu. Click Empty Recycle Bin. Confirm that this is what you want to do. Another caution: If you are using programs originally written for Windows 3.1, their documents will be deleted as soon as you drag them to the Recycle Bin.

If you go on a cleaning frenzy and then decide that you chucked one too many files into the Recycle Bin, don't have a cow — you can get that file back. Remember, it's called the Recycle Bin, not the Incinerator.

1. Double-click the Recycle Bin.

The Recycle Bin's contents appears.

2. Drag the document, folder, or program out of there and drop it on your Desktop.

You can now drag it from there to a new location.

As you can see, the Recycle Bin is great for temporarily holding files and folders that you think you may want to permanently remove at some time in the near future. However, you probably should put it off limits for the younger kids in your family because once a file is gone, it's gone.

Flipping Floppies

To take your documents on the road so you can work on them with another computer, you have to first put them on a floppy disk for safe transport. Some floppies come ready for you to do this right out of their package. These floppies are *preformatted.* (If you're not sure whether your floppy disks are preformatted, look on the outside of the box they came in. If they're preformatted, it will say so right on the box.)

Formatting a new floppy disk

Many floppy disks are not preformatted. Those disks have to be *initialized* before you can add information on to them. Here's how to do that:

1. **Insert the floppy disk into the three-inch-wide disk drive with the label side up and the metal circle down.**

   If your disk drive is vertical, put the label side away from the little button that ejects disks.

2. **Double-click the My Computer icon or open Windows Explorer.**

3. **Select the drive the floppy's in, usually A.**

   A Format dialog box pops up.

4. **Click Start to say that you want to format the floppy.**

   The status bar shows you the progress of the formatting, which is always slow. At the end, you see a report on the results.

5. **Click Close to put away the report and then click Close to put away the Format dialog box.**

6. **Put a paper label on the disk, and as soon as you put material on the disk, write the name of the document, folder, or program on the label so you will know later what's on the disk.**

Formatting a used floppy

There are two reasons why you'd want to format a used floppy (a disk that already has stuff on it):

✔ You want to quickly erase everything on the disk.

✔ You don't know where the disk has been. You have no idea what the disk has been hanging out with, which means it may be infected with one of those ugly computer viruses that are the pits for your computer.

Flopping around

Floppy disks are about the size of your palm. They come in a hard plastic case, so they don't seem very floppy. But if you slide that metal cover back, you see a flimsy piece of plastic. That's actually a circle, or disk, in shape, and it spins around inside the container while the disk drive reads what is on the disk by pushing back that metal cover and sensing the alignmnent of little iron filings inside the plastic disk.

Compared to a floppy disk, a CD-ROM is a giant: Bigger than your hand, it holds more than 600 times as much information as a floppy disk. Most people don't have the hardware or software to store their documents on a CD-ROM yet, but in a few years you will probably be able to do that.

Don't take any chances. Go ahead and format a used floppy disk before putting your precious files on it. But make sure that this disk doesn't hold some of your own work that you need to save. If in doubt, use My Computer or Windows Explorer to view the contents and then format away, using the following steps:

1. **Insert the floppy disk into the disk drive.**

2. **Click the My Computer icon or start Windows Explorer.**

3. **Choose File⇨Format.**

   The Format dialog box pops up, as shown in Figure 6-11.

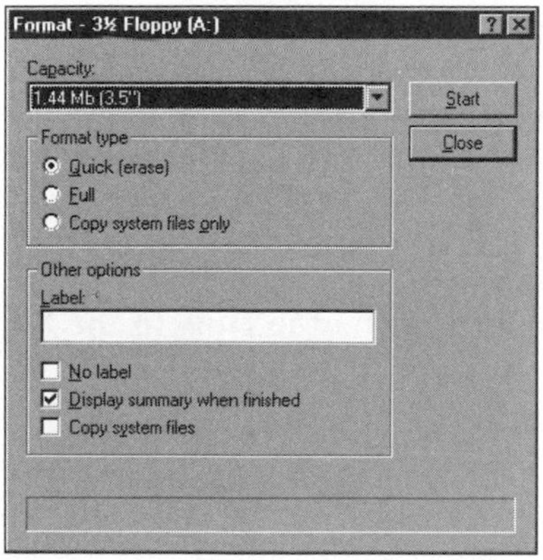

Figure 6-11:
Set your
fomatting
options
here.

4. Check the boxes that apply.

Wondering what the difference is between the Full and Quick Erase option? Quick Erase is great for saving a lot of time. It will go in and zap all the info off that floppy in no time (and you don't have to go to complete Steps 5 through 8). The downside to Quick Erase is that if this floppy is damaged in any way, you won't find out about it until after you copy a file or folder onto to it and try to use it again. As a general rule, if the disk is old, or been around a lot, choose the Full option. Ignore the Copy system file only option.

5. Type in a name (up to 11 characters) for the disk in the label text box.

6. Click Start to begin the formatting process.

When it's done, you get a note with a lot of gobblygook info in it. Smile and realize that sometimes Windows 95 can't help itself.

7. Click Close.

You go back to the Format dialog box.

8. Click Close to leave the Format dialog box.

Floppies' cases are made of real hard plastic and are very durable. But there are a few things you should never do with them:

- ✔ Never let your puppy use them as chew toys.
- ✔ Never let your little brother use one as a bathtub toy.
- ✔ Never leave them in direct sunlight or someplace where it is very hot.
- ✔ Never jerk the metal slide on the outside of the floppy back and forth when you have nothing better to do.

Copying to a floppy

People make copies of their documents or folders on a floppy disk for all sorts of reasons. Some do it so that they have a backup copy in case their computer crashes, and others want to transfer a document from one computer to another. Here's how to copy a document to a floppy disk.

1. Right-click on the file or folder you want to copy to the floppy disk, to bring up a pop-up menu.

2. Select Send To, which brings up another pop-up shown in Figure 6-12.

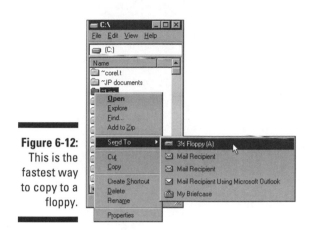

Figure 6-12:
This is the
fastest way
to copy to a
floppy.

3. Click 3¹/₂ Floppy (A).

The copying begins. You see a message showing the document being copied.
When that goes away, you can push the button on the disk drive to remove
your floppy and take it with you.

Chapter 7

Playing with the Free Programs in Windows 95

In This Chapter

▶ Scribbling away with WordPad

▶ Becoming an artist with Paint

▶ Adding it all up with the Calculator

Block head: What do you call a horse with no ears?

Smarty: Anything you want. He can't hear.

A computer without software would be as clueless as that horse. Microsoft figured out that after your family got Windows 95 installed, you'd want to do something fun and useful, so they added a bunch of free programs called *Accessories*. Accessories are like your belt and an earring or two — stuff you add on to show off.

Of course, Microsoft didn't want to lose any sales of their really big programs, like their monster word-processing program, Word. So they made these accessories, well, for kids. Accessories are trial size, like those tiny toothpastes your mom gets when you go on vacation trips or to camp.

But even though they're small, these Accessories are great. You get:

▶ **WordPad:** Lets you write so somebody else can read it, and you don't get a cramp in your hand. It isn't fancy, but it can make your homework look great.

▶ **Paint:** Lets you be a real artist with fantastic colors and weird shapes and funny pictures that make your letters, reports, and drawings really stand out.

▶ **Calculator:** Hey number lovers! If you like to keep stats on your games or add up how much money you just made mowing lawns, the Calculator program does just what your calculator does at school — like, add, subtract, multiply, and even do high school math.

Macho programmers don't consider any of these accessory programs big and powerful programs or applications, so they call them *applets*.

If you can't find one of these accessories, someone may have accidentally left it out during installation. To add an accessory, get your Windows 95 installation disk ready and then do the following:

1. Put your Windows installation disk in the CD-ROM drive.

2. Choose Start⇨Settings⇨Control Panel.

The Control Panel window opens, advertising a bunch of useful little programs, as shown in Figure 7-1.

Figure 7-1:
The Control Panel lists programs that let you twiddle the controls on Windows 95.

3. Double-click the Add/Remove Programs icon.

In a moment, you see the Add/Remove Programs Properties dialog box with several tabs, as shown in Figure 7-2.

4. Click the Windows Setup tab.

This tab displays a list of the different software components you can add to your version of Windows 95. (You have probably already installed some of these programs.)

5. Double-click Accessories to see the list of accessories.

As shown in Figure 7-3, the accessories you have already installed have check marks next to them.

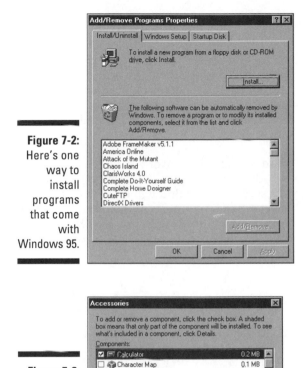

Figure 7-2:
Here's one
way to
install
programs
that come
with
Windows 95.

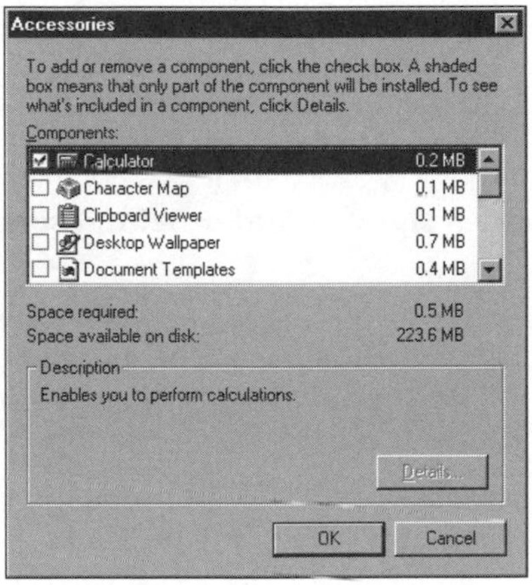

Figure 7-3:
Check
marks
appear next
to any
Accessories
you have
already
installed.

6. **Click the accessories that you want to add and click OK twice.**

   Windows 95 copies all the accessories onto your hard disk. After
   Windows 95 finishes installing, you can find your list of programs in the
   Start menu, under the heading Accessories.

7. **Click the X in the top-right corner of the Control Panel window to get
   rid of the window.**

Writing with WordPad

Hey, no more pencil! Using WordPad, you can write down the secret codes for your new game and be sure that you can read them the next day. You can list the members in your club without having to worry if your pencil's sharp. WordPad is simply slick. WordPad appears on your screen in a flash, letting you write something down while it's still fresh in your mind — and then you can print out your thoughts to show everyone.

If you've already used a "real" word processor like Word or WordPerfect, you'll notice that WordPad doesn't do some fancy stuff like columns, headers, or footers. It can't check your spelling, and, although it can look for a word you typed somewhere, it can't find a tab or paragraph mark. If you find yourself saying, "So what?" WordPad is for you. You can use WordPad and spend the money you would have put into Word on a dozen trips to fast food heaven or one all-day visit to the amusement park.

Gimme something to write on — fast!

Got the code for disarming the space geek? Call up WordPad to write it down. Here's how:

1. **Choose Start⇨Programs, which shows a folder behind some kind of open window**.

   Effect! As soon as the pointer hits Programs, a big menu opens up, with all your applications, plus stuff you may never have heard of. But — hey — here's the good news: The Accessories show up at the top of that menu. They're usually Numbah One.

2. **Slide the pointer onto Accessories, and then, in the menu that opens up, slide down to the very last item, which is WordPad.**

   Slipping and sliding? Having trouble slithering down through all these menus? That's natural. They're hard to handle. So don't blame yourself. By the way: Because each menu seems to pour out of another, like a big waterfall, Microsoft calls these *cascading menus*.

   Squint! Can you make out what that picture is on the menu? The WordPad icon is a pen on an open pad, as shown in Figure 7-4.

Figure 7-4:
The wonder that is the WordPad icon.

3. Click the WordPad icon.

Ta da! In a moment, WordPad opens in its own window, as shown in Figure 7-5. All that white space is where you can write whatever you want.

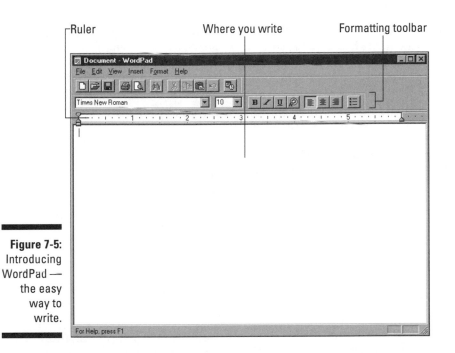

Figure 7-5:
Introducing
WordPad —
the easy
way to
write.

4. Type away.

Mess up? If you make a mistake, just back up over the typo by pressing the Backspace key. It's above the Enter key, near the F12 function key, if you have one. Backing up is the easiest way to erase a goof.

Don't throw that away! Saving what you've done

Some stuff you just write and print and *that's it!* Forget it. As Arnold says, it's history. You'll never use it again. But if you are working on a long paper, or you want to print something out and see what other folks think, you should save your work.

Saving takes what you have written and puts it on the big hard disk inside your computer for safekeeping. Saving your work means you don't have to do it all over again later if your baby brother pulls out the power cord and the computer goes dead, literally forgetting everything you wrote. You should save whenever you take a break or after you've been typing for awhile. And you should always save before exiting the program. Saving only takes a few seconds — but you'll be glad you did.

Saving 101

Here's some great news! All Windows programs let you save your document the same way. (If you get this down, you can save anything!) Just follow these steps:

1. Choose File⇨Save.

You see the Save As dialog box, as shown in Figure 7-6.

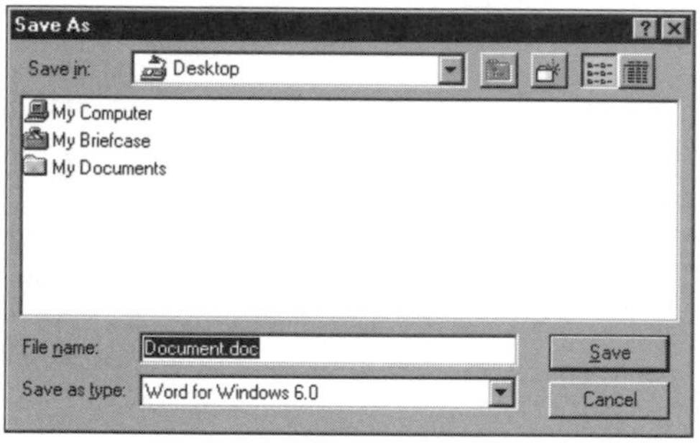

Figure 7-6:
To save, you fill in this form, called the Save As dialog box.

Save As	? ✕
Save in:	Desktop
My Computer	
My Briefcase	
My Documents	
File name:	Document.doc	Save
Save as type:	Word for Windows 6.0	Cancel

At the top of the dialog box, you can see where the program proposes to save your document. WordPad likes to save your document on the Desktop. It's really not your desk's top, but the top level of the computer, which is set up like a giant filing cabinet. (Sometimes WordPad suggests a folder called My Documents, which is okay, too.)

For now you can just accept the location suggested by WordPad. (See Chapter 6 to find out more about putting files in different places.)

2. In the box called File Name, type a name for your document and then click Save.

That's the quick and simple route. WordPad saves your document on the Desktop, or in a folder called My Documents — unless you changed the location shown at the top of the window in the Save In text box.

The first time you save, you have to invent a name for the document. But only the first time. If you do more work, luckily, WordPad remembers that name, so when you have done some more writing and want to save the new version, you don't have to type it in again.

Up to about fourth grade, kids may need you or older siblings to help with saving, mostly because this process is so verbal. Encourage kids to call for your help when they are finished using WordPad.

Saving a WordPad document for a friend — or for school

Just as a Nintendo game cartridge won't fit in a Sega machine, a WordPad file may not work in some other word-processing program. So if you want to use your WordPad file in some other program, or if you want to give it to a friend who uses some other program, you have to save it in a file format that that program can read.

You start out by saving like you usually do (back up to "Saving 101" in this chapter if you need to brush up on your saving techniques). Then, in the Save As dialog box, you have to fill in the box called Save As Type by picking a format from a list. One of the following choices should do the trick:

- **For Word users:** Use Word for Windows 6 if they have Word Version 6 or later. If not, use Rich Text Format (RTF).

- **For other WordPad users:** Use Word for Windows 6 because this format keeps all your boldface and color.

- **For people with any other program**: Use Text Document. Any decorations such as boldfacing, italics, font choices, or colors get thrown away. All that's left are the actual letters and numbers and a few characters like paragraph marks. But every word processor can read these files, and so can thousands of other programs. By the way: You'll hear other terms for this kind of file: Text Only and ASCII, pronounced *ASK-ee*.

After you make your selection in the Save As Type box, you can proceed to name your file and click the Save button. Your document should be all set to go!

Playing with the size of the type

Changing the size of various words helps your words stand out in a flyer, report, or even a letter. Look at that flyer you brought home from school advertising Little League sign-ups or swimming lessons; notice how some sentences are bigger than others. Which do you notice first?

Try this: Change the size of the characters in WordPad so that every letter typed shows up dramatically. This way, typing a whole word seems like a big deal.

1. **In the bottom toolbar, click the down arrow next to the 10 in the second text box, right next to the big B button.**

   Whoa! What's this list of numbers? Those are different sizes. The letters on the screen can be almost any size you want, as shown in Figure 7-7.

Figure 7-7:
Pick a size,
any size.

You don't have to know this. But did you wonder what the heck these numbers refer to? Like, 10 what? Well, it is 10 points. These points come out of the way printers used to measure the hot metal they poured to make up characters. An inch is made up of 72 points. So if you want a letter that's half an inch high, you would pick 36. Now, for a quarter inch — hey, I said you could forget it. Just pick big numbers for big letters, and you'll do fine.

2. **Slide your pointer down to 24 and then click.**

   The list jumps back, and 24 appears in the Size box.

   Now everything that you or your grandma type will be more than twice as large as before. Blowing up the size helps people who aren't familiar with typing. Every time they hit the right key they get a big reward. So let the hunting and pecking begin!

Putting your names in lights — together

Everybody likes to see their name on-screen. It's like being famous. Even the Spice Girls like to see their names on MTV. So, even if you aren't Buffy the Vampire Slayer, or Seinfeld, you can spotlight your name in WordPad. And if you're working together with a beginner, like Grandma, you can make the process of learning a lot more fun by focusing on, you guessed it, your names.

To make your names stand out in black and white, follow these steps:

1. **Type a letter in WordPad describing how much you and Grandma (or whomever you're working with on the computer) have figured out about WordPad.**

2. **On-screen, select your names by clicking on one side and dragging the pointer through the letters, highlighting them all.**

3. **Play with different fonts, by going to the Format bar and pointing to the down arrow to the right of the text box that starts off saying Times New Roman, sliding down to another font, and clicking it.**

To see what this font does to the names, click outside the name to remove the highlighting. (You may want to print the text and hold it up next to the screen, to spot the differences between the screen and paper versions.)

4. **For more magic, select all the letters again and click the B button on the Format bar to make the letters bold, I to make them italic, or U to make them underlined, as shown in Figure 7-8.**

Figure 7-8:
Icons for
boldfacing,
italics,
underlining,
and adding
color.

Even if you don't have a color printer, your monitor can display text in color, so select some text, click the button that looks like a painter's palette, click a color, and then click somewhere else in the white space to see the results. Presto! The text changes color!

Making smiley faces

Want to send a secret message or tell someone how you're feeling about what you just said? Use *emoticons* — that's a fancy word meaning icons that let you draw a picture showing how you feel. Most people just call these gizmos Smiley Faces. For instance, to show that you are smiling you can type **:)**

Turn this book around a quarter turn to the right: See the two eyes? See the smiling mouth? You can make smiley faces out of a lot of the characters the computer lets you type. For instance, you can add a nose to your face by typing a minus sign, like this: **:-)**

If you're shocked, you could show your open mouth this way: **:-o**

When grownups look at these things, they may just see a bunch of punctuation. It doesn't mean anything. But you — and your buds — know the secret. (Invisible ink.) To see the face, you have to tilt your head to the left to see its eyes in the right place (or print the stuff out and tilt the paper to the side).

Table 7-1 shows some smileys to try out on your friends.

Table 7-1	Way Out There Emoticons
Secret code	*Means*
:-(	I'm sad.
[]	I give you a hug.
:-x	I give you a kiss.
:-b	I'm sticking my tongue out at you.
<:-)	I'm an idiot (in a dunce cap).
B-)	I'm cool (wearing wraparound shades).
[:-l]	A robot.
$-)	I see money!

Sometimes Windows grabs the punctuation and turns it into a real smiley face (or sad face). If you just want the secret code, press the Backspace key and Windows will lay off.

Showing off with WordPad

Sometimes you just have to show off. Like if you want to put up an ad for your babysitting business or you are putting together an invitation for your birthday party. Or — bummer — if you have to create Science Fair write-ups, book reports, or meeting notes for a school club. Whatever the reason, you can make everyone ooh and ahh at the way WordPad makes your writing look.

Here are a few tricks that you can use to earn a wow — and maybe an A for presentation (content, unfortunately, takes more work):

✔ Make more room around the text by choosing File⇨Page Setup. You see the Page Setup dialog box, as shown in Figure 7-9. Type new numbers in the Margin boxes and click OK.

✔ Insert a picture or map created in the Paint accessory (see "Drawing with Flare Using Paint," later in this chapter, for the details on Paint) and copied to the Clipboard. Choose Edit⇨Paste. Nudge the graphic right by clicking to its left and pressing the spacebar. (To WordPad, art's just one giant letter.)

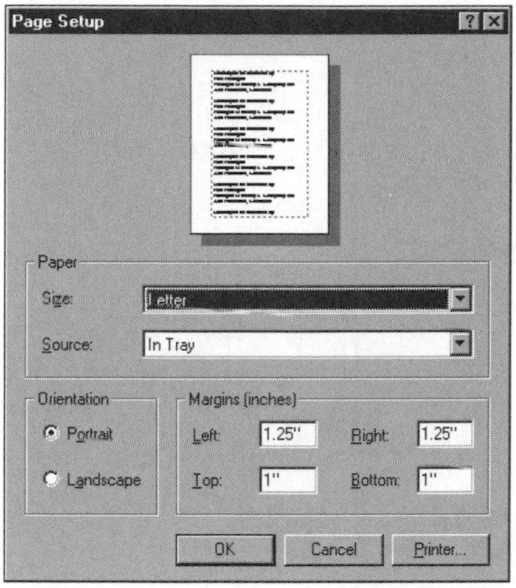

Figure 7-9:
The Page
Setup
dialog box
lets you
change
margins,
page
size, and
orientation.

> ✔ Select a few paragraphs and turn them into a bulleted list by clicking the Bullets icon on the bottom toolbar (it's the last icon on the right).

Correcting a massive error

Omygosh! You just typed your whole report on dinosaurs, and you spelled Barney's name wrong all the way through. What to do? You can have WordPad replace one word with another throughout your report, saving you endless hours. Heck, you may even save so much time that you can still catch your favorite TV show. Just follow these steps and let WordPad take care of all the work:

1. **Choose Edit⇨Replace.**

2. **Type the mistake in the Find What box.**

3. **Type the right spelling in the Replace With box.**

4. **Click Replace All.**

Opening a file in WordPad

If you have been working on a document in WordPad and try to open another one, WordPad assumes you want to put away the first document. If you want two documents open, each in its own window, start another version of the program just the way you started it the first time. That way, you have two WordPad windows open, each with its own document.

Here's how to open a file in WordPad:

1. **Choose File⇨Open.**

   You see the Open dialog box, as shown in Figure 7-10.

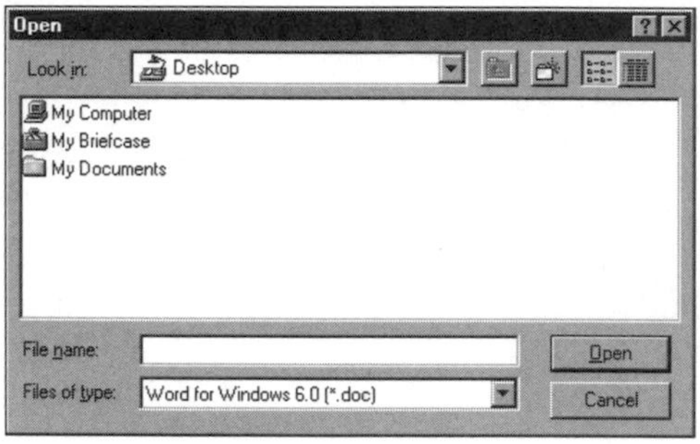

Figure 7-10:
This dialog
box lets
you tell
WordPad
which
document
to open
next.

Open	? X
Look in: 🖳 Desktop	
🖳 My Computer	
🖳 My Briefcase	
📁 My Documents	
File name:	Open
Files of type: Word for Windows 6.0 (*.doc)	Cancel

2. **Click the filename.**

   (You may have to scroll up and down to spot the file you want, or move to another location if you have saved it somewhere other than in the My Documents folder.)

3. **Click Open.**

   The file appears in the WordPad window.

So your friend wrote up all the master codes for 18 levels and five warlords — but that was on some other word processor. Ask your friend to save the document in one of the following formats that WordPad can open:

- ✔ Word for Windows 6
- ✔ Rich Text Format
- ✔ Text Document

Then you can open it in WordPad.

Get that on paper! Wow — your own printout

Printout — that's what nerds call the stuff that comes out of your printer. You can take what you see on-screen and have it put on paper in less than a minute. (Less time than it takes Nick at Night to advertise three shows.) You, too, can be an author with a published, printed body of work.

Filename tailgaters tell you what kind of file you're looking at

Wonder how to tell what format a file is in? See if the filename has a dot at the end, and three letters after that — a suffix. If that tag at the end says .txt, you have a Text Document. .rtf means a Rich Text Format. And .doc, well, that means the file may have come from Word or WordPerfect, both of which tack that abbreviation on, so you just have to go ahead and try to open it and see what happens. (The geeks and their companies have just not agreed on standards, so you have to hope you get lucky.)

If the filename has no suffix, click the Details icon at the far right of the Open dialog box and look in the column devoted to Type. In that column, you see an indication that a file is Rich Text Format, Word, or Text (covering both Text formats).

And if you're working with a beginner — young or old — printing their work makes them feel like they are getting somewhere. Just follow these steps to print out your masterpiece in WordPad:

1. **Turn on the printer.**

2. **Choose File⇨Print.**

   You see the Print dialog box, as shown in Figure 7-11.

3. **Click OK to get a printout of what has just been typed.**

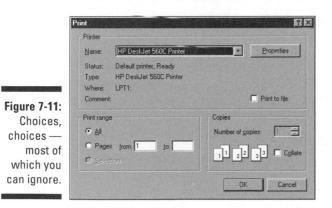

Figure 7-11:
Choices, choices — most of which you can ignore.

Drawing with Flare Using Paint

What's so cool about art, anyway? It's messy — all that paint all over, and the crumpled paper, and the cleanup. And at school, some teachers make you feel like an idiot if your picture doesn't come out looking like something real.

Well, chill. Paint makes art fun again, the way it was back in kindergarten.

Paint's electronic, so you don't have to go wash up every two seconds, and it gives you all those neat colors and tools. Like an electronic pencil that makes lines on the screen, a brush that does whole wide swatches in swirls, a spray can (don't tell the principal) that airbrushes colors, and, thank goodness, an eraser. Can't draw a straight line? Let Paint do that for you — plus perfect rectangles, ovals, circles, and squares.

Make neat posters to put up on the refrigerator. Paint a big face and then print it out for a mask for Halloween. Invent gift cards and wrapping paper.

The worst thing you can do to an artist is ask, "What is that thing?" We all may take our inspiration from the real world, but we may not have the skills to create realistic pictures. Don't discourage the artist by pointing out that tree bark is rarely purple. Instead, just ask the artist to tell you something about the picture.

Opening your Paint can

To start Paint, follow these steps:

1. **Click Start, slide over Programs, and glide up to Accessories.**

2. **Click the Paint icon, which looks a little like a scrunched-up bunch of brushes, if you have a good imagination.**

   You see the Paint window, as shown in Figure 7-12.

If you're working on the same picture over several sessions, you can open the picture from the bottom of the File menu, which lists the last four files saved. (This lets you skip the Open dialog box.)

Step back, Leonardo! You're exploring the Paint tools

Go crazy. Using Paint is like being let loose in the Art room — with no one to supervise and nothing you *have* to do. Feel free to explore the Paint tools, "just to see what happens."

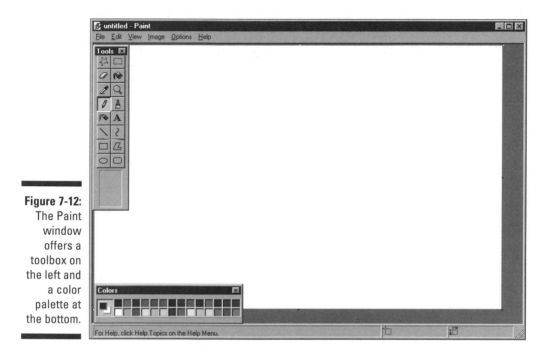

Figure 7-12:
The Paint
window
offers a
toolbox on
the left and
a color
palette at
the bottom.

The tools show up on the left of the Paint window in an area called a *toolbox*. Click any tool and move the pointer over to the big white canvas, click there, and sketch.

Table 7-2 shows the tools that most people enjoy (with their icons on the left).

Table 7-2	**Paint Tools**	
Tool	*Name*	*What It Does*
	Pencil	Makes lines. Good for a few minutes of squiggle-squaggle, but hard to draw with. A loser.
	Color Palette	Awesome! Lets you pick colors to draw with or put in the background. Click a color to draw with. Right-click to select a color for the background. Imagine there are two layers you can work with — like a plastic sheet on top of a piece of paper.
	Brush	Swoops and paints. Works more like a felt-tip pen with interchangeable tips. To change tips, click the Brush icon and then click one of the tips offered at the bottom of the tool palette.

(continued)

Table 7-2 *(continued)*

Tool	Name	What It Does
	Airbrush	Really a spray can, but renamed so you don't get the idea of spraying graffiti. The longer you spray at one place, the more color goes on. Neat idea: Try moving the airbrush around quickly, to see what happens.
	Straight Line	Yes, that's what it makes. Click to start, drag in any direction, and click to stop. For dramatic effects, change to the thickest width, down at the bottom of the tool palette.
	Rectangle	Makes a rectangle when you drag diagonally. Hold down the Shift key to make a perfect square.
	Ellipse (or oval)	Makes an egg-shaped circle. Great favorite, because it's so hard to draw one freehand. To make a perfect circle, hold down the Shift key as you drag.
	Paint Bucket	Wow! Here's a chance to pour paint all over. The paint fills up any figure like a rectangle or an oval. But if you have even the tiniest little hole in the edge, the paint seeps through and fills up whatever it can reach.
	Star (Free-form select)	Lets you carve out any chunk of the picture and move it somewhere else (leaving a hole where it was). Allows massive destruction of the original picture. Draw around whatever you want to capture and then click the shimmering selection, drag it where you want it, and click outside of the selection to drop it there.
	Select	Lets you select a rectangular chunk of the picture by dragging diagonally over an area; you can then drag the chunk elsewhere and drop it there by clicking outside the selection. You can also use the Edit commands to copy this chunk and then paste it somewhere else in the image, or in another document, as described in Chapter 6.
	Eraser	Peels away the paint on the foreground layer, revealing the background color of the moment. (Try the super size!) Very satisfying!

When encouraging timid beginners (like your younger brother or sister), you may want to demonstrate what the tools do. You may find that once they see you use it, they want to try — and they will probably want to experiment with it for five or ten minutes. When they can handle a few tools, here are some projects you can team up to try — each person does a part, taking turns.

- ✔ **Silly patterns:** Use as many tools and colors as you can.
- ✔ **Boxes on top of boxes on top of boxes:** Draw shapes that stand in front of each other.
- ✔ **Every different width and color of line:** Like pick-up sticks.
- ✔ **Window decorations:** Snowflakes, pumpkins, and hearts you can put up in a window at your house so neighbors see.

If you like colors and lines and surprises, you'll be a fan of Paint. But unless you're already an accomplished cartoonist or architect, the images tend to be a little fuzzy — colorful, but impressionistic. For pictures that look like real things, you should turn to programs aimed at folks who want to prepare home plans, diagrams, or maps; or photo-editing software; or clipart prepared by professionals. See Chapter 9 for descriptions of software for the whole family. (Check out samples on our CD-ROM.)

A neat trick: Replacing one color with another

You can erase one color and replace it with another, without affecting anything else:

1. **Click the Eraser.**
2. **In the color palette, click the color you want to get rid of.**
3. **Right-click the color you want to replace the old color with.**
4. **Hold down the right mouse button as you erase. Amazingly, the old color gets replaced with the new.**

Your friend wants to give you a picture. Can you open it? Well, you can open any *bitmapped* file in Paint — they are the ones with the extension .bmp, for, yes, bitmap. A lot of commercial clipart comes in this format, so you may be able to open a picture of a car, change its color, and then use the new version in a WordPad document, using the Clipboard as described in Chapter 5.

Psst . . . The secret behind Paint

With Paint, you are actually building the picture dot by dot. Your screen is like a theater marquee with thousands of lightbulbs. To make an image, you turn on each bulb as you need it.

Originally, programmers could make each dot with a single bit (a zero or a one, standing for on or off). Now, with color, each dot needs a few more of these computer bits to represent each speck of color, leading to terms you hear in ads: 7-bit, 24-bit, and so on, depending on how many colors you want to use. Paint is a 7-bit program, which is about as simple as it gets with colors.

But how can Paint keep track of all the bulbs that are on? Well, it keeps a map of the screen — really a grid, like old-fashioned graph paper — and marks the location of every dot you make. That chart is called a *bitmap*, because it helps the computer keep track of each bit.

What difference does this make? Well, it means that when you draw a line and let go of it, you can't easily pick it up as a unit. It disintegrates into individual dots. (In a more advanced program, called drawing software, the line would be considered a single object, and could be picked up with a click.) Like a watercolor sketch, when you make a change to a Paint picture, that's it: You have wiped out what was there before, and you can't get it back except by reaching for the Edit➪Undo.

Also, when you want the picture to be a certain size, you must choose Attributes from the Image menu and say exactly what the width and height will be, in dots. On-screen, the dots are called *pixels*. Many screens have 72 pixels per inch. So if you wanted a picture the size of a thumb, you might specify the dimensions as 72 x 72. Or you could switch to inches and use those.

Unfortunately, your printer may not make dots the same size as your screen. Your bitmapped picture may come out a lot smaller on paper, because the dots are smaller. Experiment so you know what to expect.

Really getting into Paint

If you get serious about painting with Paint, you may want to really explore some of its tools and commands.

Magnifying

If you really want to get precise, click the Magnifier and move its rectangle to the section you want to work on and then click to blow up that portion of the image. Choose the Pencil to work dot by dot, as shown in Figure 7-13.

Labeling

Use the Text tool (the big A) to add a name for a thingamajig in your picture.

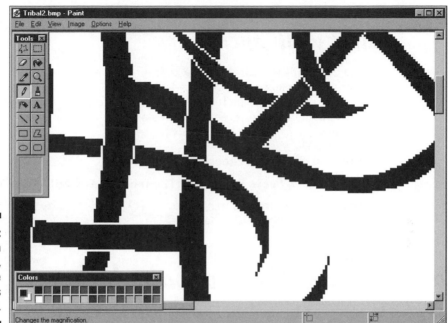

Figure 7-13:
When
magnified,
your picture
shows
every dot.

Remember, when you are finished entering letters, they (and their background rectangle) become part of the picture and wipe out whatever lies below them.

Moving or cutting chunks

When you remove a chunk of your painting, you leave a hole in the foreground, and see, well, sometimes white behind it, sometimes some other color. How come? Well, Paint fills the background with whatever color you currently have set for the background color.

Want to see more of your picture?

Click the margin of the toolbox or color palette and drag it somewhere else. You're tearing them off and setting them free to float around the screen.

Using your picture in another program

Choose Edit⇨Select All and then choose Copy on the same menu. Go to the other program and choose Edit⇨Paste. (Try this with WordPad, to spruce up your letter to Grandma.)

Hate the whole picture?

Choose Clear Image from the Image menu. You get a clean canvas, all stretched and ready to paint.

Put your picture up on the screen — and call it wallpaper!

Yes, you can point with pride to the computer screen when you turn your own picture into wallpaper so your friends see it as soon as the computer starts. You can place the picture in just the middle of the screen or have it plastered up all over the screen, like tiles on your bathroom wall. Just follow these steps:

1. **Save the picture by choosing File⇨Save.**

2. **Choose File⇨Set as Wallpaper (Tiled) or Set as Wallpaper (Centered).**

    Your picture shows up behind the Start button and any icons you have on your desktop. You are famous.

Total It Up with Your Calculator

Do you use a calculator at school? If so, here's one on the computer, and it works just about the same way.

Need to add up the costs so you can put the correct total in a letter to your team? The Calculator accessory lets you make a quick calculation, and then get back to your work in another application.

Opening your number cruncher

Pop Calculator up like you would any other accessory by choosing Start⇨Programs⇨Accessories⇨Calculator. You see the computerized Calculator as in Figure 7-14.

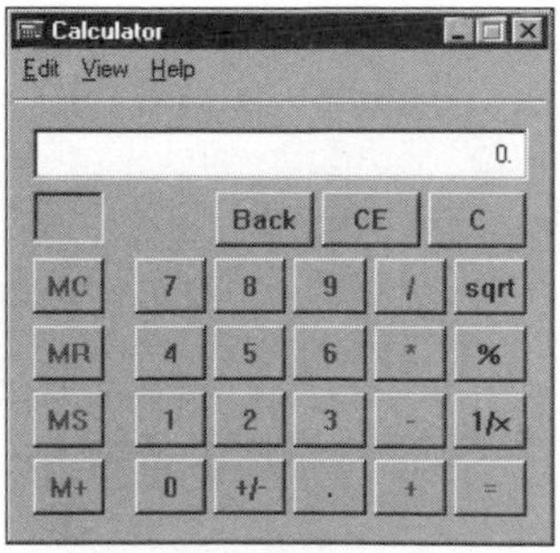

Figure 7-14:
The Calculator, when it first appears, lets you do simple calculations.

When the Calculator first opens, you can perform the following simple feats on it:

✔ To enter numbers or operators like the plus sign, point to the buttons on the screen, or Click the NumLock key and then use the numeric keypad over on the right side of your keyboard. Use the asterisk (*) for "multiplied by" and / for "divided by."

✔ To copy the results to another application, choose Edit➪Copy, go to the other program's document, and choose Edit➪Paste. Copying this way makes sure that you don't accidentally let a typo creep in when you are trying to type a number such as 3.14159265359.

Crunching your numbers

If the teacher approves, you can certainly use the Calculator to do addition, subtraction, multiplication, division, and square roots. So it's great for homework. (Many schools have incorporated calculators into the curriculum, but only on certain assignments. If in doubt, check with the teacher.)

1. **Start the Calculator and click its C button to clear the display so you can begin with a clean slate.**

2. **Type the first number, using the number keys at the top of the keyboard, or clicking the numbers shown in the Calculator on-screen.**

   Or, if you want to use the numeric keypad (the clump of keys with numbers and a plus sign and a giant Enter key), click the NumLock key, and then use the other keys in that clump.

3. **Choose a math operator, such as the plus sign, minus sign, multiplication sign (that's the asterisk *), or division sign (the slash /) to tell the Calculator what arithmetic job you want to do.**

4. **Enter the next number.**

5. **Press Enter or click the equal sign on the screen to get the answer.**

To add a bunch of numbers in a row, just keep pressing Enter, then the plus sign, and the next number. You can get some kicks out of adding up your grades, getting the total, and then dividing by the number of grades to get your average before your teacher does. Try getting your batting average the same way.

Mmmm

Wonder what those buttons on the left do? Well they help the Calculator remember stuff. The M stands for Memory. And you maybe thought the first one was the host of the show, the MC, and then there was a couple, Mr. and Ms., and their little child M+. Nope. MC clears out memory, so the Calculator will forget whatever you asked it to remember before. MR makes the Calculator recall what it memorized, displaying the number, so you can work on it again. MS forces it to store a number in memory. And M+ adds the current number in the display to whatever number you put in memory. Useful for long or complicated arithmetic, where you have to combine the result of one calculation with another.

Going exponential

If you're in high school and need more than arithmetic and square roots, you can choose Scientific from the View menu and use the dozens of extra statistical, log, and trig functions. The functions go beyond science, though, and let you do some programming and statistics as well.

Complicated? Sure. You can group terms in 25 levels of parentheses, if you want. Here's how to enter numbers in scientific notation:

1. **Choose View⇨Scientific.**

   You see the Scientific View, as shown in Figure 7-15.

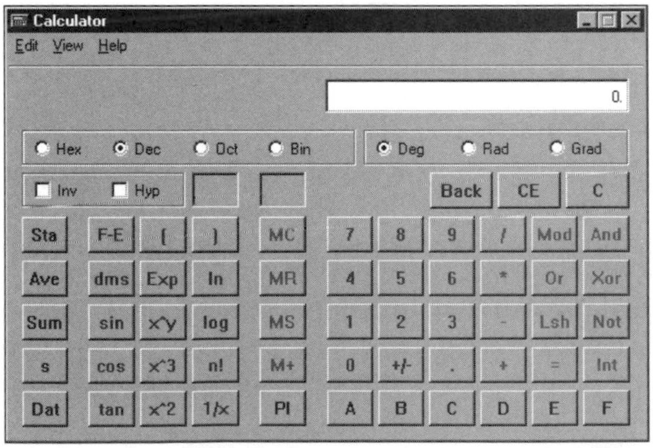

Figure 7-15: The Calculator's other face: Meet Mr. Science.

2. **Enter the significant digits (the number you want to raise to a power).**

3. **Click the Exp button.**

4. If the exponent is going to be negative, click the +/- button.

5. Type the exponent and press Enter.

Mostly we work in the decimal system — for example, dimes and dollars, tens and hundreds. But if you want to work in binary (to the base 2, that is, with just two digits, a zero and a one, to work with), octal (to the base 8), or hexadecimal (to the base 16), click the radio button at the upper left, and proceed. (Many of the Scientific Calculator buttons only work in the decimal system, but the letters A to F at the bottom of the numeric button pad on-screen are for entering the hex digits above 9, and only work when you turn on the hexadecimal system.) Aren't you glad you have a hex calculator?

A Sneak Peek at Windows 98

In This Chapter

▶ Making your desktop active

▶ Switching between a Classic Windows 95 desktop and the new Web-style desktop

▶ Clicking once where you used to have to click twice

▶ Piling up toolbars on top of the taskbar

▶ Expanding and "Webifying" the Start menu

▶ Finding people and Web sites as well as folders and files

▶ Putting Web info on the desktop

▶ Using "channels" to bring information from the Web onto your screen

▶ Browsing in My Computer and Windows Explorer

▶ Taking advantage of Outlook Express for e-mail and newsgroups

▶ Meeting on the Net

▶ Multiplying your screens

▶ Watching TV on your computer

You've heard about it. You may even have played with parts of it. Now you can find out what all the buzz is about. Here's your sneak peek at the features in Windows 98.

For an in-depth look at Windows 98, pick up a copy of *Windows 98 For Dummies*, by Andy Rathbone, published by IDG Books Worldwide, Inc.

Getting Your Machine Ready for Windows 98

You can run Windows 98 on the same machine you have now. You don't have to make any changes.

What's the Big Deal about Windows 98?

Do you have to get the new Windows right away? No. You can get along just fine with Windows 95 for another six months or a year — and that's a long time with computers. All the programs you run today will run on Windows 98.

But will you want to have Windows 98 in a year or so? Yes, because the big new games will depend on its power, graphics, and multimedia pizzazz. The newer the software you want to use, the more you will need to trade up to Windows 98 to get all the features the software vendors advertise on TV.

If you are already using the World Wide Web, you'll feel right at home with a lot of the new features of Windows 98. But if you don't have an Internet connection yet, you can postpone buying Windows 98 until you sign up for one. The big bang in Windows 98 is on the Web, so if you aren't already on the Web, and don't want to be, forget Windows 98. You don't need it.

Tempted? Here's a list of the hot new features coming in Windows 98:

- ✔ You can keep using an interface that works just the way Windows 95 does, or you can switch to an interface that works the way the Web does.

- ✔ You can put Web pages up on the desktop, so you can quickly click them and get online. That's called making your desktop active.

- ✔ You can open a file with a single click — no more of that hard-on-the-finger double-clicking.

- ✔ You can put tons more information on your taskbar if you want.

- ✔ You can put favorite sites and documents into the Start menu, and you get faster access to settings and online updates.

- ✔ You can make a Web site send you information like a TV channel beaming you the news. Later, you can log off and read the new info from your hard disk, without paying for the time you are on the Web.

- ✔ You get a new look at My Computer and Windows Explorer.

- ✔ You get new accessories like Quick View (to see what a file looks like even if you don't have the program) and a tool for making your own Web pages.

- ✔ You can finally bring together all your e-mail addresses and use a new utility, Outlook Express, to route your e-mail and take you to newsgroups on the Internet.

✔ You can set up your own chat sessions over the Web without having to use the public chat rooms of America Online or Microsoft Network.

✔ You can share a drawing with a friend as you build it together over the Web using an electronic version of the whiteboard you have at school.

✔ If you have a video camera and the right hookup, you can have a video phonecall, watching each other as you speak, over the Internet.

✔ You can even hook up your TV antenna or cable to the computer and watch regular shows next to your programs.

Some of the new features depend on your buying a second monitor, a video camera, or acquiring a higher-speed modem to connect to the Internet. Some of the farthest-out features, such as the ability to interact with a TV program via the Web, also depend on Microsoft persuading lots of other companies to support them — which may not happen.

The Weblike Desktop: You Can Turn It On or Off

And you thought your desktop was active enough, what with soda cans falling over, candy piling up, papers all over, and old socks rotting away underneath the debris. No, no, — we're talking about the other desktop — the one on your computer. And Windows 98 does make that desktop a heck of a lot more Weblike than ever before. You can jump from your desk to the Web and back, as if your hard disk were a Web site, and a Web site was as easy to open as a document on your own computer. That's hyperactive.

You get your choice. You can either look at the desktop the way you have in Windows 95 — now called the Classic Windows desktop — or check out the Weblike Desktop. The active way of looking at the world lets you see beyond your own computer to the whole World Wide Web. You can put Web pages right on the desktop so you can click one any time and go directly to those sites. It's as if you were Webmaster of the World. (You can read more about the World Wide Web in Chapter 10. Or you can pick up *World Wide Web For Kids and Parents,* by Viraf Mohta, published by IDG Books Worldwide, Inc. for more information.)

You know how, on the Web, one click on a button takes you to a new Web page? Well, in the Weblike Desktop, one click opens a document on your hard disk, too. (We'll show you how this works in "Making your mouse chill.") So suddenly every document, icon, or button on your own computer acts like, well, a button on a Web page.

You May Already Have Part of Windows 98 on Your Computer

You may have been looking at a lot of Windows 98 already, if your folks installed the Internet Explorer 4, along with something called the Windows Desktop Update. The update doesn't take you all the way to Windows 98, but it sure looks like it at first. So, in previewing Windows 98, we show you how to use the Windows Desktop Update, if you have it.

Changing your point of view

Not sure whether you already have the classic Windows 95 desktop or the Windows Desktop Update? Here's how to find out, and, if you have the Update, to twist the knobs all the way over toward the right so you get a sneak preview of Windows 98.

1. **Double-click the My Computer icon.**

   If you see a dialog box alerting you to the fact that you can either single click or double-click some items, you have the Update. The idea is that in the Classic style, you had to double-click a program icon to start the program, or double click a folder or file to open it. In the Web style, where the desktop acts the way a Web page does, a single click will do the job.

2. **To try the Web approach and get a preview of Windows 98, select Single Click and click OK.**

   If you are still using Windows 95, or if you have the Update, but have left the settings tuned to the Classic Windows 95, you see a window like the one shown in Figure Preview-1.

Figure Preview-1: My Computer, in the Classic Windows style.

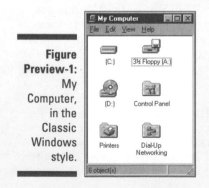

If you have the Update, but someone has chosen to keep as close to the Classic Windows desktop as possible, you see a little blue "e" in the top-right corner, signaling that you can always launch Internet Explorer to find a Web page, as shown in Figure Preview-2.

The "e" gives it away–you have Internet Explorer 4

Figure Preview-2: My Computer, in the Windows Update Desktop, set to Classic style.

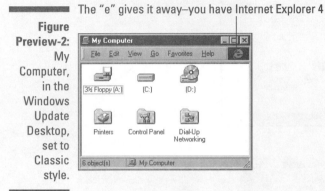

If you have the Update, and someone has chosen to use the Web style, you see a window like the ones shown in Figure Preview-3 and Figure Preview-4. Look at the difference in the labels under the icons.

Figure Preview-3: My Computer, set to be viewed as a Web page.

3. Choose View⇨Folder Options.

If you don't have this command on the View menu, you are still using the pure and classic Windows 95 desktop.

If you have some version of the Update, you see the Folder Options dialog box, as shown in Figure Preview-5.

Web style underlines the name of anything you can click to open

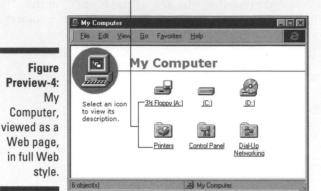

Figure Preview-4: My Computer, viewed as a Web page, in full Web style.

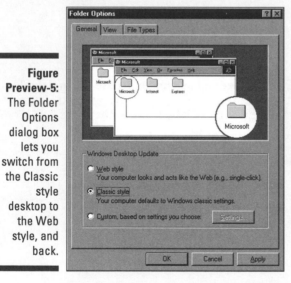

Figure Preview-5: The Folder Options dialog box lets you switch from the Classic style desktop to the Web style, and back.

4. To experience a preview of Windows 98, select <u>W</u>eb style and click <u>A</u>pply.

If asked whether you want to use single-clicking the way you would on the Web, click OK.

In a few moments, any open windows change, a list of Web sites that you can subscribe to — called channels — appears against the background, and you have entered the world of Web style.

You may find the Classic style easier for tasks like moving, copying, or renaming, because the Web style makes it easy to accidentally open the folder or Web the moment you touch it. (The key is not to let your mouse button up.)

Making your mouse chill

Do you have a nervous mouse? Does it want you to keep clicking all the time? Well, time to let your mouse chill out.

As Windows becomes more and more Weblike in the Update and Windows 98, you'll find your mouse finger can relax. Instead of double-clicking, double-clicking, double-clicking to get some action out of your icons, you can slow down and just click once. (That's the way you click a hot spot on a Web page to go to a new location on the Web.)

So if you choose to have a Web-style desktop, Microsoft changes the way most items on the desktop react to clicks (go to "Changing your point of view" in this chapter to see how easy it is to switch between the Classic and Web-style desktops in Windows 98). Table Preview-1 shows you both the old Windows 95 and the new Windows 98 way of doing things with the mouse.

Table Preview-1	Classic Style versus Web Style	
To Do This	*Classic Windows 95 Style*	*Web Style*
Select one item.	Click it once.	Just point to it.
Open an item.	Double-click it.	Click it.
Select a range of items.	Hold down SHIFT key; click the first and last items in the range.	Hold down the SHIFT key, point to the first item, and then point to the last item in the sequence.
Select a set of individual items.	Hold down the CTRL key; click each item.	Hold down CTRL and point to each item.
Drag an item (to move it to a new location).	Point to it, hold down the mouse button, and drag item to new spot.	Point to it, hold down the mouse button, and without releasing the mouse button, drag item to new spot.
Rename a file or folder.	Click its name, choose Rename from File menu, Page, and click OK.	On View menu, deselect As Web and retype. Then click the file or folder name, choose Rename from File menu, and retype.

Changing the way you click can get confusing. But don't worry. When you're using the Web-style desktop, double-clicking is usually okay, just overdoing it. And in programs that haven't been rewritten for Windows 98, you find buttons and commands still work the old-fashioned way. That is, they work like the Classic Windows 95 desktop, even when you run them on top of Windows 98. Who said using a mouse was easy?

Tickling the Taskbar

Oof! Ouch! Often, your window gets crowded, so you minimize some windows, and they shrink into little icons down on the taskbar at the bottom of the screen (or side, if you dragged the taskbar there). That was the original reason for the taskbar — to hold programs or windows until you needed to look at them again.

But in Windows 98, you can add a lot more to the taskbar than ever before inluding the following:

- **A Web-address toolbar:** You can type in a Web address, press Enter, and take off onto the World Wide Web, right from the taskbar.

- **Links:** Sports the same collection of Web site links that you see on the toolbar in Internet Explorer 4.

- **Desktop:** Icons for every item now on your desktop. (If you have more icons than will fit, you see an arrow pointing to the right or left: By leaning on the arrow, you can scroll through all the icons.)

- **Internet Explorer**: Provides quick launching of Internet Explorer 4.

Here's how to add a toolbar to the taskbar in Windows 98:

1. **Right-click any empty spot in your taskbar.**

   A menu pops up, like that shown in Figure Preview-6 or Figure Preview-7.

Figure Preview-6: The taskbar menu in your Windows Desktop Update.

| View | ▶ |
| ✓ Show Text |
| Refresh |
| Open |
| ✓ Show Title |
| Toolbars | ▶ |
| Cascade Windows |
| Tile Windows Horizontally |
| Tile Windows Vertically |
| Minimize All Windows |
| Properties |
| Close |

**Figure
Preview-7:**
The Taskbar
menu in
Windows 98.

Toolbars ▶
Cascade Windows
Tile Windows Horizontally
Tile Windows Vertically
Minimize All Windows
Task Manager...
Properties

2. Click Toolbars, to see what toolbars you can add to your taskbar.

3. Click a toolbar to add it to the taskbar.

The toolbar is squeezed into your taskbar.

Of course, if you add several toolbars, your taskbar gets pretty crowded.
You may want to organize your toolbars by doing any of the following:

✔ To make room for all the new items, drag the top border of your
   taskbar up.

✔ To rearrange items on a crowded taskbar, grab the slider next to the
   name of each type of item and drag up or down, left or right. Result: a
   stack of toolbars, as shown in Figure Preview-8. Ugly, isn't it? Well, hey,
   nobody said Microsoft could solve everything. (Just start closing some
   of those windows yourself!)

You can drag a toolbar right off the taskbar to make it into an icon on your
desktop. The question is: Do you want clutter on the taskbar, or on the
desktop?

Enter a Web address here   Click to see a list of sites you've visited already

Task button to display a program that's running

**Figure
Preview-8:**
You can
stack up
icons to a
dizzying
height in
your
taskbar.

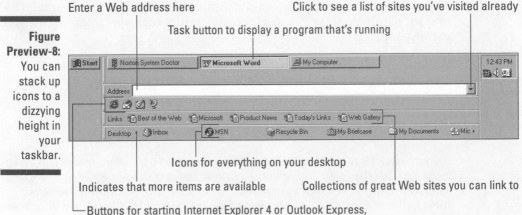

Icons for everything on your desktop

Indicates that more items are available   Collections of great Web sites you can link to

Buttons for starting Internet Explorer 4 or Outlook Express,
showing the desktop (and nothing else), and channels

You can pick a folder and turn it into an icon on the taskbar for fast access. Right-click any empty space on the taskbar, click Toolbars, and then choose New Toolbar. You then name the folder and click OK. Voilà! (To get rid of it, choose Toolbars again and deselect the folder name.)

Startling Start

Does your backpack get heavy some days? The Start button is like that in Windows 98.

You can still start programs quickly from the Start button, but in Windows 98, the Start button does so much more you could hang a car and a kitchen sink on it, and no one would notice. Figure Preview-9 shows what the Start menu looks like in Windows 98.

Figure Preview-9: The Start menu in Windows 98.

[figure: The Start menu showing Programs, Favorites, Documents, Settings, Find, Help, Run..., Log Off Jonathan Price..., Shut Down...]

Programs

You still start programs here, but the menus don't open out quite so far. The first list of folders stays in a single column rather than spreading out all over the desktop.

Neat feature: To get rid of a program, drag it off the Start menu onto the open desktop or into the Recycle Bin to get rid of it altogether.

Favorites

If you've used Internet Explorer for long, you found a lot of your favorite Web sites, and maybe even added some of their addresses to the list of Favorites. This new entry in the Start menu lists every item stored in the Favorites folder, plus some extras, as shown in Figure Preview-10. (You have your own favorites, so your list will be different from ours.) Of course, now this folder can store more than just your favorite Web sites. You can put a frequently visited folder there, too — so you can get there even faster, next time.

Figure Preview-10: The Favorites menu includes Web sites you want to revisit, plus Channels, Links, and Software updates.

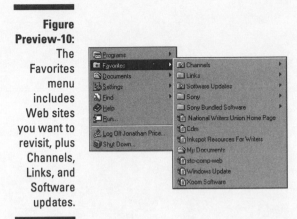

Just to fill out the list, Microsoft adds some items of its own to Favorites:

- **Channels:** Contains Web sites you may want to subscribe to so you can get alerts whenever the sites update their information. (For more info, see "Channeling the spirits of the Web.")

- **Links:** Offers the same icons as in the Links toolbar down on the taskbar: Best of the Web, Microsoft, Product News, Today's Links, and Web Gallery.

- **Software Updates:** A set of links to company sites for software that you may want to get updates for.

Documents

This folder includes the folder called My Documents and the last 15 documents you opened or created, as shown in Figure Preview-11.

Want to get rid of a document for good? Drag it over to the Recycle Bin.

Settings

The Settings menu, shown in Figure Preview-12, updates the Control Panel contents and adds new items.

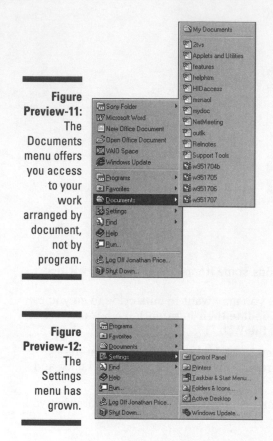

Figure Preview-11: The Documents menu offers you access to your work arranged by document, not by program.

Figure Preview-12: The Settings menu has grown.

The Control Panel

As in Windows 95, the Control Panel lets you make adjustments to just about everything in the interface. You'll notice a few new items, as shown in Figure Preview-13, and after you experiment with them, you'll find new twists to old controls.

For example, you use the Display Properties dialog box a lot in Windows 95, and the new version resembles that one but includes two new tabs, one for icons, and the other for Web-related stuff, as shown in Figure Preview-14. (You make the Display Properties dialog box appear by clicking the Display icon in the Control Panel window.) You can make Windows 98 act like a Web page and display or turn off the display of channels.

One other change you may enjoy; click the Sounds icon in the Control Panel window to open the Sounds Properties dialog box, as shown in Figure Preview-15. You see that all the events that could trigger a sound are listed at the top to let you attach a whole set of sounds or individual sounds to them more easily.

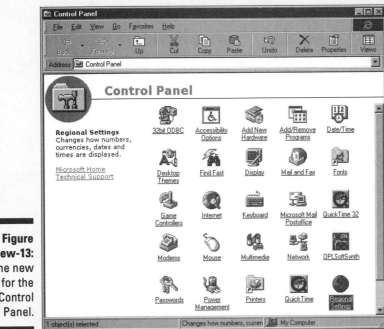

Figure Preview-13: The new look for the Control Panel.

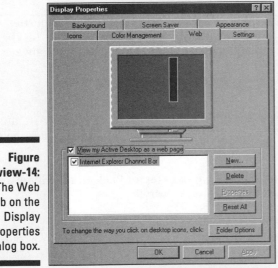

Figure Preview-14: The Web tab on the Display Properties dialog box.

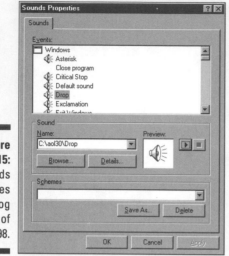

**Figure
Preview-15:**
The Sounds
Properties
dialog
box of
Windows 98.

Printers

You can add a printer without having to know what techie stuff is (like an interrupt).

Taskbar and Start Menu

This nifty little feature brings up the Taskbar and Start Menu Properties dialog box, so you can adjust the taskbar or Start menu. With the Taskbar and Start Menu dialog box you control whether the taskbar stays always on top or goes into hiding.

Folders and Icons

A new entry in the Settings sweepstakes, shown in Figure Preview-16, this dialog box lets you adjust the way the desktop displays folders, files, and icons.

You use the General tab on this dialog box to teeter back and forth between the Classic Windows 95 approach or the Web style.

The View tab on the Folder Options dialog box lets you get really picky telling the system whether or not to show a popup description for a folder or hide file extensions — probably a hot tab if you are sensitive to details like these.

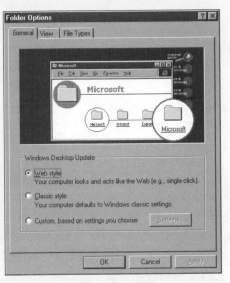

Figure Preview-16: The Folder Options dialog box opens to the General Tab, which lets you switch the way folders and icons appear and react to your clicks.

Active Desktop

Brings up a menu, as shown in Figure Preview-17, that lets you make the whole desktop act the way Web pages do. When you activate the desktop this way, the icon labels get underlined so that you can open a program, folder, or file with a single click (rather than double-clicking as in Windows 95). From here you also can jump to the Display Properties dialog box to set colors and the look of icons, bars, and other interface stuff.

Windows Update

Just like a direct line to Microsoft, this feature fires up Internet Explorer and attempts to connect you with the Microsoft site that has the latest updates for Windows.

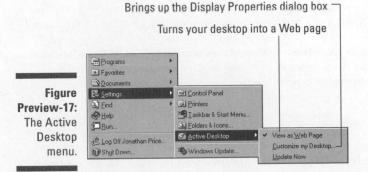

Figure Preview-17: The Active Desktop menu.

Find

With Find, you can reach out to find people, information, and Web sites all around the world — not just files and folders on your computer, as in Windows 95.

You also can look up a file even if you only know part of the name or the last date you worked on it. You can even ask for a file that happens to contain some particular phrase.

Here's how to locate a person you have lost touch with in order to get their e-mail address.

1. **Choose Start⇨Find⇨People.**

   The Find People dialog box appears, as shown in Figure Preview-18.

Figure Preview-18: The Find People dialog box.

2. **Choose a directory to search in from the drop-down list of services that list people and their e-mail addresses.**

3. **Type in the information requested if you know it.**

4. **Click Find Now.**

   You may have to OK a connection to the Internet. In a minute or two you get the results of your search. Hope you find your long-lost friend!

If you want, you can have the e-mail address transferred into your Address Book. The Address Book is a list of e-mail addresses you can use with Outlook Express for electronic mail.

Help

When you need a little help, this feature provides information as if it were on a Web page, as shown in Figure Preview-19. Click Web Help to get the latest information direct from Microsoft, over the Web.

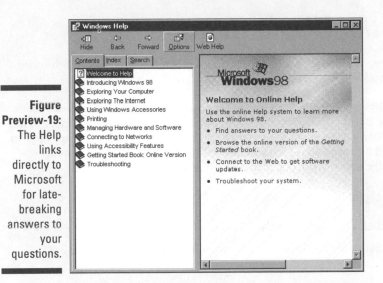

Figure Preview-19: The Help links directly to Microsoft for late-breaking answers to your questions.

Run

Lets you run a program if you know its exact name — or type an Internet address and zip right out there on the Web. The Web address trick is what's new.

Log Off

With this command you can sign off so someone else can sign on, without turning off the computer, to get their own personally arranged desktop. You get the opportunity to Close All Programs and Log On as a Different User, an option that lives in the Shutdown area in Windows 95.

Each of you can log on and set up the desktop in a personal way. So when you sign on you get your own look and feel. To set up someone as a user, choose Start⇨Settings⇨Control Panel⇨Users and click New User. You'll have to make up individual passwords for each person (and worse, remember them!). After you are set up as a user, you can use the same Users panel to change your settings, too.

Shut Down

Yes, this feature does just what it says: shuts your computer down in an orderly way. This is the way to go. No more pulling the plug and laughing. (And, yes, it works the way it did in Windows 95.)

Activating the Whole Desktop

You're active, right? You run, you jump, you go to school. How much more active do you have to be?

Well, if you like a quiet life, you can keep your desktop the way it was in Windows 95. But if you like change, you can make your desktop active. That means, you can put news flashes, stock quotes, or sports scores up on your desktop, and as long as you are connected to the Web, those will keep changing right up on your desktop as new information comes in.

To get active, you have to turn the Active Desktop on. Here's how:

1. **Right-click anywhere on the desktop.**

   The Desktop menu pops up, as shown in Figure Preview-20.

Figure Preview-20: The Desktop menu.

2. **Point to Active Desktop and when a submenu appears, make sure that View as Web Page is selected.**

Putting activity on the desktop

Here's the idea: Add objects to your desktop — but not just limp, dead objects. These objects do stuff. Some keep track of time, in a funny way. Others collect information off the Web and display it for you, keeping you up to date.

Follow these steps to put some life into your desktop:

1. **Right-click the desktop and choose Properties from the menu that appears.**

2. **Click the Web tab.**

3. **Click the New button.**

   You are asked whether you would like to select an item from the Active Desktop Gallery, which is a special Microsoft Web site with fun items to put on your desktop.

4. **Click Yes to go to the Active Desktop Gallery.**

   Internet Explorer 4 starts up, and, if you are not already connected, you need to OK a connection. When you finally get connected, you land at the Microsoft site with comic clocks (silly looking timepieces that keep real time), stock tickers, and news crawls (just like during tornado season when the TV station alerts your county) ready to install.

5. **Click an item to preview its activity.**

6. **If you like the preview, click the Add to my Desktop button.**

7. **Follow the directions given at the site.**

   Each gizmo has its own installation process, which may take a few seconds, or 15 minutes, depending on the complexity of the software and the speed of your modem.

8. **Click OK to accept the new item and put away the Display Properties dialog box.**

Result: you now have a new gizmo on your desktop, waving at you, alerting you to breaking news, or just acting silly.

Channeling the spirits of the Web

A channel is a Web site that's been set up to send you the latest information, or notify you when the information is updated on the site rather than sitting around waiting for you to visit. Part of the benefit of subscribing (you don't pay, but they send you information) is that you can read it after you hang up the phone, so you are not charged for connection time while you read. Here's how to set up a channel so that it's active:

1. **Click the Channel Guide in the stack of channels on your desktop.**

   If you don't have a list of channels on the desktop, click the icon of the satellite dish on your taskbar, or launch Internet Explorer 4, and click the icon there.

   Internet Explorer 4 appears with a list of channels on the left. If you are not connected to the Web, you are asked if you want to — so click Connect.

2. **Click a vendor or a category to get a list of Web sites that can act as a channel for information about that subject.**

3. **Click a channel.**

   Your system starts up Internet Explorer 4, and if you weren't connected, asks you to help connect, which you should do.

4. **Explore the Web site for a while to see if you are interested.**

5. If you would like to keep up with the site, click the button Add Active Channel on the site somewhere.

In a dialog box shown in Figure Preview-21, Windows 98 asks whether you want to subscribe or just add the site to your channel list. (Subscribing means that when you connect to the Web, you receive updated information from the channel — stuff you can look at later when you drop the connection to the Web.)

6. Select an option and click OK.

If you subscribe, the updates may start pouring onto your disk at any moment.

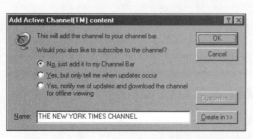

Figure Preview-21: You can make the channel active, get notices of updates, or get the updates themselves, so you can read them offline.

Browsing in Hyperspace (And Your Computer)

In the Windows Update and in Windows 98, almost everything begins to act as if it were on the Web — even when you are just looking at folders on your computer in your home. As in Windows 95, you have two tools for inspecting your folders and files, but both let you look at icons for Web pages as well. So you can get information from your own computer or the Web, all in one view.

Take My Computer, for example

My Computer looks great now, with lots of white space, and the large icons floating out there with their labels underlined, as shown in Figure Preview-22.

Underlined labels ⌐

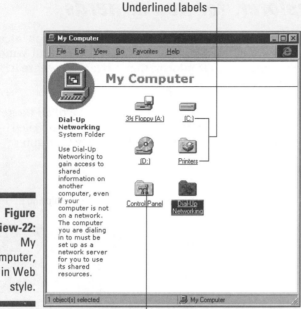

Hover here for more information

Underlined labels mean you can open whatever is underlined with a single click, as on the Web.

When you hover over a folder, you may even get an explanation of what's inside, over on the left, under the gigantic icon of, you guessed it, a computer.

You can now look at some new items, which get stuck onto the standard My Computer like wings on a buffalo:

✔ Your list of Favorites (which used to be just Web sites, but may now include folders and files on your own computer, as well)

✔ A History of all the Web visits you have made today or during the last few weeks

✔ A list of the Web sites you have chosen as channels

✔ A direct link to some search engine on the Web

These extra items extend your view forward and back in time, and way out over the Web.

Windows Explorer, for power nerds

Windows Explorer has exploded to include tons of Web information, as well as news about what's on your computer. Here's what is great about Windows Explorer: You can easily see all of your information, no matter where it exists, as in Figure Preview-23.

But many folks find Windows Explorer a little scary, because of all those lines and pluses, and what is the connection between the left and the right, anyway? If you find Windows Explorer a little much, use My Computer instead.

Folders on your hard disk   Files and folders you're exploring

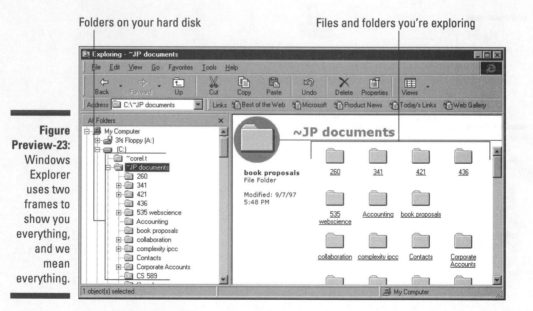

Figure Preview-23: Windows Explorer uses two frames to show you everything, and we mean everything.

Improving Your Outlook

Microsoft has issued so many e-mail programs so fast that they sometimes trip over each other's feet. But Microsoft swears that with Microsoft Outlook Express they have a strong program that will help out with electronic mail from Internet Explorer 4, Microsoft Network, America Online, CompuServe, and You-Name-It.

So Outlook Express started life as a kind of universal In-Box. You know those trays people have in offices, marked In and Out? Well, that's what this program does on your computer. It accepts mail from electronic mail programs, information services, whatever, and it hands over the outgoing mail.

But Outlook Express does a lot more: Yes, you can read mail here, but you also can read news from folks who band together for a common interest, and share an electronic bulletin board, or a newsgroup. You can compose mail, look up someone's address in your address book, and search through the whole Web to find someone's address when you don't know it, all from your base in Outlook Express.

Here's how to start Outlook Express and get a sense of what it can do for you:

1. **Choose Start➪Programs➪Internet Explorer 4➪Outlook Express.**

   In a moment you see the Outlook Express welcome screen, as shown in Figure Preview-24, with full-color icons promoting what it can do for you.

   Windows 98 may ask you if you want to make the connection to the Internet.

Area where message lists and messages will appear

Different tasks you can do with Outlook Express

Figure Preview-24: The Outlook Express welcome window.

2. **Click OK to make the connection, if necessary.**

   A school, government agency, library, nonprofit group, or for-profit commercial vendor may act as the post office for your electronic mail. Whoever does this for you has given you a phone number to dial and a password to enter upon arrival. Without the number and password, and the connection, you can't get beyond your own desktop. Better ask Mom or Dad.

3. Click Read Mail on the right frame.

The righthand frame splits into two panes that display your Inbox. The top shows a list of recent mail, the bottom displays the text (and pictures, and Web links, if included) for the message that's highlighted, as shown in Figure Preview-25.

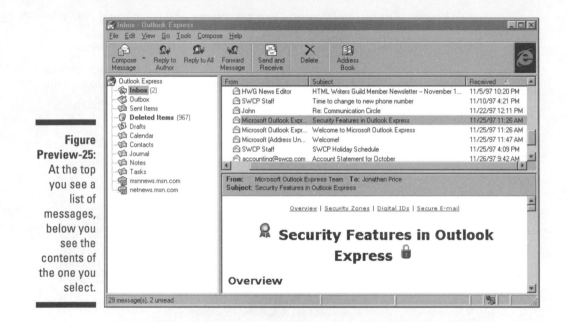

Figure Preview-25:
At the top you see a list of messages, below you see the contents of the one you select.

4. Click the Send and Receive button to send out any messages you have recently written and pick up any that have come into your electronic mailbox.

A message appears telling you how many messages are being sent and received. The incoming mail piles up in the list above, with a line describing the sender, the subject, and the date and time received by your electronic post office.

5. Click the title of a message to see its content displayed in the pane below. (You may have to scroll up to see the new messages.)

6. If you want to reply, click Reply to Author, type your comment, and click the Send button.

You get a message, warning you that although you said to Send the message, it really isn't sent until you click the Send and Receive button again — just to keep you off balance.

You can forward a message to someone else using the Forward button, too.

7. **If you know you don't want to read a message (for example, a message with the title Earn Big Bucks Stuffing Envelopes with Your Home Computer), click Delete.**

   Very satisfying!

8. **To print a message you want to save or ponder, choose File⇨Print and click OK.**

Making up a message

You can follow these steps to tell the world what you think about things, all from within Outlook Express:

1. **Click the Compose a Message button or pick a graphic style from the drop-down menu of formats next to the button.**

   You get a form in which you can compose your message. For example, the Technical look features a graph paper background in light blue, as shown in Figure Preview-26.

2. **If you remember the person's e-mail address, type it into the To box. If you need help, click the Select Recipients button (it looks like an open address book).**

   You see the Select Recipients dialog box with a list of the e-mail addresses you have added to your address book.

   Click the name, click the To button to move the name to the To box on the right, and then click OK.

3. **Type a subject in the text box next to Subject.**

4. **Type your message in the large area at the bottom of the message window.**

You can include Web links in messages you send to folks who are using Outlook Express. When you type a Web address, the program automatically underlines it and changes it to blue to make it clickable. If this doesn't happen automatically check the Format menu and make sure that Rich Text (HTML) is selected. Similarly, you can include pictures as long as the Tools menu shows Send Pictures with Message selected.

5. **Click Send.**

Outlook Express warns that although you asked the program to send your message, it merely holds onto it until you again click Send and Receive.

6. **Click Send and Receive to really send the message.**

Nosing out the news

Newsgroups are clubs, where everyone, more or less, has a common interest. One person posts a message and others chime in with answers. You can dial in and read all the messages and then make your own.

You can find more than 20,000 newsgroups on subjects from aardvarks to zoos. Here's how to subscribe and visit some newsgroups:

1. **In the list in the frame on the left of the Outlook Express window, click** msnnews.msn.com **or** netnews.msn.com **to get a list of all the newsgroups that Microsoft Network has collected on its server. (Or choose Go⇨News.)**

You may be asked for a Microsoft Network password.

You get a message saying that the server is sending you a long, long list of the names of various newsgroups. (Just sending the list may take five minutes.) When they have all arrived, you see the first dozen or so in a dialog box.

2. **Type a topic into the text box at the top.**

When you stop typing, you get a list of newsgroups whose names include whatever you typed.

3. **Select a likely newsgroup and click Subscribe. Keep doing this until bored and then click OK.**

The newsgroups you chose to subscribe to now show up on the left.

4. Click a newsgroup.

In a moment, a list of its messages appears at the top on the right. To read a messge, just click it.

To respond to a message, click Reply to Group, fill in subject, type your comments, and then click Send.

You can spend many long hours reading tons of drivel on newsgroups. Keep hunting around for a group you like. Skip the ones that have no messages for the last few weeks, or too many ads, or surveys by marketing companies. Eventually, after a few weeks of hunting, you will probably find two or three newsgroups that discuss topics you really care about. We like `misc.creativity`, `misc.education.science`, `misc.kids.computer`, and, for our goldfish Joe, `rec.aquaria.freshwater.goldfish`. Two or three are plenty if you have a daytime life.

Meeting and Showing Off on the Net

Do you like talking on the phone? Well, with Windows 98, you can talk to someone else, send video pictures of yourselves back and forth, and type messages all with Net Meeting, a new program that takes gossip onto the Internet. Of course, you need more gear to use this, so you may not be able to chat right away.

To talk back and forth, you need the following:

- ✔ A sound card and speakers
- ✔ A microphone

To hold a face-to-face video conversation, you also need:

- ✔ A video capture card that works with Video for Windows
- ✔ A video camera

Here's how you get Net Meeting ready to do your bidding:

1. Choose Start⇨Programs⇨Internet Explorer⇨Net Meeting.

If this is your first time using the program, you need to fill out some background information and take an audio test.

2. In the wizard, agree to whatever directory is suggested or type in a particular server that can handle these conferences; then click Next.

3. Fill in your first name, last name, e-mail address, city, and zip code; then click Next.

4. **Settle on a category of conversation, personal is probably best. (Not adult!) Click Next.**

5. **Take the audio test to make sure other folks can hear you over your microphone. Click Next and then Finish.**

   Eventually you see the main screen for Net Meeting, as shown in Figure Preview-27.

Figure Preview-27:
Net Meeting turns your computer into a meeting room.

Chatting with Net Meeting — by type and by phone

Gab, gab, gab. You can talk on the phone, er, the microphone attached to your computer if you want, or you can chat the way you do on an online service by typing. Unfortunately, you can't do this with just anyone.

If you really want to try out Net Meeting, you need to get the other folks who will be meeting with you to register with the same directory server as you have signed up for. The directory server is a computer that acts as the giant switchboard, connecting everyone who wants to talk during the meeting. So the other folks need Net Meeting 2.0 and a registration at the same server. You should probably also agree with everyone (by e-mail) about the exact time everyone should sign on.

1. **Connect to the Internet and then choose Start⇨Programs⇨Internet Explorer⇨Net Meeting.**

   The software goes out and makes a connection with a special server called a Directory Server, which is where everyone gets together. You see a list of servers (computers hosting Net Meetings).

2. **Click a server in the Server list and then look on the Directory tab for a list of people who are running Net Meeting.**

3. **To place a call, double-click the name of the person you want to call.**

   You can do this on the Directory, SpeedDial, or History tab. In a moment, you see a notice of your connection.

4. **Talk and wave. Then on the Tools menu click Switch Audio and Video and click the name of the person you want to hear and see you.**

5. **When you're tired of talking and waving, go to the Current Call tab and click the icon of a loudspeaker next to the person you no longer want to receive your voice and picture.**

6. **To hang up, choose Call⇨Hang Up.**

To chat by typing while connected, click the Chat button on the toolbar to make the Chat window appear, as shown in Figure Preview-28. Then type the message and press Enter.

Figure Preview-28: Net Meeting lets you chat by typing.

Using the Whiteboard together

Writing on the blackboard isn't much fun at school. But imagine your screen is a whiteboard and you can draw on it, and so can the person at the other end of the line. You can make a picture together, even though you are both at home. (You can write words, too. You can talk and draw, both at the same time, as if you were sitting next to each other at a desk, coming up with a project for the rainforest, or a mural for the school dance.)

1. **Connect to the Internet and then choose Start⇨Programs⇨Internet Explorer⇨Net Meeting.**

2. **Click the Current Call tab and then click Whiteboard on the toolbar.**

   You see a painting and drawing program come up on your screen, like that shown in Figure Preview-29. Your friend does, too. You can both draw on the same space.

3. **Use the tools to draw, letter, and illustrate your ideas.**

Figure Preview-29: The Whiteboard lets you both draw and see the results at the same time on your computer screens.

Trading video shots

If you have your video card and video camera all hooked up, and running, you can send video images of yourself (you can receive video without having the camera):

1. **Connect to the Internet and then choose Start⇨Programs⇨Internet Explorer⇨Net Meeting.**

2. **Choose Tools⇨Options.**

   You see the Options dialog box.

3. **Click the Video tab.**

   You see the Video tab, as shown in Figure Preview-30.

4. **Make sure that there is a check mark next to Automatically send video at the start of each call.**

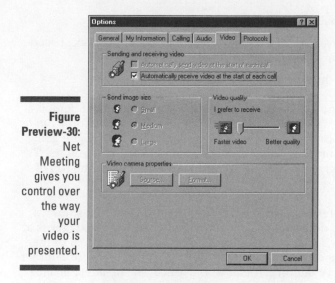

Figure Preview-30: Net Meeting gives you control over the way your video is presented.

5. **If you are already in a call, click the button at the bottom of the My Video window. To receive video, click the button at the bottom of the Remote Video window.**

   Now you can see the other person and your picture appears on their screen at the same time.

Watching TV on Your Computer (Maybe)

Yes, you can now combine your favorite screen activities — playing a computer game and watching MTV — at the same time. The idea is that you can bring the TV signal right into your computer screen, the way you do for TV.

Okay, so it turns out this isn't as easy as you'd think. (Or else it would have been done long ago.) And, yes, it probably costs so much you won't get to do this until your family decides to buy the next computer. But just so you have an idea how it works, here goes.

To watch TV, inside the computer you need:

✔ A video capture card following the standards known as DirectShow 2 and WDM, and the standards of American National TV System Committee (NTSC)

✔ Software known as a video driver, following the same standards

✔ A screen that can manage a resolution higher than 640 x 480

Connected to the computer you need one of the following:

✔ TV reception from a DIRECTV direct broadcast satellite service, broadcast captured on an antenna

✔ Cable TV, plugged into the back of your computer

Using software called the TV Viewer, you get a TV Toolbar on your screen, and you can sign on to watch TV. You get a Program Guide just like *TV Guide,* so you can pick shows by time and channel. (You switch channels by going through the Program Guide, picking a favorite channel you set up on the TV toolbar, or going through a set of Channel buttons you set up at the top of the screen.)

You can also use the Internet to send e-mail to the producers of a show while it is on, chat with other folks about what should happen next, guess at the ending on the show's Web site. Neat. But for most folks, the cost of the hardware and hookup means these features aren't really in place for another few years. So keep an eye out for a friend who likes to get the latest gizmos before anyone else.

Chapter 8

Playing with Games, Music, and Video

In This Chapter

▶ Fun and games that come with your computer

▶ Playing and making music and sounds

▶ Looking at video

*W*e like all kinds of music — rap, rock, country, and hiphop. You probably have a lot of music CDs, too, and video tapes and games gathering dust under the TV. A lot of times just buying Microsoft Windows 95 means that your folks can't afford any big-time games, and you can't rent a video for a few weeks. Knowing this, Microsoft threw in some free little goodies — to make owning Windows 95 fun, on the cheap!

Included in Windows 95 you get the following fun stuff:

✔ Games to play when you need a break from homework

✔ Music to listen to when the computer's beeps and boops are getting boring

✔ Video to watch when your little brother is hogging the TV

Let the Games Begin!

Windows comes with three card games (Hearts, Solitaire, and FreeCell) and a very quiet war game called Minesweeper. These games are all designed for solo play unless you have a network designed at home, which isn't very likely. But after you discover these games and figure out their rules, you'll beg for more time on the computer.

Hearts

The object of the game is to be the player with the *lowest* number of points. The deck of 52 cards is evenly divided among four people. (You can play by yourself against three "virtual" players that the computer picks or against three real friends.) You pick a card and "throw" it on the table. Everyone else has to throw a card down that's the same suit (diamonds, clubs, hearts, or spades) as the one you used — if they have one. Whoever tosses out the highest card has to pick up all the cards that everyone threw. You keep this up until someone is out of cards, then you total up everyone's score.

You score each card according to the following scale:

- Each heart counts as one point.
- Queen of Spades is 13 points.
- If you get the Queen of Spades and all of the hearts, you "Shoot the Moon," which gives each one of your opponents 26 points — and you zero!!

You start by selecting three cards and passing them to the left. You get three cards from the person on your right. Then the player with the Two of Clubs starts the game by tossing it on the table. The computer plays all three other hands, following suit where possible, but otherwise dumping hearts onto the table. The highest card in the correct suit wins the hand.

If you don't have any cards left in that suit, that's a good time to dump your high cards in other suits. But of course you don't always want to win the hand, because hearts count against you. (You'll be astonished at how fast the computer plays.)

Don't worry about remembering all of the rules. The game gives you little prompts at the bottom left of your screen telling you what you have to do next.

To fire up the Hearts program, follow these steps:

1. **Choose Start⇨Programs⇨Accessories⇨Games⇨Hearts.**

   The Hearts Network Dialog box appears, as shown in Figure 8-1.

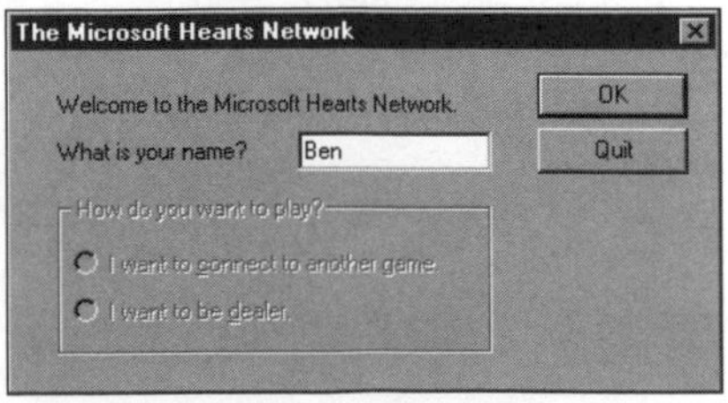

Figure 8-1:
The game
wants to
know who
you are.

The Microsoft Hearts Network

Welcome to the Microsoft Hearts Network.

What is your name? Ben

How do you want to play?

○ I want to connect to another game

○ I want to be dealer

OK

Quit

The game's designed to be played over a network, but you probably don't have a network at home yet. Without a network, it's you against the computer.

2. Type in your name.

3. Click OK.

The game board appears with your hand on the bottom of the screen, as shown in Figure 8-2.

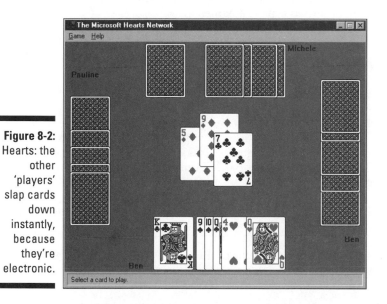

Figure 8-2:
Hearts: the other 'players' slap cards down instantly, because they're electronic.

4. Click the cards you want to pass to the person on your left.

As you select the cards to pass, the cards pop up.

5. When you are satisfied with your selection, click the Pass Left button.

The cards swoosh over to the left and you instantly get three cards from the hand on the right. Click OK.

6. If you have the Two of Clubs, toss that card in by clicking it. If you don't have the Two of Clubs, the computer automatically tosses it in for you.

The person who "wins" the hand gets all the cards in the trick and selects the next card to play by clicking it. Keep going until one person is out of cards. The game automatically tallies everyone's score (no chance to cheat).

7. Click OK to start a new game.

Here are some tips to help you win at Hearts:

- ✔ When you pass cards to the next player, include aces and face cards, which forces that player to "win" a few hands.

- ✔ Play high cards early, while opponents may still have a few cards in your suit.

- ✔ Expert players recall which hearts have been played and which spades.

- ✔ To assign names to the computer players, choose Options from the Game menu and then type the names in.

Solitaire

Here's a game that's simple enough for grown-ups to follow and challenging enough for everyone. The aim of this classic game is to eventually transfer cards from the seven card stacks to four suit stacks (from the ace to the king, in each suit) on the top of the screen. But to get to the cards underneath the upturned cards in the card stacks, you have to move them to the other rows. To move one of those cards from one row stack to another, drag it to the appropriate row.

Wait — there's more to this game. You can only move a card to another row in the card stacks if:

- ✔ That card is the opposite color of the card at the bottom of the row.

- ✔ That card is one lower than the card at the bottom of the deck.

After you finish dragging all of the cards you can, click the deck in the upper-left-hand corner for some more cards. You can play the card on the top by either dragging it to the appropriate card stack, or, if it is an ace, double-click it to send it to the one of the suit stacks.

Give your cards a new look

You can change the card backs of your deck if you don't like the default picture:

1. **Game⇨De_c_k.**

2. **Click the picture you like.**

3. **Click OK.**

To play the game, just follow these steps:

1. **Choose Start⇨Programs⇨Accessories⇨Games⇨Solitaire.**

   A new game instantly appears, as shown in Figure 8-3.

2. **Begin to play by double-clicking any aces (you may not have any) that appear in the card stacks.**

   Drag the cards around to the bottom of the various card stacks until you have moved all the cards you can move.

3. **Click the deck of cards.**

   Three cards appear. Drag any playable cards to the card stacks and double-click any that can go on the suit stacks.

   Keep playing until you run out of options and then deal again.

   If you get all of the cards into the suit stacks, you win.

TIP

Prefer to deal one card rather than three? Want to change the way you score? Choose Game⇨Options and play it your way.

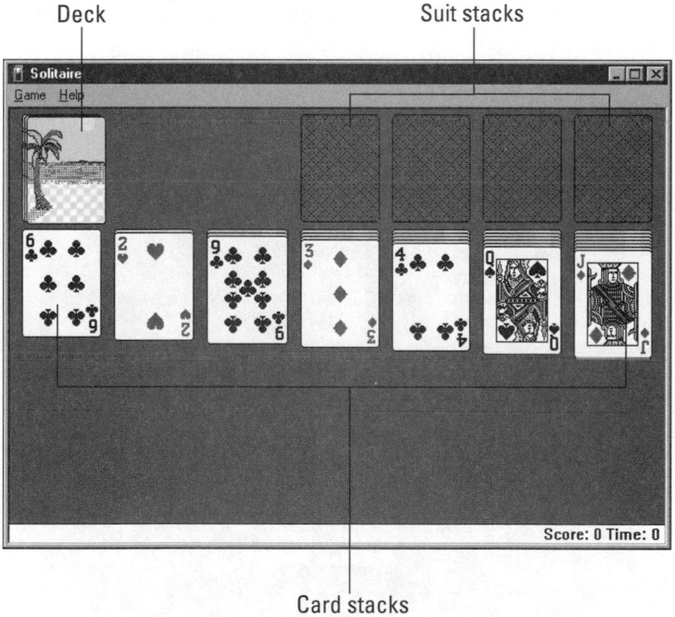

Deck   Suit stacks

Figure 8-3: Warning — this game is addictive.

Card stacks

FreeCell

After you get tired of playing Solitaire, move up to FreeCell. Here's a variation on Solitaire that starts off looking easier, but isn't. Your aim is to arrange the cards from Ace to King in each suit in four rectangles, known as the home cells, on the upper right. In this game you are given four holding or free cells on the upper left to temporarily hold your cards until you're ready to use them.

The rules are a little different from Solitaire:

  ✔ To move a card, click it and then click the area you want to move it to.

  ✔ You can always place an Ace in an empty home cell. But in moving other cards to a home cell, you have to go lowest to highest, in the same suit. And in moving a card to the bottom of another column, you have to go highest to lowest, alternating red and black suit colors.

  ✔ To move a card into a free cell, double-click the card.

Here's how to start the game:

  1. **Choose Start➪Programs➪Accessories➪Games➪FreeCell.**

     The FreeCell window appears, as shown in Figure 8-4.

Free cells   Home cells

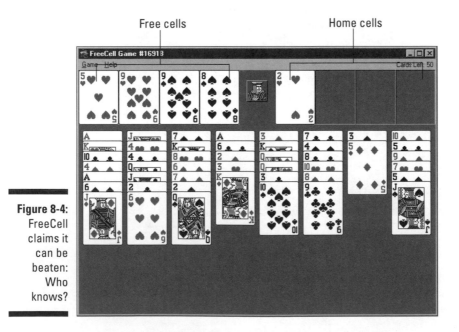

Figure 8-4: FreeCell claims it can be beaten: Who knows?

2. **Click the card you want to move and then click the area where you want to place that card.**

   You can either move that card to a free cell, to a home cell in order of lowest to highest all in the same suit, or to the bottom of a card stack, from highest to lowest in alternate colors.

   What mostly sets this game apart from Solitaire is that you can use the free cells to temporarily hold cards. Use these free cells when you are stuck.

3. **Keep going until you finish.**

Microsoft estimates there are 32,000 possible variations on this game. You're probably saying, "No way!" But according to Microsoft, it's "Yes way!" Oh well, look at the bright side, you won't get bored easily.

The computer refuses to let you move a card to an incorrect spot if you don't follow the rules. If you move the wrong card by accident, press F10 to undo the move. But do it right away. If you make another move, F10 will undo that one.

Minesweeper

Your challenge: to figure out where the mines are buried in a mine field. You click a square, and if you don't get blown up, you know that square is safe; that square also tells you how many mines are in neighboring squares. You can then guess which squares contain mines and which don't. If you guess wrong, all the mines blow up, and, well, you lose. You win when you place flags on all the hidden mines without detonating the field.

To play the game, follow these steps:

1. **Choose Start⇨Programs⇨Accessories⇨Games⇨Minesweeper.**

2. **Right-click any square to see if it is mined or not.**

   The game ends in a hurry if the square is mined as shown in Figure 8-5.

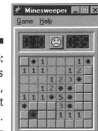

Figure 8-5:
If you guess
wrong,
you get
blown up.

3. Keep going until you flag all of the mines.

Here are two strategy tips to help you with your game:

- ✔ If you figure that a certain square must have a mine in it, right-click the square to put a flag there.

- ✔ If the square you uncover is near the edge of the minefield, it has only five neighbors. If it's in the corner, it has three. But if it is out in the middle of a minefield, it has eight neighbors.

Let's Party with Some Tunes!

Besides playing games, you can also play music CDs on your computer. In fact, you can listen to Aerosmith while you're busy not blowing yourself up playing Minesweeper. You can also make your own recordings and compile a list of your favorite tunes. And when you want to have some wacko fun, you can mess around with the variety of sounds Windows 95 comes with. (If you want to jump to making sounds and your own recordings go to the section "Listening to audio CDs" a little later in this chapter.)

But first things first. Although Windows 95 gives you the means to play audio CDs and other sounds, you have to first make sure that your computer has the right stuff.

If you're bummed at your parents for the moment, or at life in general, why not chat 'n' chill with other fans of music groups you like? Go online (see Chapter 10) and do a search for your fave group. If the group has more than one word in its name, like Smashing Pumpkins, make sure that you put quotes around the whole name, like this — "Smashing Pumpkins." You get a list of sites where fans gather and talk and, with many groups, you can download all or parts of their songs that will go into your computer as wave files.

You have to have this junk on your computer

You need a CD-ROM drive to play audio CDs, no duh, and you need to have a sound card installed in your computer. External speakers, while not 100 percent necessary, greatly enhance the sound quality.

A CD-ROM drive

To play audio CDs on your computer, quite simply, you need a CD-ROM drive either attached to your computer or just part of it. If you don't know whether any of those disk drives on your computer are for CDs, press the button just under the drive. If a drawer slides out and you see a depressed circular shape that a CD fits into perfectly, then you have a CD-ROM drive on your computer.

If you already have a CD-ROM drive, then Windows 95 probably has shaken hands with it, given it a thumbs up, and is ready to make rad music with it.

If you want to make sure that Windows 95 recognizes your CD-ROM drive, pop in an audio CD and click the My Computer or Explorer icon. You see a list of drives, as shown in Figure 8-6, including the name of the CD in the CD-ROM drive. If the CD-ROM drive doesn't show up, reinstall the drive following the drive's manufacturer's instructions.

Figure 8-6:
Here's a list
of usable
drives.

If you don't have a CD-ROM drive and want to buy one, make sure that you buy one that is specifically advertised as "Plug and Play-enabled" or "Designed for Windows 95." That way you can plug the CD-ROM drive in and Windows 95 should recognize it, shake hands with it, and give it a donut.

Boring stuff about Plug and Play that you really don't need to know

So just what is Plug and Play? In the old days, like before Windows 95 came out for PC users, or in the *really* old days before the Macintosh came out for Apple users, life was very hard for anyone trying to install hardware (like a CD-ROM drive, or a modem, or even a joystick) or upgrade existing hardware. You had to contend with switches called DIPs and Direct Memory Access channels, whatever they are, and generally you were out of luck unless you lived next door to a friendly nerd. Windows 95 did away with this mess, for the most part. So, if you want to add any hardware to your computer, before you buy it, always look on the box and make sure that it says, "Plug and Play-enabled."

You should know that techies rather affectionately (some of them are really a sick bunch) call this new technology Plug and *Pray*. So, if after you plug some piece of hardware in your computer, like a new sound card or CD-ROM drive, and it doesn't work, put your hands together, close your eyes, and do what everyone else does next.

CD-ROM drives are different from the other drives on your computer because you can't copy anything to them. In fact the ROM in CD-ROM means Read Only Memory. That means you get info from it but you can't add anything to it or take anything off of it. By the way, if you were wondering, the CD in CD-ROM stands for compact disc.

A sound card

If you want to hear something more than some clicks and beeps, you need a sound card installed in your computer. If you already have one, skip this section and go to the next one.

If you don't know if you have a sound card installed, you can check by choosing Settings⇨Control Panel. If you see a little Sound icon, then you know you have a sound card installed.

A sound card is really a circuit board that slides into the guts of your computer. If you're going to buy a new one, make sure that you get the kind that also lets you record your own voice and music and, of course, is Plug and Play-enabled.

If you've installed Windows 95 onto an older computer with a sound card, Windows 95 may not recognize the older card and therefore the sound card won't work. It's like trying to get a Sega game cartridge to play in a Nintendo machine. If this happens, you're out of luck and will probably have to buy a new sound card. Unfortunately, Windows 95 isn't very friendly to older hardware.

Listening to audio CDs

You can pop in the latest CD from Pearl Jam or Brooks & Dunn and listen to it as you play Solitaire or work on a book report.

Windows 95 has a built in CD player that works a lot like the CD player in your bedroom. The quality of the sound is as good as your sound card and your computer's speakers. How good is that? Pop in your favorite CD as shown here and find out for yourself:

1. **Open the CD-ROM drive by clicking the button near it.**

2. **Put a music CD in that drive and then click the button to shut the drawer.**

Most of the time Windows 95 starts playing the CD in a few seconds. If you've been staring at silent speakers for over a minute, choose Start⇨Programs⇨Accessories⇨Multimedia⇨CD Player. The CD Player window appears, as shown in Figure 8-7.

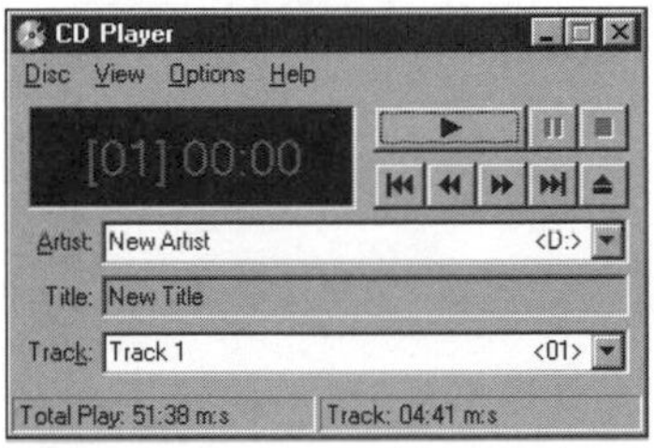

Figure 8-7:
Hover over each button to find out what it does.

CD Player

Disc View Options Help

[01] 00:00

Artist: New Artist   <D:>
Title: New Title
Track: Track 1   <01>

Total Play: 51:38 m:s   Track: 04:41 m:s

If you're looking for a certain song but forget its name, pull down the Options menu and select Intro Play, which plays the first few seconds of every song until you find the one you're looking for.

Do it your way — makin' your own hit list

When you listen to an audio CD on Windows 95, the CD Player makes a list of all of the songs on that CD. It's in the exact same order as the songs on the CD. That's okay for a start, but when did you ever listen to a CD when all the songs were winners? There's always one or two that sounds like they were recorded on Mars or came by way of the Borg. So, when you listen to that CD again, why not skip some of those dud songs? You can do that by excluding those songs from the *play list* (the list of songs), and you never have to listen to them again. You can also change the order you listen to the songs or program it to listen to the same one over and over again. But before you make your own hit list, you should label the CD and the songs. That makes it much easier when you start deleting and repeating.

Labeling the CD and its songs

When you start to mess around with the order of the songs, you want to make sure that you're working with the right songs. When you edit the play list, Windows 95 just gives Track numbers to the songs, so the first thing you should do is label the songs with their title or a more personal title that you make up.

To label the CD and its songs, just follow these steps:

1. **Open the CD Player.**

   If you forgot how to do this, look back a few pages to the section, "Listening to audio CDs."

2. Choose Disc⇨Edit Play List.

The CD Player: Disc Settings dialog box appears, as shown in Figure 8-8. The CD Player: Disc Settings dialog box isn't very smart when it comes to picking up on the names of the songs on the CD — it just calls the songs Track 1, Track 2, and so on. Totally boring. You better label the songs so that you can tell the good ones from the bad ones. You can get the names of the songs off the CD.

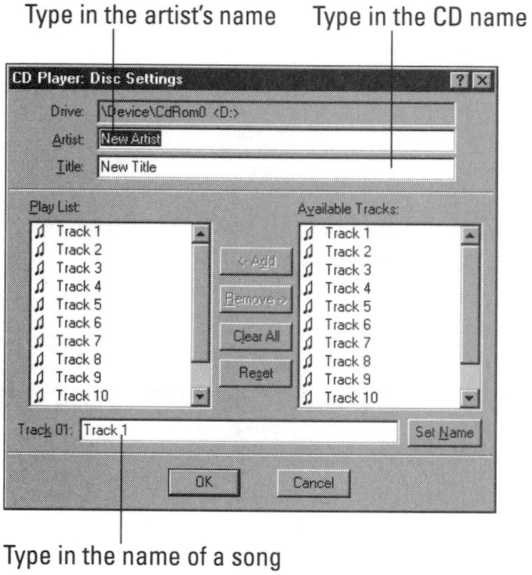

Type in the artist's name Type in the CD name

Figure 8-8: The songs on the CD are not named when you edit the play list until you type in their title.

Type in the name of a song

3. Type in the title of the CD in the Title box.

4. Type in the name of the group or singer in the Artist box.

5. Click a track number that you want to rename in the Available Tracks list.

Track 1 corresponds to the first song on the CD, Track 2 is for the second song, and so on.

6. Type in the track's title in the Track text box.

7. Click the Set Name button.

Notice that the renamed tracks appear in the Play List.

8. Repeat Steps 5 through 7 until you rename all of the tracks, as shown in Figure 8-9.

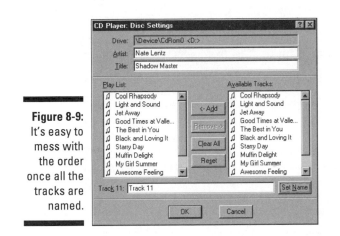

Figure 8-9:
It's easy to
mess with
the order
once all the
tracks are
named.

Playing only the songs you want to hear

Great! Now that you're organized, it'll be easy to make your own personal play list. Notice that all of the tracks appear in the Play List. Check out the list and see if there are any duds. If there are, delete them so that the next time you play that CD, those songs will be gone:

1. **Select the song you want to delete by clicking it's title once in the Play List.**

2. **Click Remove.**

    Poof! It's outta there.

If you really like a song and would like to listen to it more than once, that's easy to do, also:

1. **Select the song from the Available Tracks list.**

2. **Click Add.**

If you *really* like that song, repeat Steps 1 and 2 over and over again.

Ordering your songs around

Now that you've jetted the songs you hate and repeated the songs you love, it's time to play around with the order:

1. **Select the track you want to move by clicking its title with your mouse.**

2. **Keeping the mouse button down, move the title to the right spot.**

3. **Repeat Steps 1 and 2 until you have the order just right.**

If, after changing the order around, you decide that you really liked the way it was set up in the first place, don't fret, you're entitled to change your mind. Just click Reset. If you want to start from scratch with no songs in the Play List, click Clear All.

Getting funky with the Sound Recorder

Your computer occasionally makes beeps and blats, to alert you to something or other. In the same way, you can play hundreds of different digital sounds — that is, sounds or music that have been computerized. You can even record your own, if you have a microphone attached to your computer. Just follow these steps:

1. Choose Start⇨Programs⇨Accessories⇨Multimedia⇨Sound Recorder.

The Sound Recorder window appears, as shown in Figure 8-10.

Figure 8-10:
From the Sound Recorder window you can record and play music.

2. Choose File⇨Open.

The Open dialog box appears.

3. Navigate to the C drive, open the Windows folder, and then open the Media folder. Click any sound file you want to listen to.

The Sound Recorder picks up that sound file as if it were a track on a CD or a song on a tape. Not sure where to start? Try the file called Tada.wav.

If this is the first time anyone's looked in the Sound Recorder you won't find any sound files yet, so head over to the Media subfolder and select one of the files that comes with Windows 95.

4. Click the Play button.

If you want to skip a part of the sound, use the slider bar to jump to the end or the beginning of the sound.

Ready for the big time? Recording sounds

You can make a tape of yourself as a DJ at a hip radio station, make recordings of your own music, or just get a bunch of your friends together and record silly sounds. The choice is up to you. The steps to your recording career are simple.

But first you have to make sure that your computer has a sound card and you have a built-in microphone, or one that can be attached to your computer (many microphones come with the new sound cards and newer computers).

Now you're on your way to your recording career or, more probably, to some hootin' fun.

1. **Start the Sound Recorder.**

   Go back to "Listening to audio CDs" in this chapter if you need some help with this.

2. **Choose File⇨New.**

   If this is your first time recording, you may want to go for the lowest quality sound, which takes up the least amount of memory. If you want to do this, choose Edit⇨Audio Properties; in that dialog box, choose Telephone Quality. If you're ready for the big time, select CD Quality. But remember it uses up gobs of disk space.

3. **Click the Record button (the red circle) and go for it.**

   Speak! Play a drum! Hum.

   The Record button is dimmed if your sound card doesn't support the Sound Recorder.

4. **Click the Stop button (the black square) when you finish.**

5. **Click the Play button to hear your masterpiece.**

6. **If you like what you hear, choose File⇨Save.**

7. **Type in a name in the Save As dialog box.**

8. **Click Save.**

Want to add some kooky effects to your sound recording? Pull down the Effects menu as shown in Figure 8-11, and have some fun:

- To sound like an old man or a little twerp, select either Decrease or Increase speed.
- To add an echo, select Add Echo.

Figure 8-11:
Make
weirdo
sound
effects.

Putting It All Together on Video with the Media Player

Media Player is a conglomerate that can do lots of different things. Media Player can play your audio CDs, electronic music files from instruments that have a connection to the computer known as a MIDI connection, a bunch of sound files, and even video files. All together, these files are called multimedia, because multi sounds a lot better than one, and the computer is acting as if it were a CD player, musical instrument, and TV, all at once.

Even though you can play your audio CDs from Media Player, you'll have more options if you use the CD Player for this. (See "Listening to audio CDs" for more information on working with the CD Player.)

Check out Media Player to watch your favorite digital video.

1. Choose Start⇨Programs⇨Accessories⇨Multimedia⇨Media Player.

You see the Media Player window, as shown in Figure 8-12.

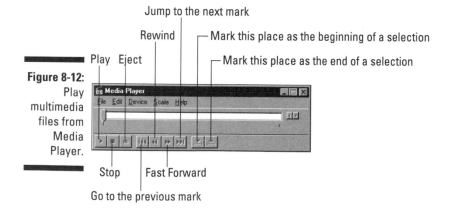

Figure 8-12:
Play
multimedia
files from
Media
Player.

Remember, if you don't have our book next to you and you wonder what the buttons do: Hover over the buttons to see what they do.

2. Choose Device⇨Video for Windows.

You can watch *digital videos,* which are computerized versions of the videos you rent from the video store, on your computer. Some video rental places rent or sell CD-ROMs with digitized video versions of films, along with the regular old-fashioned video tapes that you pop in the VCR. There isn't the variety yet in digital videos, because they didn't look so good on the computer until just recently. But in 1997, video-to-computer technology took one of those quantum leaps forward and created all the bells and whistles needed to watch great quality video on your computer. Now you can see Jim Carrey tell lies in focus and in true color.

3. Select the title of the video you want to watch.

Hint: Look on the C drive, and inside the Windows folder, open the Help folder, and then click any file that ends in .avi.

4. Click Open.

In a moment, the window expands, and you see the first frame of your video. If you chose one of the Help videos, you are about to witness the re-creation of some exciting task, such as cutting and pasting.

5. Click the Play button.

To pick up neat videos of movies, visit `www.hollywood.com/trailers/`.

Chapter 9

Sharing Software with the Rest of the Family

· ·

In This Chapter

▶ Family software that draws parents and kids together

▶ In and about the house

▶ At home

▶ Organized and disorganized sports

▶ Computer crafts

▶ Digging deeper

▶ Stepping out

▶ How to test before you buy or browse

· ·

*T*hanks to some amazing software programs, the computer offers unlimited fun activities you all can do together. From selecting the right breed of dog for your family to planning a great birthday party, software has taken out a lot of the guess work and has given you the tools to let your creative juices flow freely.

In this chapter, we look at some family activities that are enhanced by the use of programs that you run on your computer with the help of Windows 95. In some cases, we even put a demonstration of what the software program can do on the CD that comes with this book, so that you can try out some of the software.

Look for the On the CD icon to get a peek at many beneficial and fun programs. (And if a particular piece of software piques your interest but is not on the CD, read the section "Testing Before You Buy or Browse" at the end of this chapter.)

Software for Family Projects

When we first started writing about family software several years ago, there were only a few good titles out. Most of the programs were dull, hard to use, and, in most cases, very user unfriendly. Our test for a good program then was the same as it is now; we look and see if the computer adds something to the particular task or activity. If not, then why bother? (And why spend the money?)

All of the programs mentioned in this chapter not only use the capabilities of the computer in a creative way — they are also easy to use, right from the start.

You see an enormous amount of software designed for the education and entertainment of kids, commonly known in the biz as "edutainment," which is a blend of educational and game programs that, hopefully, entertain. Parents, you've probably helped your young kids install and use these programs. Kids, you've probably warned your parents about deleting your games. However, family software doesn't fit the edutainment category.

We only list our favorite software programs in this chapter. If you'd like to find out more about kids' software, read *Great Software For Kids & Parents* by Cathy Miranker and Allison Elliott, also published by IDG Books Worldwide, Inc.

We're not talking about programs with macho sounding names, such as Excel, Access, or PowerPoint. While these programs make working on spreadsheets, databases, and brochures a lot faster, they won't put a smile on your face or help you decide where to go on vacation.

This category of software is designed for the rest of the stuff you do with your computer — cooking, gardening, parties, and any other activity that is shared by a number of family members, regardless of age. Great software for Windows families helps kids join parents in activities around the house and on the road.

Quid est computare in familia? (Translation: What is home computing?)

While we're talking about family computing software, it may interest you to know that the word *computer* is not a new term. Like so many words in the English language, it has its derivation from Latin. In this case, the Latin word is *computare* meaning "reckon together," which made its way up to Old French as *compter*. As best as anyone can tell, the word *computer* was first used in the 17th century and meant a "person who computes."

Enhancing Your Surroundings

If you're like us, you spend a lot of time fixing up the inside and the outside of your home. Some people are naturals at this (they are all probably related in some way to Martha Stewart). However, if you fall into the vast majority who need a little help in the house and garden department (like us), you can find a wide array of software available to help you achieve your goals around the home.

Trying out new rooms with interior design software

Many years ago, when we bought our first home, we bought some graph paper with little quarter-inch squares and cut-out shapes for our living room and bedroom furniture. We moved the paper couch and paper desk endlessly trying to figure out just the right place to put everything. Our older son did the same thing with his bedroom furniture. When moving day finally came, despite all of our planning on paper, we found that the things didn't fit where we had envisioned them, and we had to play around with them amongst the packed boxes.

Well, deciding where things should go in the new room is a lot easier with design software. You can not only get a 3-D look at any room in your house, you can also play with different colored walls and carpets. You can go back and forth between contemporary and early-American sofas, and you can browse through the different looks of shades, blinds, or curtains. These programs also help you with your design questions when you want to remodel a room or put an addition onto the house.

Remodeling with 3D Home Architect

Broderbund is well known to parents and kids for its innovative children's computer software, such as Grandma and Me, Kid Pix Studio, and the Carmen Sandiego series. What many of you may not know is that Broderbund is also a pioneer in the home-design software market.

Three years ago, we looked at 3D Home Architect, Broderbund's premier home-remodeling program, for the first time. We thought the program was very good and was far and away the best one on the market. While other programs have caught up with 3D Home Architect since then, the newest version continues to add features to an already easy-to-use program.

The most recent version of 3D Home Architect allows you to design an addition or make changes to an existing room. The program guides you through all the necessary steps and warns you if your design is faulty in any way. It also comes with hundreds of fixtures and sample furniture styles so you can get a good idea of what your design will look like when it is built.

Make sure you take accurate measurements of the room you want to re-model or the space you want to build an addition onto before using this or any other program. Without accurate measurements you may find a door-knob smashing into a window.

Spiffing up a room with 3D Home Interiors

Two years ago there were about 20 interior design titles available. Now there are only a few because, as the song says, only the strong survive. To be good, the program needs to be easy to use and have lots and lots of materi-als, colors, textures, designs, and fabrics to select from.

One such program is 3D Home Interiors from Broderbund. This program also offers templates and specifications for fixtures and furniture from major manufacturers, such as Bigelow, Congoleum, Hotpoint, JCPenney, and Wallpapers To Go. This is great because you don't have to imagine how, let's say, different wallpaper patterns, as seen in Figure 9-1, will look like in your bedroom, because you can view it right from your home on your computer. If you have a modem and an Internet browser, you can link to these manufac-turers' Web pages directly from the program for more info and to order online, if you wish.

Figure 9-1:
From a sports' motif to a Southwestern theme, select just the right wallpaper for your bedroom right from your computer.

Refinancing or buying a new home

If you can look at this category and say, "Been there, done that," then you know that this is *the* most stressful event of your life except for when your dog gets skunked right before your child's teacher comes for her home visit — but we digress.

Mortgage software describes, in plain English, terms such as *points, sweat equity, earnest money, and real money.* This software helps you figure out how much of a mortgage you qualify for before you start to shop for a loan. And, best of all, mortgage software lets you figure out which deal is the best in the short and long run.

One mortgage program we like a lot is HomeBuyer 2.0, which helps you find the perfect mortgage for your finances. You can find a demo of HomeBuyer 2.0 on the CD that comes with this book.

Many finance software packages, such as Quicken, have a feature that allows you to compare various mortgage options. You type in the interest, downpayment, mortgage length, and the total purchase price, and then Quicken figures out your monthly payments.

Now that you have all of the financial arrangements taken care of, it's time to get cracking on actually finding the house you want to buy. Just follow these steps for successful home shopping:

1. **Turn off the computer.**

2. **Gather everyone in the car.**

3. **Go house hunting!**

Planning and ordering the garden together: LandDesigner

We are happy to report that we know of a superb gardening program called LandDesigner by Sierra Home. Try out a demo of this great program from the CD that comes with this book. You find the following features to help you indulge your green thumb:

- ✔ A large database of trees, bushes, flowers, and grasses

- ✔ Good photos so you can see what each plant looks like

- ✔ A drawing feature that lets you outline your existing garden so you can add the various plants from the database to this drawing

- ✔ A "grow feature" that lets you see when and if that sycamore tree nudges up against the electrical lines and how long it takes for the passion flower vine to cover up the ugly retaining wall

- ✔ A troubleshooting section on bugs, fungus, and other plant ailments

- ✔ Online ordering that lets you select your plants from the program and then, if you are hooked up to the Internet, enables you to order directly from the nursery

LandDesigner, which has a database of over 2,100 plants, lets you design a sprinkler system to keep them all well watered! You can walk through your design in 3-D, and if you just want the program to tell you want to do with all that dirt in your backyard, LandDesigner offers many templates and design advice to help you get started.

When you finish drawing your creation, you can either print out the list of plants or e-mail an order to White Flower Farms in Connecticut, which works with the makers of LandDesigner to provide the same plants found in the plant database. We ordered, and our plants arrived fresh and in great condition.

We had a ball with our kids this spring designing a vegetable garden. Each of us picked two things to grow in the garden. We searched through the database looking at various vegetables. As parents, of course, we oohed and aahed over all the veggies. Our kids, of course, crunched up their noses at a lot of them (especially eggplant, which we think suffers unduly from a funny name, shape, and its purple color). But this is a great activity for the whole family. Here's how we did it:

1. **Before you do anything, measure your garden plot to determine how many varieties each family member can select.**

2. **Go through the program's database (as shown in Figure 9-2), look at the pictures, read the descriptions, and pick the vegetables you want to grow. (You can do this with a flower garden as well.)**

Figure 9-2:
Choose a plant group and start digging!

3. **After you make your selections, print out a seed shopping list and take it to a store that sells vegetable seeds. (Many programs, including LandDesigner, give you an approximate cost of any design you're contemplating.)**

4. **Print out the vegetable design plot and plant your seeds accordingly.**

5. **Water and feed according to the directions on the seed packet.**

6. **Eat the ripe vegetables before the bugs do.**

We can say with great experience that if your kids decide that they want to plant pumpkin seeds, design a spot just for them because these viney squashes tend to take over in no time flat.

Making Up Menus and Cooking Together

You can find up to 100 electronic cookbooks on the market today. Most of these cookbooks are general, all purpose books — and then there are many, many specialty titles. Depending upon what your tastebuds are like, you can find electronic cookbooks dedicated to sushi, French pastry, pasta, crab, cookies, low-fat, low-cholesterol, and even one devoted just to chocolate.

When we first tested some of these cookbooks a few years ago, we were a little dubious about their efficacy. Would they really be better than our tried-and-true, yellow-around-the-edges paper cookbooks? Well, for starters — yes. We found it fast to search for recipes in a number of ways, such as by low-fat, short prep time, and by ingredients (which was a lifesaver when we had barrels of zucchini ripening in our garden).

We also like that with many of these cookbooks, you can type in a list of ingredients that you have on hand and the cookbook comes up with some suggested recipes based on what you have in the cupboard, saving a trip to the grocery store. With the flick of the mouse, you can instantly resize recipes and printout shopping lists according to the recipes you selected.

One of our all-time favorite electronic cookbooks is the Betty Crocker Cookbook by Lifestyle Software. It is visually very attractive and easy to use, has lots of ideas for quick and kid-pleasing recipes, and has all the features we want in an electronic cookbook.

We use the Betty Crocker Cookbook to plan the birthday party meal for each member of our family because of the neat party plan menus it offers, but you can use any all-purpose electronic cookbook to plan a special event (or even supper for a weekday).

1. **First, if your cookbook has a photo slide feature, have the birthday kid look at photos of various recipes, marking all of the possibles for further review.**

2. **Search the recipes you marked and narrow down the selection.**

   Figure 9-3 shows a typical search.

   Kids, if the birthday person is your mom, this selection process may take a long time.

3. **After the final selections have been made, resize the recipes according to the number of people you expect to have at the party.**

4. **Print out each recipe and the shopping list.**

   Use a magnet to attach the paper recipes to the top of the venting hood over the range so you can easily refer to the recipe when cooking.

5. **Put on your chef's hat, tie on the apron, and start cooking.**

6. **Eat.**

Figure 9-3:
You can use
all sorts of
criteria to
search for
just the
yummiest
recipes.

Inside Fun

When your belly is full, it's time to settle in to some home-bound pleasures. Your computer can do so much from helping you plan a party to selecting the right breed of dog for your family. Why, it can even help you stick with your diet.

Picking the right dog

Sometimes it's fun to stoke up the fire, put on some pretty music, get on your comfy slippers, and read a good book. Unfortunately, if you have a new puppy, you'll probably have to forgo the comfy slippers part.

But because they are cute and filled with so much unconditional love, we tend to put up with this eat-everything-in-site phase of our puppies until they are trained to eat only dog food and the occasional beetle that creeps across the bathroom floor. Of course, because this cute puppy will grow up to be an adult dog, it's very important to select a breed that works well with your family. Some breeds are great with kids; others are more adults-only oriented. Then there are breeds that need to be walked a lot and others that excel at being lap dogs.

Best of Breed—The American Kennel Club's Multimedia Guide to Dogs by Macmillian Digital Hybrid is lots of fun to use. It helps you select the right breed of dog by asking you a lot of questions, and it also helps you to name your new puppy. It's also chock-full of info and includes a space to keep your doggie records and shows many videos and photos to help you to train your new pooch. Best of Breed also connects you with several canine friendly Web sites that put you in contact with other dog lovers.

For pet lovers only

If you are a true animal lover, meaning that your pets are part of the family, you should go on the Web and check out some of the sites compiled by loving owners and breeders.

When you go out on the Web looking for information about your favorite type of animal, you'll be surprised at the number of sites devoted to pets. We found everything from the helpful to the unusual to the real cute — all the way up to the incredulous.

Here are some of our favorite animal sites to get you started with pets on the Web:

✔ The San Francisco SPCA (www.sfspca.org): The City of San Francisco has an ordinance that no stray dogs can be put to sleep, so they put pictures and descriptions of their adoptables up on this site.

✔ A Real Life Ace Ventura — Sherlock Bones (www.sherlockbones.com): This guy's been helping folks find their lost pets for over 20 years.

✔ Adorable Downloadable Dog Screensavers (www.dogsaver.com/screensaver.html): The beagles are especially adorable, but we're a little biased.

✔ Toilet Training Your Cat (www.rainfrog.com/mishacat/toilet.shtml): This site is a must for adults having a bad day and for 7-, 8-, and 9-year-old boys who still live for this stuff.

Board games go electronic

Some things are just more fun to do at home than anywhere else. Playing board games is one of them. While you can't sit around the computer rolling the dice and counting out the money, you can get lots of help from the program, zooming around the virtual board in ways you only dreamed of before, and yes, you can also cheat, as seen in Figure 9-4.

Figure 9-4:
Use Scrabble's "hints" to level the playing field.

A classic board game that's been successfully adapted to the computer is Scrabble. One of the things our family likes about this electronic version of the popular board game is that it helps people of different ages play together by providing hints and assistance so even the youngest member of the family can play.

Punt, Pass, and Climb

Hardly any sport has been neglected in the software department. You can find software to play almost anything — from baseball to football to soccer all the way up to mountain climbing. You can even find some neat programs available for parents who have taken the thankless task of coaching their child's sports team.

Tracking and perfecting sports

We've coached many of our kids' various sports teams over the years. Using a spreadsheet helps track various things, such as each player's stats to see how they are progressing and where they may need a little more help. We use a database to keep track of their phone numbers (including Mom and Dad's work number, the mobile phone number, the babysitter's number, and Grandma's number), which is extremely important when you have to cancel practice. Both ClarisWorks and Microsoft Works are naturals for this.

If someone in your family has a burgeoning baseball card collection, you may want to check out Sport Card Organizer Deluxe from Ninga Software, which helps you evaluate and keep track of your inventory.

Working together on fitness and nutrition

You wouldn't think that your computer could help you with your diet or help you keep fit, would you? But we find that the computer is actually quite well suited to this. It was a real eye opener to our kids to see where they stood on the nutritional scale. Thanks to these programs, our kids found out that Mom really wasn't a liar when she said that broccoli is the king of the vegetables.

You really aren't what you eat, but sometimes you look like what you eat. Don't think so? Notice how if you eat a lot of pizzas your middle and rump (not to mention your face) start looking like a pizza? And if you eat lots of apricots, you skin starts to turn a little orange? Well, some programs allow you to enter everything you eat (including those double burgers from the double arches), and they will not only tell you how many calories you ate in a day, they will calculate all of the minerals and vitamins you ate, too. Some will even go a big step further and let you enter in all of the exercise you had in that day to calculate if you ate enough calories to gain weight, lose weight, or stay the same.

Two nutrition products we like are NutriBase Personal Nutrition Manager by Cybersoft and Expert Diet by Expert Software. These programs have a large food database and are easy to use.

Having a Party

In the past few years, a plethora of software has come out for printing all sorts of things from party invitations to family albums.

Because your computer lends itself so naturally to printing party supplies, there are many, many good products devoted just to this. One of the best is Print Artist 4.0 by Sierra On-Line. What we like about this program is the colorful, playful templates (you get over 10,000 graphics to choose from), its ease of use, and its adaptability to many skill levels.

You can make gifts for your friends, family, and teachers with printing software:

    1. Select a graphic that fits the personality of the recipient.

2. **Print out a calendar with that graphic on the top and any special days.**

   You put the picture at the top of the page, just like those mountains you see in the calendars you get at the dry cleaner. Then the program puts the dates below that.

3. **Make a letterhead using that same graphic and print out the letterhead.**

   Choose from many different grades of paper. When you make these kinds of gifts, such as stationery with a nice letterhead, it's better to use the heaviest weight of paper you can find.

4. **Now print out thank you notes by using the graphic and typing "thank you" over it.**

5. **Depending upon what's available on the program, print out placemats, envelopes, memo paper, and anything else that's appropriate.**

   Some programs, such as Print Artist, give you a list of things you can make, as shown in Figure 9-5.

Figure 9-5:
You can design and print almost anything.

6. **Find a large box and place all of the coordinated items in it.**

7. **Print out wrapping paper with, you guessed it, that same graphic, and wrap the box.**

Now that makes a great gift for almost anyone.

Picture Perfect

Even with all of the wonderful graphics available in many different programs, you may want to add a photo to a document, greeting card, or make
a family album.

Using your camera

You can take pictures from your camera, pick out the negatives you like, and
ask your photo developer to put them on a disk. Then you can use the
electronic image to copy and paste it into your document (see Chapter 4.)
Or a cheaper option is to have the entire roll put on a diskette.

Kodak has a new service. When you bring your film in to them to be developed, they can develop it either digitally or regularly. (Check with your local
developer, too. Many are jumping on the digital bandwagon.)

Scanning to capture printed pictures electronically

You can only do this if you own a scanner. Scanners used to be very big,
cumbersome pieces of equipment, but now there are scanners that are no
bigger than your hand.

If you want to paste pictures this way, first get your roll of film developed.
Then put the desired photos through the scanner and place it in the appropriate document.

Making albums, calendars, cards, and more using electronic snapshots

Several programs can help you transfer your photos into a document on
your computer.

We like Photo Creations from Creative Wonders, because it is so versatile
and easy to use — kids from about 11 can use it by themselves. You can
scan photos or have them digitally inserted. Then you can make newslet-
ters, cards, or calendars using those photos.

Use a program, such as Photo Creations, to make an album of some special event or events. Start by making an album cover, as shown in Figure 9-6, for albums that cover special happenings in your family's life, such as this year's Little League games or pictures of one whole school year. It's easy to make a digital photo album; here's how:

1. **Take lots and lots of pictures.**

2. **Scan or digitally paste the photos onto album templates.**

3. **Write a caption for each photo. (If the program has sound capabilities and you have a microphone for your computer, add narration instead.)**

4. **Use the drawing portion of the program and decorate the borders of each page.**

5. **E-mail the album to relatives who have a computer and e-mail. For relatives with no computer, print out each page and compile the papers into an album. (Don't forget to make a cover.)**

Figure 9-6:
Create a digital photo album of your life.

Web sites overflowing with info

You can find out about almost anything on the Web. Want to know the lyrics for that song that's been going around and around in your head? How about what was going on in this day in history? It's all there and then some. The tricky thing often is to find it. When you are doing a search remember to use the words *and* or *not* in your search.

(If you would like some more great searching tips, check out *The World Wide Web For Kids and Parents,* by Viraf Mohta, published by IDG Books Worldwide, Inc.)

Let's say you want to find out all you can about the explorer, Columbus. If you just type in Columbus you'll find thousands of listing such as the Chamber of Commerce for Columbus, Ohio, Columbus, Georgia, Columbus, Indiana, Columbus, Nebraska, as well as the Knights of Columbus, Columbus Day sales, and many, many more.

So, if you are searching for the explorer Columbus, it's better to type in Christopher and Columbus or Columbus not Chamber of Commerce.

Fantastic Encyclopedias

It used to be that there was only one decent electronic encyclopedia and that was Microsoft's Encarta. It still is a fantastic encyclopedia, but many have caught up and one, The World Book Encyclopedia 98, by IBM, is especially good for homework.

This encyclopedia always had a huge amount of information, but its previous versions didn't take full advantage of what the computer can do. In this latest version, IBM incorporates lots of photos and video and have aimed it at elementary- and middle-school-aged children. One of the new features is a Homework Wizard, as shown in Figure 9-7, which gives step-by-step instructions (taking notes, writing a draft, design visuals, creating a bibliography, and writing the final paper) to the student for completing his homework.

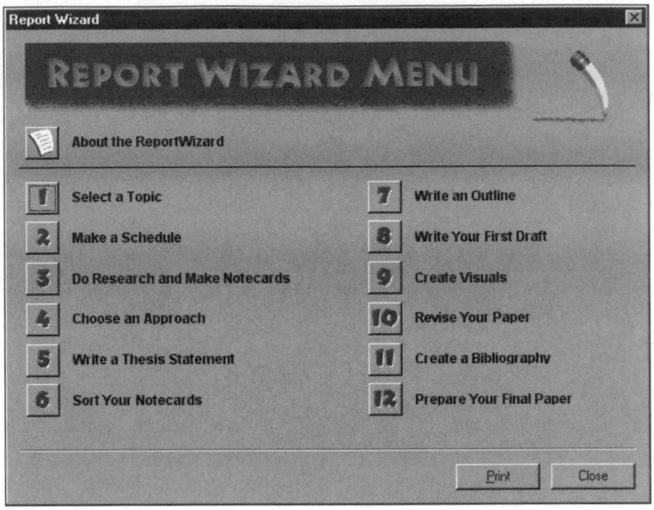

Figure 9-7:
Students
can use the
Report
Wizard to
keep their
reports on
track.

Taking a Trip

All of the other activities that we talk about in this chapter are home related in one way or another. But what about when you want to get out and go on a trip? Well, your computer can help you there, too.

Travel software was great from the beginning, and it's gotten even better with each tweeking. Our favorite from the start has been TripMaker from Rand McNally, and the 1998 Deluxe edition continues to be our favorite. It has many different ways to plan your itinerary whether you are traveling by car or by airplane. It also helps you figure out how much your trip will cost. (But all travel programs do that.) What really makes TripMaker stand apart from the pack for families is that it has a huge list of kid attractions near or on any route you're taking and it gives you a list of kid-friendly hotels and restaurants and even supplies some kid travel games. You'll still have to answer the ever present "Are we there yet?" question, but maybe it won't be asked quite so often.

This activity works well if you are planning to drive to someplace at least 300 miles away. All travel software will be able to do this.

1. **Once you decide where you are driving, get out a paper map and have everyone in the family take a guess at how many miles it will take to get to your destination.**

2. **Then, still looking at the map, have everyone select a route that they think will take the least amount of driving time.**

3. **Using your travel software (TripMaker works well but others do also), type in your place of origin (your hometown) and your destination and ask it to tell you how many miles apart they are from each other.**

4. **Select quickest route. The program calculates the fastest route and you can see who the winner is.**

Testing Before You Buy or Browse

When you buy a new car, you open and shut the doors, check that the windows work properly, kick the tires, and take the car for a test drive to see if you like the feel. But when you want to buy software, you're usually faced with a shrink-wrapped box or a shrink-wrapped CD case. The most you have to go on is reviews, which basically only tell you what the reviewer likes. So how do you take software for a test drive before you buy?

Arranging to watch a software demo

Some software stores and some bookstores that sell software allow you test new programs on a well-worn computer. This is pretty good unless the store is crowded and some parent has left Junior in front of this computer while they browse the rest of the store.

A better way really is to test drive software in your own home on your own computer. Let's say you're interested in reading edutainment software, but you're not sure which one would be right for your child. (There must be at least 100 titles in this category alone!) You can download demos and then watch how your child uses it. This way you won't waste $49.95 on a program that your kid thinks is "dumb."

Where to find downloadable demos

Check out the Web — it's software demo heaven:

- **Software manufacturers' Web sites:** Most vendors now have Web sites with demos. To find the Web address of a manufacturer, do a search with the company name in quotes, such as "Broderbund."

- **Online software sales stores:** Some software store sites strictly sell software; others write reviews and features and offer demos, such as Thunderbeam (which you can find at www.thunderbeam.com).

- **Computer magazines' online sites:** Such as Family PC at www.zdnet.com/familypc.

Part III
Opening a Window to the Internet

The 5th Wave   By Rich Tennant

"TELL THE BOSS HE'S GOT MORE FLAME MAIL FROM YOU-KNOW-WHO."

In this part . . .

Take a cruise on the Internet. Windows 95 comes with your passport and ticket for a trip around the World Wide Web. Seasoned travelers will want to make their own itinerary and fly directly to the Internet Explorer. The newcomers may want to take the more leisurely route via the Microsoft Network (MSN) or America Online (AOL). And one of the neatest things about this trip is that you won't need a stamp when you e-mail your postcards to your friends and family.

Chapter 10

Surfing the World Wide Web with Internet Explorer

• •

In This Chapter

▶ Understanding a web browser

▶ Starting Internet Explorer

▶ Going from place to place on the Web

▶ Looking for information on the Web

▶ Keeping track of pages you want to go back to

▶ Sending electronic messages to your friends

• •

*I*f webs are for spiders, and browsing is something you do at the store, then why do you need a web browser?? In this chapter, we tell you all the cool stuff you can find on using a popular program called Internet Explorer.

Browsing for Stuff on the Internet

Well, it's casual. You don't go to the mall to exercise. You just stroll along, and, well, browse.

Internet Explorer, software that comes with Windows 95, lets you browse through the biggest mall of all — the World Wide Web. The World Wide Web is part of a large group of computers, as shown in Figure 10-1. You sit at your computer at home, dial out along the phone lines, through the phone network, and perhaps over satellites, and through various other networks, to get to another computer, which serves you some information in the form of a Web page. What kind of info? Pictures, text, video, sound — you name it.

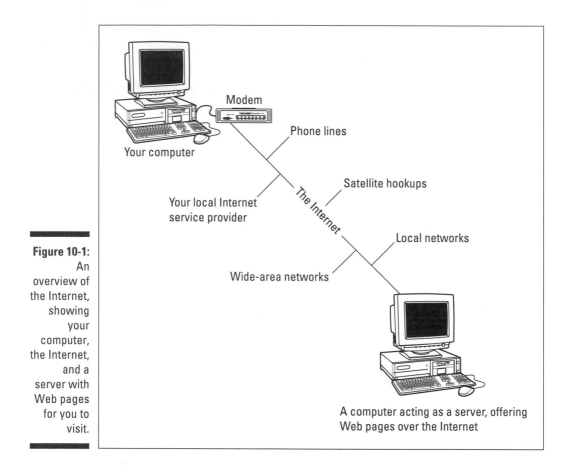

Figure 10-1:
An overview of the Internet, showing your computer, the Internet, and a server with Web pages for you to visit.

Wow! The Internet is the Big Momma of all networks. Originally, a network was the wire connecting a bunch of phones so people could talk to each other locally. Then every town had a phone network, and then every state, and every country. Soon companies built their own networks to pull together their own computers and phones in a wide-area network. Now the Internet pulls together every phone system in the world, plus a ton of communications satellites, fiber-optic cables, and company-wide networks. Because of the Internet, you can connect your one home computer with thousands of networks that can link you to millions of computers.

Your computer connects to the Internet through a gizmo called a *modem,* which dials across your phone lines to an Internet service provider, who plugs you into the Internet itself. Your parents have probably already gotten a modem (maybe it came with the computer), but they need to make the deal with the Internet service provider before you can get on the Internet from home. (For more info about modems, please check out *Modems For Dummies,* by Tina Rathbone, published by IDG Books Worldwide, Inc.)

Lots of people make their computers available to the public. These computers serve up all kinds of info, so they are known as *servers*. Each server has its own address on the Internet.

To make pictures, sounds, video, and text available on a server, people put them into Web pages and post the pages on the server. The idea is that the Internet is like a giant spider web, and at every place the strands cross, there is a server with a lot of Web pages you can explore. Each person's set of pages is known as a *Web site*. (Most companies, schools, and government agencies have their own Web sites.)

You use a Web browser, like Internet Explorer, to go to a particular address on the Internet and pick up Web pages to display at home. That's called *surfing the Web*.

So what's Netscape?

Netscape Navigator and Netscape Communicator (usually called Netscape 4 for short) are the leading web browsers — meaning more people use them to cruise the Web than use Internet Explorer or Microsoft Network. But that's this year. Next year, the year after . . . as a company, Microsoft intends to take over any area it competes in, and we anticipate it will gradually put Internet Explorer on more desks than Netscape. In the meantime, do you need Netscape?

Not necessarily. If you just want to surf the Web, then Internet Explorer will suit your needs just fine. But Netscape does allow you to do a few other cool things beyond just regular surfing — things that may make you want to ask your parents if you can get Netscape.

The most important thing that Netscape Communicator does, which can't be done inside Internet Explorer, is let you create your own Web pages by using a part of the program called Composer. It's like a word processor. You just type and format and drop in pictures, and voilà — you've got a Web page. (Composer makes it easy to create simple Web sites, but not easy to tweak them, or make

them, well, just a little special.) To compete with Composer, Microsoft offers FrontPage Express with the latest version of Internet Explorer 4; this program does just about what Composer does, with the same limitations. To create fancier pages, you need something stronger: Adobe PageMill, Claris HomePage, or Microsoft FrontPage.

The less important plus: Netscape can read certain Web codes that Internet Explorer can't. Of course, the reverse is true, too: Internet Explorer reads other codes that Netscape doesn't. So what? Well, not much. The result is that whichever browser you are using, you will miss out on a few special effects. Not a big deal.

Historically, Netscape comes from some of the folks who created the first browser for the Web, something called Mosaic. The team's independent, cranky, and aggressive. They were there with a browser before Microsoft paid any attention. If you like the idea of keeping Microsoft honest, or at least keeping it from complete dominance, go online to www.netscape.com and download a copy of Netscape Communicator.

If your family is just starting to explore the Internet, you may want to consider limiting the time each child uses the Web in order to keep down the cost of connection time. Some families post a schedule, showing exactly which hours the kids can use the Web. Or, if you can't yet anticipate how much time each person may really want to use it, ask your Internet service provider about a sliding scale, in which you pay for some base number of hours, and only pay for extra hours if you really use them. Most providers also offer, for $20-$30 a month, unlimited access, but most parents find that too expensive, unless they can justify it through work at home.

Getting the Right Address

When you're calling a friend, you have to know his or her phone number. Well, you have to have a similar piece of info, called a Web address, to get to a Web site.

A Web address tells your browser what point on the Web you want to travel to (see "Browsing for Stuff on the Internet" for more information on browsers). Here's an example of what a typical Web address looks like:

```
http://www.theprices.com/circle
```

What the heck are all those abbreviations and slashes and dots? Most Web addresses are similar in construction. Here's a translation of the different parts of a Web address, piece by piece:

- **http://:** Starts every Web address and tells the Internet and your browser, "What follows is a Web address."

- **www:** Announces that what follows is a Web site. Most, but certainly not all, Web site addresses contain this phrase.

- **The actual name of the site:** In the preceding address, this would be `theprices`.

- **The type of site:** In the preceding address, this is `.com` (com means commercial). There are several different types of sites, which we tell you about in "Dit dit dot dot" in this chapter.

- **A specific page on that site:** In our address, `circle` is the page that welcomes you to our site.

Dit dit dot dot

The dot and the letters at the end of a Web address tell you what kind of site you are looking at. Every address in America has some kind of three-letter code afterward, as shown in Table 10-1.

Table 10-1	Types of Web Sites	
Code	**Type of organization**	**Example**
.com	Commercial	www.levis.com
.edu	Educational institution, such as a school, college, or university	www.harvard.edu
.gov	Government agency	www.whitehouse.gov
.mil	Military	www.navy.mil
.org	Nonprofit organization	www.ets.org
.net	Internet service provider	www.worldnet.att.net

Countries other than the United States have their own two-letter code, such as uk for the United Kingdom. That gets tacked on their end of their addresses. For instance, to find the PC User Group in the U.K. you would go to www.ibmpcug.co.uk.

Slashing through the Web

Sometimes you see a bunch of extra slashes and rashes of text after the site's name. Those direct your browser down to some page deep within the site. Essentially, each new phrase after a slash takes you down a level, as if you were opening folders using My Computer or Windows Explorer.

For example, if you wanted to look at an excerpt from another of our IDG books, you might have to type an address like this:

```
http://www.idgbooks.com/bookstore/excerpts/3099-2.html
```

That means that on the IDG Books site, there is a folder called Bookstore, and within that is another folder that contains excerpts from various books. Our particular excerpt is inside that folder; its name is the exciting 3099-2.html.

Getting Ready to Use Internet Explorer

Software changes as fast as sneaker styles. So you may have the latest and greatest version of Internet Explorer — Version 4 — or you may still have an earlier version — Version 3 —which is perfectly okay, but looks different. IE4 is like having IE3 with air pumps.

What version you have on your computer may depend on when your folks got the computer (or bought the Windows 95 package and added it to the computer):

- ✔ If your folks bought your computer or the Windows 95 package before October 1997, they got Internet Explorer 3.

- ✔ If your folks collect updates, they may have gotten the new version — Internet Explorer 4 — some time after October 1, 1997, and installed it.

- ✔ If you got the computer or a Windows 95 package after October 1, 1997, it probably came with Internet Explorer 4.

How can you tell which version you have? Look for one of the following two icons on your desktop:

- ✔ If your desktop shows an icon of the world with the phrase "The Internet" underneath, you have Internet Explorer 3.

- ✔ If you see an icon that looks like a weird lowercase *e,* labeled "Internet Explorer," you have Internet Explorer 4.

Depending on how it gets installed by your folks or the computer maker, Internet Explorer 4 may *also* make a lot of little changes to the Windows 95 desktop, adding icons inside of windows, and taking over a lot of windows, adding a line for a Web address, and adding another toolbar. The idea is to make the computer itself a window on the Web. So if your windows have more icons than we show in other chapters, or different toolbars, you may be using a version of Windows 95 that has been tweaked by IE4. Congratulations! You have a mutant.

Starting Internet Explorer

You probably know how easy it is to get lost when you start a new space-adventure game. Well, get set — the Internet's a super galaxy, with lots of great things to see and do, but it takes a lot of click-click-clicking to find your way past the lame to the awesome. So chill. Exploring can be such fun that you don't mind spending time — in fact, you don't even notice the time go by. So don't worry if starting your web browser seems a little slow the first time; after a few launches, you'll be right at home in hyperspace.

Because everyone's connection to the Internet has slight variations, we can't predict exactly how your kids should make the connection. Can you show them the drill? What follows is our best guess, which should cover most situations. You may want to read through it, and make sure that we're on target for your setup.

If your folks say that you need to connect to the Internet before starting Internet Explorer, then follow these steps to get up and running. If you don't need to connect before starting Internet Explorer, then skip down to Step 3:

1. Double-click My Computer and then Dial-Up Network, and finally, click the name of your Internet service provider.

You see the Connect To dialog box, shown in Figure 10-2.

Type in your secret password here

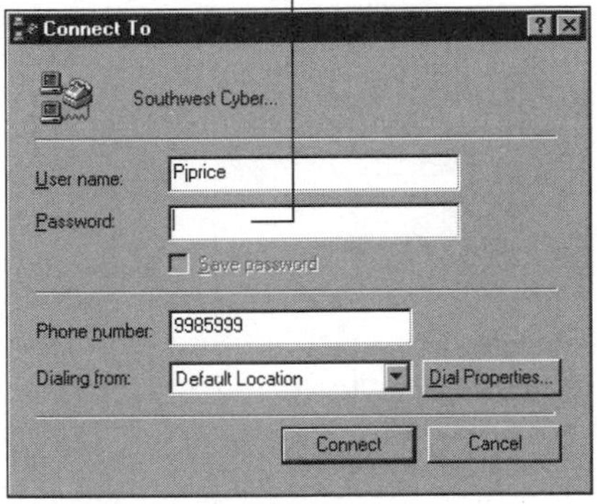

Figure 10-2:
The
Connect To
dialog box.

2. Enter your password and click Connect.

In a few moments, you see a message telling you that your computer is dialing, you hear your modem dialing, clicking, whizzing, and whirring, and finally you get a message saying you are connected. Now that you have the connection to the Internet, you can start browsing with Internet Explorer.

If there's a problem connecting, don't freak. You may get a nerve-wracking message that the computer is not getting a response from the modem, or that the computer you were calling isn't answering. No biggie. Just try again. If your modem sits in a box outside the computer, try turning it off and then on so it forgets its troubles. If your modem is hidden inside the computer, shut everything down and restart. (For the dope on shutting down, see "Stop: Turning Your Computer Off without Breaking Anything," at the end of Chapter 1.) If you keep getting these messages, shriek like George in the jungle. No, no, no. Just politely ask your folks if they will call the Internet service provider to ask for help.

3. Double-click the icon for The Internet or Internet Explorer on your desktop.

A dialog box may appear asking if you want to make the connection to the Internet through your Internet service provider or Microsoft Network. If so, click OK. You now see the Connect To dialog box, shown in Figure 10-2. Enter your password and click Connect. The software goes out, dials the right phone number, makes the connection to the Internet, tells you that it has connected, and then launches Internet Explorer.

In a moment, you see the Internet Explorer window, and gradually the details fill in. You are connected to a Web site — that is, a spot out on the Web, full of different pages of information.

The first site you go to is known as your Start page. Internet Explorer is set up by Microsoft to take you to the Internet Explorer Start page, whose address is www.microsoft.com. That address tells Internet Explorer to use the HyperText Transfer Protocol to go out on the World Wide Web and go to the site belonging to a company called Microsoft. The HTTP is just a code telling your computer to treat whatever comes in as a Web page, which is full of links (known as hypertext).

Wandering in Cyberspace

Websters like hot spicy food. Web pages are full of hot spots — buttons, little icons, blue underlined text — standing for other places in the World Wide Web. These items are hot because you can click them and go to the places they stand for. For instance, look at the IDG home page shown in Figure 10-3 — they're the folks who brought you this book.

How can you tell what's hot? Move your pointer over any item you think may stand for another Web page and, if clicked, take you there. If the pointer turns into a hand, you've found a hotspot. If you click the item, you go right to the Web location described in the text or represented by the picture.

Click-click-clicking along

You can surf almost anywhere by clicking hot spots on the screen and letting Internet Explorer zip you to their locations. Those locations may be deeper in the page you are now looking at, in another page on the same site, or in a page on some other site. Here's what to click.

- ✔ Click anything that looks at all like a button within the Web page (not up in the toolbar) to go to a new location.

- ✔ Click any underlined text to go to another part of the current Web page or to another Web page.

- ✔ Click any graphic — it may be a button, just waiting to take you to another location. The picture usually gives you an idea of where you will go.

Hot spots to click in the text

Menu buttons - click and go

Graphics may be hot spots, too

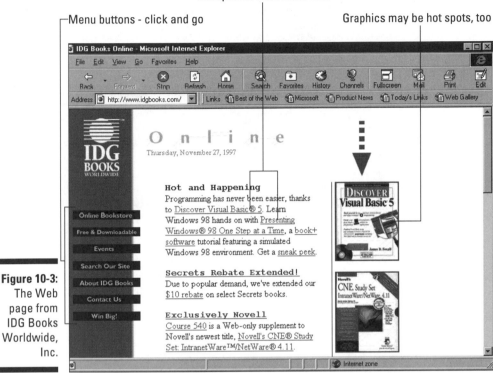

Figure 10-3:
The Web
page from
IDG Books
Worldwide,
Inc.

Sometimes a button, graphic, or underlined text doesn't do anything. No blame. It ain't your fault. The people who made the site may have forgotten to hook that button up to some other page, or they never intended to. Just keep on clicking until you find something that takes you somewhere.

Tooling around with the toolbar

So you're cruising through hyperspace. Internet Explorer's toolbar acts like the instrument panel on your spaceship. We show the Internet Explorer 3 toolbar in Figure 10-4, and the toolbar for Internet Explorer 4 in Figure 10-5.

The address of the page you're currently viewing

Figure 10-4:
The Internet
Explorer 3
toolbar
lets you
navigate
the Web.

Internet Explorer menus

Tools for moving around on the Web
and working with Web materials

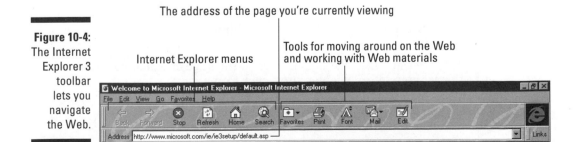

Figure 10-5:
The Internet
Explorer 4
toolbar
lets you
navigate
the Web.

The address of the page you're currently viewing

Internet Explorer menus

Tools for moving around on the Web
and working with Web materials

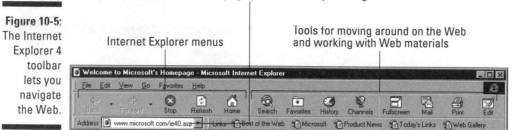

Here's what you can do, using the various tools on the toolbar to zip around. You know how to click a button to go to another page. These tools help you go back and forth among the places you have already visited, and then go to new places, too:

✔ Really loved that site you saw a minute ago? You can go back to a site you've already visited. To back up, page by page, after you have gone hither and yon, click the Back button up on your Internet Explorer toolbar.

✔ Backed up enough? Time to shift gears, so you can go forward to a site you've already visited. After you have backed up enough, click the Forward button to go through those sites again, in the same order you originally visited them.

You are not actually revisiting pages. Internet Explorer has saved each page on your hard disk, in an area called a *cache*, and just displays them again when asked. But the Back and Forward buttons let you go forward and back through the material you have already viewed — a real convenience.

✔ What's new? To go to a new location, type the address (if you know it) in the Address box and press Enter.

✔ Whoa! If you have clicked an underlined hyperlink, or button, or typed an address and asked Internet Explorer to go to that location, you may get stuck waiting and waiting and waiting. If you grow impatient, stop the process by clicking the Stop sign.

✔ If you think the page you are looking at may have changed (like, if the site advertises the latest sports scores, and you think the game may have just ended, but you still don't see the score), or if the page did not fill up the window, click the Refresh button to fetch a fresh version of the page.

✔ There's no place like Home. To go to the page at which you generally start your Internet adventures, click Home.

✔ To search for a particular fact on the current Web site, or the Web as a whole, click the Search button, type the topic you want to find, and then click the Find or Search button. (See "Searchin' and Surfin'" for more information on finding what you want.)

✔ Want to visit some of Microsoft's Favorite Sites? Click Favorites to see a list of sites — some set up by Microsoft and its allies, some just plain fun. Click one to go to it. (After you have used the Web for a while, you will add your own favorites to the list.)

TIP

If you are using Internet Explorer 4, you have a few extra buttons on the toolbar:

✔ **History:** Lets you pop up a list of every site you have visited; click a site and go.

✔ **Channels:** Brings up a list of preselected Web sites that you can do more than visit. You can also do something called *subscribing* to these sites. Subscribing to a site turns it into the equivalent of a TV channel, pouring information out at you over the Internet. If you subscribe to a company's site, the company either pumps new info to you when you are online or sends you an e-mail note alerting you to changes when they occur.

✔ **Fullscreen:** Expands the Internet Explorer window to take over the whole screen.

Print It!

Sometimes you want to preserve the great info you find on the Web, like a picture of your favorite star or the stats on your team. You can print the page to put in your scrapbook by following these steps:

1. **Click the Print button on the toolbar.**

   You see the Print dialog box, shown in Figure 10-6.

2. **If you want more than one copy, type the number in the Number of Copies text box.**

3. **Click OK.**

Some pages don't print well. White letters on black background come out as a mess, for example. If you really need the text, but it doesn't print well, you can copy the text from the Web page, paste it into WordPad, and print out the text from there (turn to Chapter 7 if you need some help working with WordPad). Just go back to the page, click at the top, and drag down through the whole text. Then press Ctrl+C (both keys at the same time) to copy the text. Start WordPad and press Ctrl+V to paste the material into the WordPad document. Then print from WordPad. If the page has different frames of information (like a box on the left and a box on the right), and you ended up printing the wrong frame, go back to the page, click in the text you want to print, and then click the Print button again.

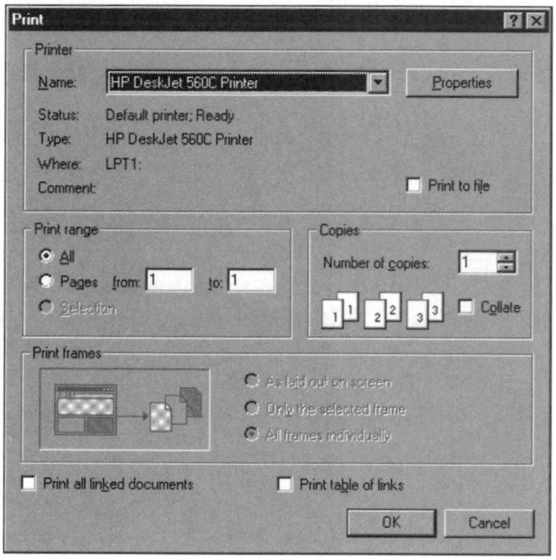

Figure 10-6:
You can print almost anything you find on the Web.

Searchin' and Surfin'

How many of your buds share your love for a certain music group, actor, or TV show? You can find hundreds, maybe thousands, of other folks out on the Web, all just as obsessed as you. Searching helps you find them or anything else you want to find.

If you get homework on biology and want to look up flies, or frogs, the Web has more info than you ever wanted. Ditto on almost anything in school. So searching's fun, and a great way to waste hours on a rainy day.

Here's how to find information you want — and a lot you don't care about, too:

1. **With Internet Explorer up and running, click the Search button in the Internet Explorer toolbar; and in the frame that appears on the left, choose List All Providers from the Providers list.**

   If you have trouble getting the Search frame, or if you are using Internet Explorer 3, type the following address into the address box and press Enter.

`home.microsoft.com/access/allinone.asp`

In a moment, you see a form for looking up a topic on the World Wide Web. In the top left you see a list of today's *search engines* — different programs for combing through the whole Web looking for whatever topic you type in. The bottom of the form offers more specialized search engines.

For example, if you know you want to look up your favorite music group, you can click Music, under Specialties, so you don't get a lot of sites that just happen to have the same word in their name.

2. **Click a search engine, if you see one that you like or one that seems to focus on the topic you are interested in.**

How can you tell which one to use? Well, at first, you guess. Each offers special features, including different ways for you to enter your topic and different ways to show you the results of the search.

Good news! Each search engine offers you some categories of information so you can hone in on the general topic area before asking for a search. Why bother to pick a category? If you just search the whole Web, you get thousands of "hits," but most will be duds. In other words, if you want to find out about tomato seeds, you can type tomato, and you'll likely get a long, long, long list of sites dealing with tomato paste, tomato bugs, tomato sauce, pizza, spaghetti, farms that grow tomatoes, trucks for hauling tomatoes, a town that calls itself the Tomato Capital, and oh yes, a few sites dealing with tomato plants, and, occasionally, a company that sells tomato seeds. So you may choose the Garden category to rule out all those recipe sites.

Each time you look something up, try a different search engine so you can discover which works best for you. For now, just throw a dart and guess.

3. **In the text box, type the topic you want to find.**

Be very, very specific if you can be. There are literally tens of thousands of sites dealing with music, thousands with rap, but only a few dozen focusing on your favorite group.

If you want to find information about a person or group, put their full name *with capital letters* in quotation marks, like this: "David Hasselhoff." That way, you only get sites that have those words, in that order, together — not sites that happen to have something about Haslo Hasselhoff the Hungarian HipHop King, or David Goliath and His Favorite Gerbil Photos.

If you want to make absolutely sure that a site has information about a topic, put a plus sign in front of it, like this: "+David Hasselhoff." That makes David a "must have." The site must have that word or phrase, or else it isn't shown to you in the list of results.

4. **Click the button next to the text box.**

   Depending on the search engine, this button may say Search, Find, Seek, or Go For It!

   You see a list of the first ten sites found by the search engine. Usually there are hundreds, even thousands, more waiting for you to peruse. But the engines don't want to waste their time telling you about all those if these first ten don't seem even close.

   Occasionally you get news that no sites were found. Don't be discouraged. Try again, adding a few other words that may come closer to describing what you want to know about.

5. **If a particular site looks interesting, click its name or address to go there.**

   Remember, if you don't like it, you can always click the Back button in the toolbar to come back here and try another site.

Playing Those Old Favorites

Love it? Found an awesome site? Great — but do you know how you got there? Can you find your way back? To keep track of your favorite sites, you have Internet Explorer memorize their addresses. Here's how:

1. **Go to the Web site you like.**

2. **Choose Favorites⇨Add To Favorites.**

   The Add Favorite dialog box appears asking you to give your own name to the site, as shown in Figure 10-7.

Figure 10-7:
The Add
Favorite
dialog box.

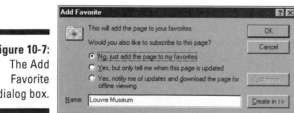

3. **Type in a name for the site.**

4. **If you want to put this site's address inside a folder, click Create In. (If you don't want to put the address in a folder, just click OK, and you are done.)**

You may want to do this if you are collecting a whole bunch of sites that deal with soda cans, and then another bunch dealing with fast food. To keep from getting confused, you can create a folder called Fast Food and another called Sodas I Have Known.

The Add Favorite dialog box extends, as shown in Figure 10-8. You can see that the bottom gets bigger to make room for more information.

Figure 10-8: In its expanded form, the Add Favorite dialog box lets you pick a folder you want to save the address in, or create a new folder for it.

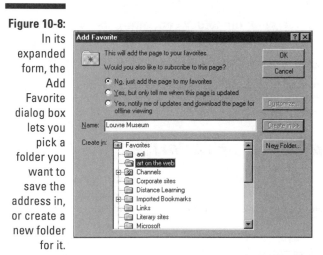

5. **Click a folder to open it. Or, if you want to create a new folder, click New to see the dialog box shown in Figure 10-9, and then type the name of the folder and click OK.**

   The folder you create this way will hold your address.

6. **Click OK.**

   The address is placed in the Favorites list in whatever folder you specified.

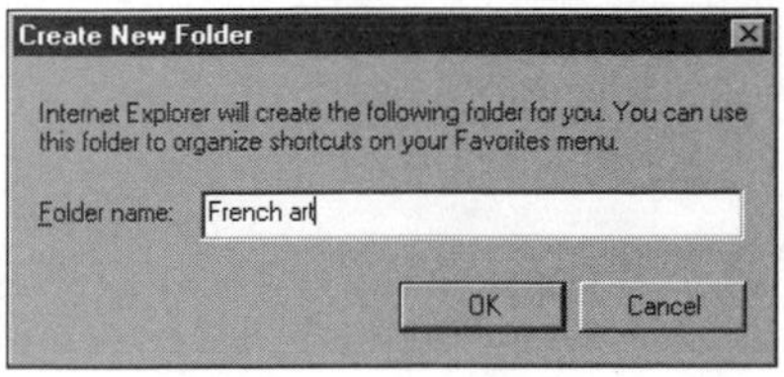

Figure 10-9: You can create a new folder to hold the address.

Getting where you want to go — fast

Whenever you want to go back to your favorite site, you can get there faster than you thought humanly possible (and you'll never have to mess with the Web address again). All you have to do is the following:

1. **Choose Favorites.**

   A menu of your favorite sites appears.

2. **If your site is in a folder, click the folder containing the site you want.**

3. **Click the site.**

   Internet Explorer puts that site's address in the address box and goes out on the Internet to look for it without any more work from you.

Cleaning up after your favorites

Chill out. You can collect a ton of favorites. But after a while, your list of favorites gets quite long, and it's hard to figure out where stuff is. You can reorganize it the way you would change the view of the documents in a folder.

1. **Choose Favorites⇨Organize Favorites.**

   You see the Organize Favorites dialog box, as shown in Figure 10-10, with a list of the names of the sites.

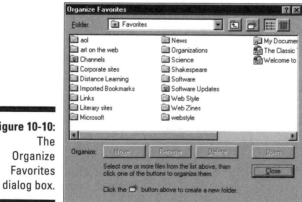

Figure 10-10:
The
Organize
Favorites
dialog box.

2. **Move the site to a different folder, delete the site, or rename the site (or a folder).**

   • To move a site from one folder to another, select it and then click Move, and in the list of folders, click the folder to put it into.

   • To delete a site or folder, select it and then click the Delete button.

   • To rename a site or folder, select it, click the Rename button, and type a new name.

If you want to see the sites as icons, or in more detail, right click in the white space next to the list, and then, in the menu that appears, choose View⇨Small Icons or Details. Or, using the Arrange Icons command, you can have the list arranged by name, type, size, date, or date you last visited. You can also use Line Up Icons to get the icons into a neat grid.

Going back in time

If you forgot to put a site on your list of favorites, but now want to go back to it, you may be able to find it on your History list — a list of sites you have visited recently. To use the History list, just follow these steps:

1. **Click the History button.**

   A list of recently visited sites shows up on the left, as shown in Figure 10-11.

2. **Click the site you want to revisit.**

   The address appears in the address box and Internet Explorer goes off to find that site for you.

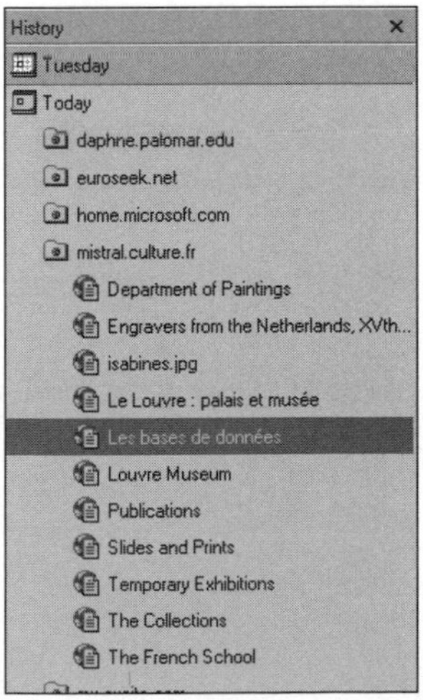

Figure 10-11:
The History list shows where you've been, so you can click and go back in time.

History   ×

- Tuesday
- Today
  - daphne.palomar.edu
  - euroseek.net
  - home.microsoft.com
  - mistral.culture.fr
    - Department of Paintings
    - Engravers from the Netherlands, XVth...
    - isabines.jpg
    - Le Louvre : palais et musée
    - Les bases de données
    - Louvre Museum
    - Publications
    - Slides and Prints
    - Temporary Exhibitions
    - The Collections
    - The French School

Using Electronic Mail to Talk to Grandma (or Your Friends)

Fast and fun — that's e-mail. Not like the kind where you put a stamp on an envelope, and write DDLDSDB (Deliver duh lettuh dah soonah da bettah). That's *snail mail*.

Now that your grandma and grandpa are hooked up to the Internet, they can send and receive mail electronically — and you know, that means you both can keep in touch better. (Who wants to get out a pen or pencil and write a thank you on paper?)

Since 1995, Microsoft has sent out one e-mail program after another with different versions of Windows 95. These programs all do about the same thing, but they don't all work well with each other, and often the same program needed by Internet Explorer 3 does not work well with Microsoft Network. Here we describe how to use the most recent, and most bugfree, package — Outlook Express, which is delivered along with the Internet Explorer 4 package, but looks a lot like Outlook, which came with Internet Explorer 3.

Please set up an electronic mail account with your Internet service provider, and, using their instructions, set up the correct software to send and receive from Internet Explorer or Microsoft Network. If you have decided to use America Online for electronic mail, send your kids to Chapter 11 to find out about e-mail through AOL.

Reading your mail

Here's how to read your mail, if you have received any:

1. **In Internet Explorer, choose Mail⇨Read Mail.**

   If you are not already connected to the Web, Explorer asks if you want to connect.

2. **If asked whether you want to connect, click OK, and if asked for a password, enter that.**

   In a moment, you see a message saying you are logged in. Then you see Outlook Express.

3. Click Send and Receive.

You see a message indicating that the software is going to your electronic mailbox and picking up the mail.

When all mail has been sent and received, you end up in the Inbox area, looking at a list of electronic mail you have just received.

Writing back

Now that you have made contact with your electronic post office and received mail, as described in the preceding section, you have a list of messages and are ready to read them.

1. **Select a message in the Inbox (by clicking the subject of the message) and read it in the open area below.**

2. **To get rid of a message, select it and then click the Delete button in the toolbar.**

3. **If you would like to print the message you are reading, choose File⇨Print and click OK.**

4. **To answer someone's e-mail, click the Reply button on the toolbar, type your answer, and click Send.**

   You'll get a message saying that the message will be sent whenever you next click the Send and Receive button.

5. **Click the Send and Receive button in the toolbar.**

   Your reply is sent off.

Sending a new message

You just heard some great gossip. Or you can't wait to tell your big news. You have something important to tell a friend: like who's going out with whom, or what the class thinks of your substitute science teacher. You are itching to make up an electronic message and send it. Just follow these steps to get your message across:

1. **To start a new message, click the Compose Message button.**

   In a moment you see a form you can fill in, as a message.

2. **Click in the To text box and type the e-mail address of your best bud, or Grandma, or whomever.**

3. **Type the Subject.**

   Like Circus in Science. Or Silly Bellbottoms.

4. **Type your message in the large area at the bottom.**

5. **Click the Send button on the toolbar.**

6. **Click the Send and Receive button.**

   You see a message indicating that your mail is being sent, and if you have mail waiting, that it is being delivered to your own Inbox.

Chapter 11

Cruisin' the Online Services — Microsoft Network and America Online

● ●

In This Chapter

▶ Starting Microsoft Network (MSN)

▶ Changing MSN's look and feel

▶ Jumping around MSN

▶ Going On Stage with MSN

▶ Chatting on MSN

▶ Browsing the bulletin boards on MSN

▶ Exploring the Channels on America Online (AOL)

▶ E-mailing on AOL

▶ Chatting on AOL

▶ Setting parental controls on AOL

● ●

Spiderman: My web is bigger than yours.

Spider: But yours can't catch flies.

*T*he World Wide Web sure is big, but it doesn't always catch flies. If you've already been tooling around with Internet Explorer, you've seen that the electronic Web is awesome, confusing, enormous, fun, and a mess. Sometimes you have to wait and wait to see a Web page, and then you get a site that has nothing interesting on it — a dud.

One way to get more out of the Web with less trash is to cruise on over to an online service like the Microsoft Network. MSN, as it's known, grabs neat features from all over, invents its own new shows like a TV channel, puts up fab pix for fans, links you to tons of prescreened sites on the Web, helps you send electronic mail all over, and lets you talk, talk, talk, until you have to go to bed. MSN also lets you launch into the rest of the World Wide Web. By putting together first-rate info on one site and acting as a guide to the rest of the Web, MSN has made itself home base for a few million Web surfers.

How is MSN different from America Online (AOL), the other hot online service? (Did you just throw away another disk that came in the mail from AOL?) Well, like AOL, MSN is an information service. But it's a lot smaller than AOL, more compact, and so MSN is a little easier to explore. And don't forget the MS in MSN. Microsoft itself has put a lot of money into creating neat services, funding new online magazines, setting up places to chat, and generally using MSN to experiment on the always-surprising Web.

In this chapter, we tell you everything you need to know about getting started with these two powerhouses of the online world. First you find out how to use MSN, and then we tell you all about AOL.

Zipping All over the Internet with MSN

Psst! Time to call your parents. Ask them — politely — to make the connection with Microsoft Network and then to show you how to connect so that they don't need to help you every time you want to get on MSN from then on.

Setting up to use MSN

You can probably skip all the rest of this section, and jump to the next one, which tells you how to tweak the way MSN looks and feels. But just in case you haven't already installed the components for MSN, read on to see what you need to check in with Microsoft Network. There are several pieces and they all need to be present for the magic to happen. That's why we suggested the kids call you.

To use Microsoft Network, you must *already* have:

> ✔ **Installed Internet Explorer, which is the rocket on which MSN rides onto the Web.** (Your computer vendor may have already installed Internet Explorer. Make sure that it is on the list of programs you see on the Start menu.)

✔ **Installed Microsoft Network.** Again, your computer vendor may have already installed it. If you have an icon with the initials MSN on your desktop, the product is already installed. If you see an icon begging you to Install MSN, click and go. If you see none of these, reach for your Windows 95 CD and install MSN from there.

✔ **Made some arrangements with an Internet service provider (ISP).** The ISP can be a local company offering you "20 hours of Internet time for $20," or something like that. You get a phone number for your computer to call, to connect to the ISP's computer, and then you can talk through that computer with the rest of the Internet. Or you may have accepted Microsoft's offer to use its own service, which is — with deliberate ambiguity — also called Microsoft Network. Whatever ISP you signed up with gave you instructions for connecting, either through Dial-Up Networking or through Internet Explorer and Microsoft Network software.

Please make the first connection and show your child how to do it. We give you some general instructions here; depending on the way MSN was installed on your computer, and depending on your Internet service provider, your way of connecting may be different. Please write variations from the following steps in the book so your kid can make the connection easily next time.

To get up and running with MSN, follow these steps:

1. **If you normally have to make the connection to your Internet service provider before launching a web browser such as Internet Explorer, use Dial-Up Networking to connect.**

2. **Double-click the MSN icon, which you should see on the desktop. If you don't see the icon there, choose Start⇨Programs⇨MSN.**

   If you connect through an independent Internet service provider but don't normally connect before launching a browser, MSN asks you if you want to make the connection to the Internet. If asked, click Connect.

   In a moment you see the sign-in screen.

3. **If necessary, enter your name and password. (They may already be entered for you, if you chose that option during installation.)**

4. **Click OK or Connect.**

5. **If asked whether you will accept a cookie, click Yes, to allow the cookie to be downloaded.**

   You may be asked whether you will accept a cookie or two from Microsoft. In general, you ought to be wary of these little treats when they come from unknown sites, because they are, in effect, bits of information that jump onto your hard disk and describe you or choices you have made to the site the next time you visit. The cookies sent by Microsoft Network, though, are innocent enough, and you can accept them by clicking Yes.

In a moment, you see the first screen of the Microsoft Network.

6. **If it's your first visit, the program asks you to give your name, address, and a credit card number and then choose a membership level (premium simply adds some special services that cost more per month).**

After you get past signup, click the Guided Tour, Navigation Practice Bar, or Helpful Hints, for orientation. If you want to skip that introduction, click Exit to MSN.

You now see the welcome screen, with the menu bar, as shown in Figure 11-1, and beneath that, an ever-changing series of commercials for locations on MSN. You may want to browse to see what is new and hot.

Figure 11-1:
The
Microsoft
Network
menu bar
helps you
navigate
the MSN
site and
the Web.

 Occasionally, you see a little button-ad telling you that MSN comes to you best with Internet Explorer. That is, MSN works best "on top of" Internet Explorer or as a companion to it. You are already using Internet Explorer behind the scenes, so you don't need to pay attention to this ad. You do not need to download another copy of Internet Explorer because you already have a copy on your Windows 95 CD and on your hard disk. Basically, when you choose to run MSN, Microsoft automatically launches Internet Explorer and runs it in the background while you are looking at the Microsoft Network window "in front" or "on top."

 After you have used Microsoft Network to connect to the Internet, you can switch from the MSN program viewer to the Internet Explorer window, if you want. (No real need to do so, but it can be done.) Just launch Internet Explorer by double-clicking its icon in the programs list, or by double-clicking the Internet icon on your desktop.

Whose network is this? Customizing MSN

When you get fast food, do you take it off the tray and arrange it just so? If so, you may want to redo the window that brings you MSN. Think of the window as a big tray, with stuff to move around in any way that makes the window easier for you to use.

Yes, Microsoft brings you the giant Web site known as MSN, but you get to adapt the window. When you first look at the welcome screen, you see black everywhere (as of this writing). (Wait a few months, and some other color will get the nod from Microsoft designers.) But as your eyes adjust to the darkness, you notice a bunch of icons and words along the top of the window.

And, surprise! The MSN logo at the top-left corner of the window is actually a menu called View, which offers you ways to adjust the window size, set options for the way you connect to Web sites, and to end an online session by quitting MSN.

1. Choose MSN⇨Options.

You see the Options dialog box, shown in Figure 11-2.

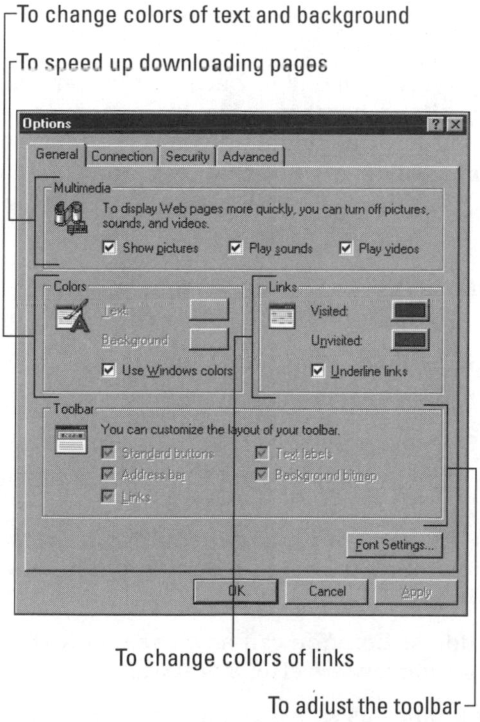

To change colors of text and background

To speed up downloading pages

Figure 11-2:
The Options dialog box lets you adapt the way you receive material over the Internet.

To change colors of links

To adjust the toolbar

2. **If you want to speed up delivery of pages from Web sites on the other side of the moon, click the General tab, and deselect Show pictures, Play sounds, and Play videos. (Click the check box to remove the check mark.)**

   This makes the pages much duller, but much faster.

3. **If you want to change the color of text or backgrounds, click the General tab and change options in the Color area.**

   These changes affect the way that every page gets displayed, unless the people who created the page wrote special codes that say, in effect, we want it our way, not yours.

4. **If you want to change the color of links (the text you click to go to another Web site) or the color of links you have already visited, click the General tab and change options in the Links area.**

5. **To add or subtract items in the toolbar, click the General tab and deselect or select items in the Toolbar area.**

6. **If you want the protection of a certification program, assuring you that the publisher has been vetted so that you can feel confident downloading some software from them, choose the Security tab and explore Certificates.**

7. **If you want to be warned of any activity that may violate your privacy or endanger your computer, leave the Warnings on in the Advanced tab.**

   Turning the Warnings on is a good idea, because you can't always tell when an unrestrained site manager may feel like sending a program down to your hard disk that would foul up your system or make an unwanted connection, particularly one that may show up later on your phone bill.

Jumping jack!

Did you ever play hopscotch? Jump, jump, and jump again! That's part of what's fun about the Web. You get to jump from one Web page to another in a few seconds (or minutes, on a slow day). You just have to tell your web browser, in this case, Microsoft Network, the address of the Web site, out in hyperspace. Here's how to jump around on the Web by using MSN:

1. **To show the address of the Web page that you are on in the address box, click the down-pointing triangle next to the MSN logo at the top-left corner of the window.**

   This brings up the address box. You can now use that text box to type in a new address to go somewhere else, if you want.

   You see the Internet toolbar, as shown in Figure 11-3.

Figure 11-3:
The Internet toolbar lets you type in the address of another Web page.

Click to enlarge the type size

Click to print the current page

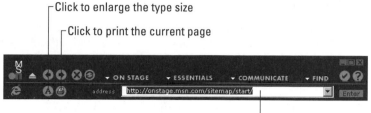

Type the address here and click the Enter button to go to another Web site

Table 11-1 lists all the buttons that you see in this toolbar and what they can do for you.

Whenever you want to hide this toolbar, click the now up-pointing triangle.

Protecting your family from offensive content

If you want to protect your family from sex and violence on the Internet, you can turn to the Content Advisor, which blocks sites that have been rated as offensive due to language, nudity, sex, or violence, and, if you want, blocks sites that haven't been rated, just in case. (A group called the Recreational Software Advisory Council creates the ratings for many sites.)

Here's how to set up your own jamming system for offensive content:

1. **Choose MSN⇨Options and click the Security tab.**

2. **Under Content Advisor, click the Settings button.**

3. **Type your regular password, or a special password to be used just for Content, twice, and then click OK.**

   You see the Content Advisor dialog box, open to the Ratings tab.

4. **Click a key for language, nudity, sex, or violence and then in the dialog box that appears, use the slider to establish the level you are willing to accept (from none to extreme).**

   You can set up controls for all four topics.

5. **On the General Tab, if you want to override these restrictions for your own viewing, check the box indicating that the supervisor (that's you) can type a password to allow users to view restricted content.**

6. **Click OK to close the Content Advisor dialog box.**

7. **In the Content Advisor part of the Security tab, click the Enable Ratings button. Enter your password and click OK.**

   The program tells you that your content advisor is turned on and watching.

8. **Click OK to dispense with this message.**

2. Do one of the following to get where you want to go on the Web.

- To go to a Web site for which you know the address, or Uniform Resource Locator (URL), type the address in the Address text box (at the top of the window) and then click the Enter button over on the right. (The URL is that weird string of characters that begins http:// and sometimes goes on and on.)

When a whole bunch of people get on the Web at the same time, getting to a particular Web page can be slooooooooowwwwwww. Often, dialing into the Web from home, you find that you have to count to 100 and then start over before you get to look at a particular Web page. No matter how fast your modem is, network traffic slows to a crawl just when you want to sign on, because everyone else signs on then, too, and no one gets new pages very quickly. To help you move around, browsers such as Internet Explorer and its companion, the Microsoft Network program viewer, store images of the pages you have already viewed in a folder called a *cache*. Then, if you want to go back and look at a page, the browser picks it off the hard disk, rather than going back out to the Internet and reloading it, which makes things a whole lot faster.

- To go back to a page you viewed earlier, click the Back button (the arrow pointing to the left). Then, when you have gone back, use the Forward tool to return to the present.

- To cancel the downloading of a page that seems to be taking forever or a page you linked to by mistake, click the Stop button (the big X).

- If a Web page seems to have died before fully loading, or if you think it may have changed since you loaded it, click the Refresh button (the two arrows spinning around inside a circle).

- For a list of entertaining sites within Microsoft Network, click the On Stage menu button. (For more, see "Dancing on stage . . . it's showbiz!," later in this chapter.)

You see a drop-down menu of channels, and if you click one of those, you see shows on that channel. A channel is like a channel on TV, except that the shows are Web sites, with tons of different pages all about the same theme or by the same company; it's as if instead of spending all day watching one show after another, you can explore all the shows at once, by going from page to page on the site.

- For a menu of practical services and informative sites within Microsoft Network, click the Essentials menu button.

- To communicate with other folks via e-mail, chat, or newsgroups, click the Communicate menu button and click an option. (For details, see "Chatting, blabbing, and conversing," later in this chapter.)

- To locate a topic on the Microsoft Network or out on the rest of the Internet, click the Find menu button and click an option.

- To go to a favorite site, click the Favorites button (the check mark at the right) and then click the site on the list. If you particularly like a site you are visiting, and want to return, choose Favorites⇨ Add a Favorite and click OK.

  If you've used Internet Explorer before and put favorites up on the list there, you'll notice that you are looking at the same list.

- For support, help, and member services, click the question mark button at the far right. You'll find answers to common questions, a way to e-mail the staff for help, and other helpful information.

Table 11-1	Microsoft Network Toolbar	
Icon	*Name of Tool*	*Function*
[MSN icon]	MSN	Lets you control the size of your Microsoft Network window, set options for displaying text and links on Web pages, and close the program.
[eject icon]	Show or Hide Internet Toolbar	Displays or puts away the toolbar showing the Internet Explorer icon, a tool for changing font size, the Print tool, and the address box, which you can use to type in the address of a Web site you want to visit.
[back arrow icon]	Back	Get set! Takes you back through pages you have already visited during a session.
[forward arrow icon]	Forward	Takes you forward through pages that you have visited during a session, up to the page at which you first started going back. Yes, it's confusing!
[stop icon]	Stop	Cancels the loading of a Web page (useful if the page is taking forrrr-evvvvvvv-er).

(continued)

Table 11-1 *(continued)*

Icon	Name of Tool	Function
(Refresh icon)	Refresh	Start over! Loads the current page all over again (useful if it only loaded part of the way before or if information has changed since you last loaded it).
ON STAGE	On Stage	Click to see channels of entertainment; click a channel to see the Web sites available. (A channel on the Web is similar to a channel on TV.)
ESSENTIALS	Essentials	Click to see a list of information pages and services in categories such as personal finance, computers, travel, shopping, automobiles, reference, and the People Finder.
COMMUNICATE	Communicate	Click to see a menu of communication options, such as electronic mail (e-mail), topical forums, chat sessions, and bulletin boards.
FIND	Find	Use to locate information about a topic on MSN or the rest of the Web.
(Favorites icon)	Favorites	List of your favorite sites, so you can revisit them quickly.
(? icon)	Support and Member Services	Help, subscription information, and answers to frequently asked questions.

Dancing on stage . . . it's showbiz!

When you visit Microsoft Network, after your initial orientation, you land at the On Stage area, which is kinda like TV. On Stage gives you a bunch of channels, and you surf the channels to find the good stuff. The On Stage menu offers games, online magazines, jokes, and chances to interact with the creators of these sites. On Stage is an electronic newsstand, a TV network, and an arcade, all rolled up into one.

Here's how to get to the On Stage area if you have gone somewhere else:

1. **Click the On Stage menu button in the toolbar if it is not already lit up and magnified.**

   If it is already lit up and magnified, you are already in the On Stage area, and looking at the menu, duh.

   A menu drops down.

2. **Click a channel to see what shows it offers.**

   For example, look at Channel 2, which features *Star Trek Continuum, Entertainment Tonight,* and *Duckman Presents.* Or try Channel 3 — the Internet Gaming Zone.

3. **If a submenu opens for the channel, click a particular show.**

   The title, On Stage, lights up and expands, and you see the welcome screen of that particular show.

These channels have even more changeable lineups than the TV networks, because Microsoft is still experimenting, trying out shows for a while, canceling some, expanding others. Every few visits, you may want to go through the On Stage menus, looking for new shows.

If you'd like fresh news on your screen when you come back from lunch, check out the MSNBC News Front Page, available in On Stage, under Channel 1. Accept the NBC News Browser. Choose Personalize this Page to pick what kind of news you want displayed next time you visit the page (or have them e-mail you news alerts).

Chatting, blabbing, and conversing

Are you a chatterbox in school? Does the teacher keep telling you to be quiet? Microsoft Network lets you chat all you want, without getting in trouble.

On Microsoft Network, chatting means typing messages back and forth with other folks who are connected to Microsoft Network at the same time you are. A kind-of conversation unrolls on the screen, with what you say and what they say labeled with nicknames. You get to say, well, maybe a sentence at a time, and then other peoples' sentences appear, answering what someone else (or you) said earlier in the conversation. If someone is interested in what you contribute, you see an answer after half a dozen or more messages go by. Not as good as chatting in person, but fun enough to keep typing for hours.

Getting on the horn at Chat Central

There are so many conversations going on all the time that you could spend all night just wandering from one chat to another; that's why MSN suggests you start at Chat Central, to join a conversation that has room for another person, and then, if you want, go off to another chat:

1. **On the Communicate menu, choose Chat Central.**

   You see a set of empty boxes, where chatting will take place. Before you plunge into the conversation, though, you need to create a nickname for yourself.

2. **Type a nickname in the bar at the bottom of the conversation and click the Join the Chat button.**

   Pick a nickname that says something about stuff you like or hobbies you enjoy. Don't say something that your parents would disapprove of and don't pretend to be someone you are not. If you have a favorite movie or TV character, though, you can use that name as a nickname, because everyone understands that the character is not really there and that you have taken the name because you like the character.

   You see an ongoing conversation, with the names of participants (and *lurkers,* that is, people who read but do not type anything) along the righthand side. Generally the conversation is all text: You see a name, and then a brief phrase, which scrolls up very fast as many other people type in a word or two.

3. **To get into the swing of the conversation, type in a comment or question, and click one of the speech balloons over on the right.**

4. **When you can't stand it anymore, click the Leave the Chat button.**

What do you want to talk about?

You can find someone to talk with about almost anything, at least during the early evening, compared to mid-day, when fewer people are online. There are tons of topics to discuss. Here's how to find something that you want to chat about:

1. **In Chat Central, click the Chat Search button to see lists of all Microsoft-sponsored chats and member-started chats.**

   You see two tabs, one open to MSN Chats, that is, chats sponsored or set up by the network itself, such as those devoted to politics, game discussions, and romance. The other tab is for chat rooms set up by members, and these are often about hobbies or private interests.

2. **If you want to focus on chats sponsored by MSN, you can leave its tab open. If you prefer to explore member chats, click that tab.**

3. **On the left, click Show All Chats (for a complete list) or Show Top Chats Now (for the most popular chats), or if you want to see whether a particular topic is being discussed, type the topic on the left and click Search.**

   You are asked if you want to send confidential information (your choice) over an open line. Don't worry. It's not as if you are a spy or talking about nuclear war. To protect yourself, just don't say anything about your home address, phone number, or school — anything that would allow a total stranger to track you down. Be Mr. or Ms. Anonymous.

4. **Click Yes to tell MSN your choice.**

   You see a list of relevant chats in the tab on the right. The names give you an idea what everyone is talking about.

5. **When you decide which chat to join, click the chat room name.**

   In a moment, you go to that chat room. At this point, the conversation is probably taking place through cartoon panels in a mode called Comic Chat. Yes, it looks just like the strip of funnies in the newspaper. Each part of the talk has a character or two, and what they say appears in a speech balloon overhead. You are assigned a cartoon character. It's as if you were jumping right into a comic book, and whatever you type appears over your head. Rad, huh?

6. **Type a comment in the only text box you can see in the window, click an emotional expression for your character over on the right, and then click any speech balloon you like, to include your idea in the flow.**

7. **To whisper to one particular participant, type a comment, click the name in the list on the right, and click the whisper speech bubble (the fuzzy one on the right). You see your comment, and the person to whom you are whispering sees it, but no one else does.**

Finding more than you expected

Got some homework on biology or space capsules? Want to find out about your favorite music group? Wonder where you can preview the next hot flick? The Web has tons of info. The trick is to find it.

Use the Find area to see what's new or to investigate some idea that just occurred to you. You can look at topics arranged by categories, or you can search for information about a particular topic on the Microsoft Network and on the Internet.

These searches work best if you stay open to serendipity — that is, to the unexpected but intriguing possibilities that pop up to view, as you look for something else.

To explore from the top level of Microsoft Network down to the smallest little detail, that is, starting with large topics and narrowing down your search to more and more specific details, just follow these steps:

1. **Choose Find⇨Browse All of MSN.**

   Top down is like looking at the school library and figuring out the main sections, like science, fiction, math, and then going to a section, to find a particular book. Browsing helps you find stuff when you aren't sure exactly what MSN calls it.

   You see the Find home page, with three tabs showing on the left: Word, Subject, and Calendar. You are on the Subject tab, which allows you to start with a broad category and narrow the search down.

2. **Click a category on the left.**

   A new set of subjects appears on the right. If there are more than one page's worth, you see arrows at the bottom. You can click the Next arrow and go through all MSN areas and plunge into Internet sites related to the subject.

3. **When you hit a site title that interests you, click it to go to that location.**

To pinpoint a subject, click the Word tab, type the word in the text box, and if you want to search the whole Internet, rather than just MSN, click one of the search engines listed on the right. (Otherwise the search will just take place within the Microsoft Network.) Then click Enter. In the list that appears on the right, click a site that interests you.

If you are feeling very brave, and want to know, really, how many Web sites mention a particular word or phrase, then choose Find⇨Search with Alta Vista. You type in your word, choose what language you want the site to be in, and click Search. You get about 10,000 hits for anything like "music" and even a few dozen for a music group's name. That's why we say you have to be brave to go through all the possibilities. Maybe, though, what you really need is a lot of sugar and caffeine — not that you should eat over the keyboard.

Playing around on an MSN bulletin board

Do you read ads for garage sales? Posters selling used guitars? Do you like gossip? Electronic bulletin boards give you a place to paste up a question and get an answer or at least a sympathetic response.

Using an electronic bulletin board is like exchanging e-mail with the ozone and getting an answer, just because there are other folks browsing the list of messages posted every day. In fact, you may find you stumble upon a question you can answer.

Here's how to read and post on an MSN bulletin board:

1. **Choose Communicate⇨Browse MSN Bulletin Boards or click any button titled Bulletin Board on any page you find within Microsoft Network.**

   You may just stumble on these buttons by accident. For example, if you are looking at a Web page that discusses a game and there is a bulletin board for folks to use talking about that game, you may find a Bulletin Board button there.

   In a few moments, you see a new window, courtesy of another application, called Internet News, as shown in Figure 11-4.

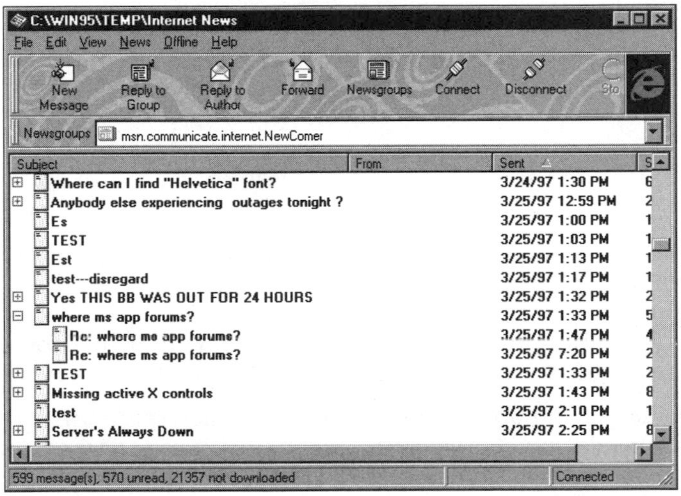

Figure 11-4: Check it out — it's an Internet News window!

2. **Scroll through the list of messages.**

   Each bulletin board lists all messages posted; if responses come in to a posting, they are stored underneath it, and a plus sign appears next to it, indicating that there are more messages.

3. **When you see a message with a subject you are interested in, double-click the message to read it.**

   If the message has a plus sign to the left, click the plus sign to reveal the responses to the original message, and then double-click whatever message you find most interesting.

   You see the message displayed in its own window. The toolbar offers tools especially designed for bulletin boards, as shown in Figure 11-5.

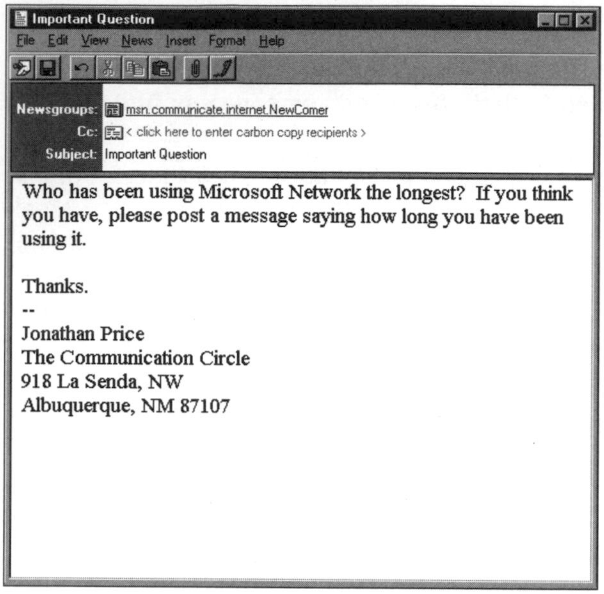

Figure 11-5:
The
message
appears in
a special
window,
with tools to
help you
work with
the mes-
sage or
respond.

If you just love what the person says and want to save the text as a file, click the Save icon (it looks like a floppy disk).

- ✔ If you want to print the text, click the Print icon (which looks like a printer with a piece of paper coming out of it, if you know what I mean).

- ✔ To respond in public, click the icon of the newspaper with the arrow pointing down; this way, your response goes to the whole group. In a moment, you get a message form. (The exact icons available in the message form depend on which application Microsoft Network finds on your hard disk; it looks for Microsoft Outlook, but, not finding that, may turn to Microsoft Exchange or, last, Internet Mail.)

- ✔ To reply privately, click the icon of the open envelope with the down-pointing arrow, so your response just goes to the writer, not the public. In a moment, you get a message form.

- ✔ To forward this message to someone, click the icon sealed envelope with the arrow pointing up. You get a message form so you can write a message to go along with the forwarded text and fill in the name of the person you are forwarding it to.

Sometimes you may want to start a conversation of your own, without responding to someone else's message. But stay on topic! Nothing drives people madder than when you put up some totally irrelevant message. If you aren't willing to talk about the main subject for the bulletin board, go elsewhere. Don't mess this one up with stuff that most people will think is, like, from Mars. To put a new message on a message board, just follow these steps:

1. **While looking at the list of messages, click the New Message icon.**

   In a moment you see a message form, already addressed to the people in this newsgroup, that is, the people who are looking at this bulletin board.

   To send the message to someone who is not looking at this bulletin board, click to the right of the CC, and replace the dummy text with the address of anyone you want to send a copy to.

2. **Type a subject.**

3. **Click in the body of the message and type your ideas. (Your name and address may already have been pasted in for you.)**

4. **To post the message, click the tack, the first icon in the toolbar.**

Your message is posted. Depending on how many people are using the MSN computers, you may see your message appear in a few seconds, or it may take 15 minutes.

Surfin' America Online

America Online (or AOL) is a great way to get your feet wet online. You get to read a lot of neat stuff and look at great pictures, all under their roof. That means you don't get lost as much as you might out on the World Wide Web, and all the content is, well, pretty good, whereas on the Web it is sometimes wonderful, sometimes stupid. Plus, from AOL you can easily jump into the World Wide Web itself whenever you feel like it. Also, AOL has five times as many members as Microsoft Network and a ton more content. It's a wonderful world of its own that lets you launch off on the waves of the World Wide Web.

(MSN, for sure, comes with Windows 95. AOL doesn't necessarily appear on the computer that came with Windows 95; you may have to get your folks to install it.)

Ask your folks if they have already gotten AOL set up so that it is ready for you to use. If they haven't set it up, but are willing to, urge them to read the next section while you make yourself a snack.

A lot of computer vendors pack America Online on the computer when they ship it, so you may already have the AOL software on your hard disk. If not, wait a few days, and a disk will come in the mail, or you'll see an ad in a computer magazine. (Or call 1-800-827-6364 and have AOL ship you a disk.) To get started, slip the CD-ROM or floppy disk in the drive, run the Setup program, and use the registration number and password they give you. You'll dial out over your modem to connect to an 800 number, answer a few dozen questions, set up a payment plan, and get a local number to call for all subsequent connection. Surprisingly, the setup process is quick. If you do have trouble, call the America Online's technical support at 1-800-827-3338.

Signing on to (and off of) America Online

Yea! After your account is set up, you can use America Online right away. So turn on your speakers, if you have some, because AOL likes to talk to you, and you'll soon be talking to AOL.

Ask your parents for the password beforehand, and write it down somewhere where you can look it up if you tend to forget stuff like that.

Ready, set, go:

1. **Choose Start⇨Program⇨America Online.**

   You see the sign-on window, as shown in Figure 11-6. The idea is that you have to check in with a screen name and your password, and if that all checks out, you're allowed in. Sort of like saying "Here!" when the teacher calls your name on the roll.

   Don't worry if your screen looks a little different from our pictures. The thing is, AOL keeps improving, and updating, and changing the way things look. So from month to month, you see new stuff, which is cool, but, hey, it means that your screen may not exactly match ours. On the other hand, you can still do everything we mention here.

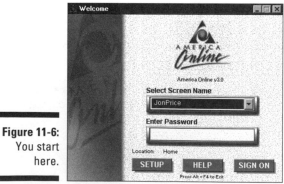

Figure 11-6:
You start
here.

2. **If your folks set up different screen names, pick yours from the drop-down list.**

3. **If the vertical bar is blinking in the box called Password, type your password. (You may not be asked for a password if your folks set up the software that way.)**

If you fear that one child will grab another child's screen name and go online and cause trouble under that name, you should require each kid to have his or her own screen name and a unique password for each. If the kids don't bug each other, you don't need to take this precaution.

4. **Click Sign On.**

You see a lot of messages, and you hear your modem dial, and buzz, and click, and hum. If all goes well, you get a voice saying, "Welcome." You may see an advertisement, up front. (If so, click No Thanks to get rid of it.) Then you see a welcome screen advertising some of the big events of the day, and behind that, a list of the current channels (channels are online stuff grouped around a theme like computers or travel).

5. **Close the AOL Today screen by clicking the X in the top right of the window.**

You see the list of channels, as shown in Figure 11-7.

Figure 11-7: AOL offers a bunch of channels, just like cable TV.

6. **Click Kids Only to see what's up today, just for kids.**

You see a screen like the one shown in Figure 11-8. You find magazines, teasers for kids' movies, and bulletin boards for bad jokes, paintings, and stuff like what's hot and what's not.

7. **Done? Choose Sign Off⇨Sign Off, or just click the giant X at the top-right corner of the AOL window.**

AOL shuts all its little windows, then closes down, detaching you from the phone connection to AOL, and then going to sleep.

E-mailing your friends and relatives

Pssst! Here's the biggest reason most grandparents buy a computer: to get e-mail from their grandkids. And most kids tell Grandma and Grandpa: Get on America Online. It's the easiest for old folks to use because the form for sending a message looks like a sheet of paper and they can figure out how to use it faster than with a lot of other e-mail programs. (Of course, your friends won't mind hearing from you every once in a while, too, especially if you know the latest piece of gossip that's way too hot to tell at school.)

Before trying to e-mail Grandma, call her, and get her to spell out her exact e-mail address, so you don't end up writing to someone else's grandma by mistake.

1. **Choose Mail⇨Compose Mail.**

   You see the e-mail form, shown in Figure 11-9.

2. **Type Grandma's e-mail address in the To box.**

   If Grandma is a member of America Online, you just need to type her nickname, or handle, here. If she belongs to another service, such as MSN, you have to put her e-mail name, plus an @ sign, and the name of the service or organization. For example, if she belongs to MSN, you would have to type grandma@msn.com. If she gets e-mail at her job at Acme, you would write to grandma@acme.com. If she gets e-mail at her school, you would write to grandma@school.edu. (Ask your parents if you have any questions about the address.)

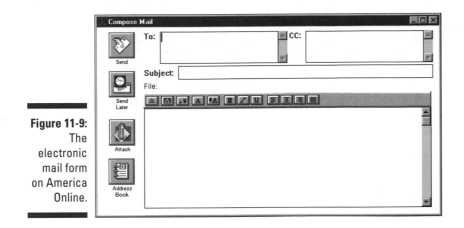

Figure 11-9:
The
electronic
mail form
on America
Online.

3. **Type a word or two on the Subject line.**

   Yes, you have to have a subject. That's because Grandma will see a long
   list of e-mail messages and delete all the ones that have as a subject
   something like "Earn $$$ at Home" or something else that she doesn't
   recognize as a message from you. Don't get deleted!

4. **Type a little note in the big box at the bottom.**

   That's your message. If Grandma is also on AOL, you can use the tools
   just above the box to color the background or the letters, to increase
   the size of the letters, and to emphasize some with boldface or italics. If
   she isn't on AOL, don't bother: None of this formatting will get outside
   the door.

5. **Click Send.**

   After a moment, AOL tells you that your mail has been sent.

Reading Grandma's reply

So you just got a phone call from Grandma. She says she's sending an answer
to your e-mail. You go online and want to get her message. Here's how:

1. **On the Welcome screen — the one that also says AOL Today — click
   You Have Mail, down in the left corner.**

   You see a list of messages for you.

2. **Click the message that you want to read.**

3. **Click the Read button at the bottom of the screen.**

   You see the message, like the one shown in Figure 11-10.

```
┌─────────────────────────────────────────────────────┐
│ Good news                                    ⌄ _ □ ✕  │
│  ┌────┐  ┌──────────────────────────────────────┐▲   │
│  │ 📝 │  │Subj:   Good news                     ││   │
│  └────┘  │Date:   97-11-23 22:22:03 EST         ││   │
│   Reply  │From:   JonPrice                      ││   │
│          │To: JonPrice                          ││   │
│  ┌────┐  │                                      ││   │
│  │ 📝 │  │The report is finally done.  Wait til you see it!│   │
│  └────┘  │                                      ││   │
│  Forward │Best,                                 ││   │
│          │                                      ││   │
│  ┌────┐  │Al                                    ││   │
│  │ 📝 │  │                                      ││   │
│  └────┘  │                                      ││   │
│Reply to All│                                    ▼│   │
│          └──────────────────────────────────────┘    │
│            ┌─────┐                                    │
│            │ ⬅   │                                    │
│            │Prev │                                    │
│            └─────┘                                    │
└─────────────────────────────────────────────────────┘
```

Figure 11-10:
Your e-mail
message
has buttons
for replying
and
forwarding.

4. **If you want to answer, click Reply and fill out the e-mail form, and then click Send.**

   If you want to forward the message to someone else, click Forward, type in the address of the other person in the To box, add a note explaining why you are sending this message along, and then click Send.

   To see the message on paper, choose File⇨Print and then click OK.

Chatting up a storm on AOL

Chatting online is a little weird because you can't see anyone else, and you do all your talking by typing. Plus, there may be a dozen people all typing at once, so you see parts of what one typed, and then parts of what another typed, and then you type, and then, in a few seconds, you see what you typed going up on the screen. Still, for all the weirdnesses, kids love chatting about school, friends, what's in, and what's out. There are hundreds of chats going on all the time, in different imaginary chat rooms, all over AOL.

Here's how to join in:

1. **While connected to AOL, double-click the icon of the two faces chatting in the toolbar.**

   You see a window with text on the left. That's the ongoing conversation. The host usually types something like, "This is Chat Room 100," so you have some idea where you are. You've landed in the first available chat room, so the conversation is, well, likely to be stupid (or at least not what you wanted to talk about).

2. **Click List Chats to find a more specific topic.**

   You see a window that lets you navigate through all the chats now going on, as shown in Figure 11-11.

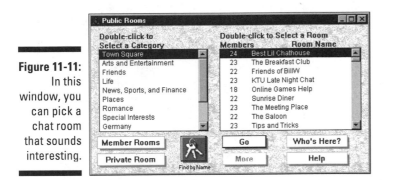

Figure 11-11:
In this window, you can pick a chat room that sounds interesting.

3. **In the window on the left, double-click a category that you think may be interesting.**

   You see a list of chat rooms dealing with that topic. For example, you may find a bunch of people talking about math homework, some talking about romance, and others talking about the weather, politics, or movies.

4. **On the right, double-click a chat room.**

   If there is space available for you to join the conversation, you see the chat appear on-screen. Your handle (screen name) shows up on the right. If the room is full, you get told sorry, and you can try another room.

5. **Type a question or comment in the text box at the bottom of this window and then press Return.**

   In a moment, your words appear in the chat and scroll upward as others keep answering each other and, eventually, you.

   Remember smiley faces? Here are some online abbreviations to use:

   - **Laughing Out Loud:** LOL
   - **Rolling On The Floor (laughing):** ROTF
   - **By The Way:** BTW
   - **In My Humble Opinion:** IMHO
   - **Great Minds Think Alike:** GMTA
   - **Face to Face:** F2F
   - **Ta Ta For Now:** TTFN

Never, never give someone else your password (they can act like you and cause lots of trouble for you, even getting you kicked off AOL). Don't swear, but, more important, don't give away your phone number or address, so creeps don't show up at 2:00 in the morning. If someone says something you don't think they should say to a bunch of people, you can have AOL send someone by the chat room to listen in, and, if necessary, yank that person out of there. Just click the Notify AOL button and fill in the form.

To find out about someone else in the chat room, double-click the screen name on the right and then click Get Info. If that person filled out a member profile, you see it now.

If you want to fill in a Member Profile, choose Members⇨Edit Your Online Profile and follow the directions. You can tell people what city you are in and what your hobbies are, but, as we said about chatting, don't put in your phone number or street address. In fact, you don't have to fill in any line on the form, if you don't want to.

 6. **To leave a chat room, just close the window by clicking the big X.**

Setting controls

Hey — the online world can be a scary place, so you'll be happy to hear that you can insert some control. Just click the Keyword button on the toolbar, and type in **Parental Controls** then click Go. You see the Parental Control screen. You can control whether or not to accept Instant Messages from other members — Instant Messages are neat because if a friend realizes you are online, he or she can send you a private e-mail by Instant Message, and you can reply right away. On the other hand, Instant Messages offer a way to chat privately, with no one else listening in; so, if you fear that someone may try to get away with unseemly talk with your child, nix these. You can block access to all chat rooms or just to member-created chat rooms (the ones where people can invite kids for a private chat). You can also set access levels for Web materials.

Part IV
The Part of Tens

The 5th Wave   By Rich Tennant

SEVERAL HOURS PASSED BEFORE WAYNE DISCOVERED THAT HE WAS LOOKING AT HIS SCREEN SAVER AND NOT OUT THE SUBMARINE'S PORTHOLE

"IT'S INCREDIBLE! I'M SEEING LIFE FORMS NEVER BEFORE IMAGINED!! BIZARRE, COLORFUL, ALMOST WHIMSICAL!!!"

In this part . . .

This is the place to look if you forget how to do something simple, such as starting a program or finding a file. And for some wild surfing fun, browse through ten great family Web sites. But if you make a mistake and have a wipe out, don't sweat it because you can also look up the answers here to find out what to do about those unearthly error messages.

Chapter 12

Ten Easy Answers to First-Timers' Questions

In This Chapter

▶ Finding the Start button

▶ Starting a program

▶ Finding a file, folder, or program

▶ Installing a new program

▶ Adding programs to the Start menu

▶ Straightening up all those icons on the desktop

▶ Changing the name of a file or folder

▶ Copying a file onto a floppy disk

▶ Copying a floppy disk

▶ Checking for available space on your hard disk

*W*hen you go to sleep during math class one day, the next day is totally useless because you have no idea what the teacher is talking about. That's because your teacher's building on what he talked about the day before, when you were busy catching some ZZZZZs. Well, we hope you weren't catching some ZZZZZs instead of reading every word of every chapter of this book, but just in case, here's a quick reference for those gotta-know-how-to-do things. If you know the answer to these ten questions already, pat yourself on the back and take a nap.

Where's the Start Button, and What's It Good Fer?

It's always a good idea to start at the beginning. The majority of everything you do with Windows 95, like starting programs, finding lost documents, and deleting applications, starts from the Start button.

If you don't see the Start button in the lower-left corner of your screen, then someone has hidden it (turn to Chapter 2 for more information on hiding your Start button). To make the Start button reappear, just drag your pointer down to the very lower left of your screen and the Start button will pop up.

How Do You Start a Program?

Click the Start button, glide up to Programs, and then click the program you want to start.

If you don't see the program you want on the menu, click the folder that contains that program. More often than not, you find several files in a program folder. If you still can't find the program you want to start, read the answer to the next question.

How Do You Find a File, Folder, or Program?

Click the Start button, glide up to Find, and click Files or Folders. You see the Find All Files dialog box. Type in the name of the file or folder you're looking for in the Named list box, and then click the Find Now button.

What if you forgot the name of the file or folder? Don't sweat it. If you know the date, give or take a few days, when you first created the file or folder, click the Date Modified tab in the Find All Files dialog box and select Between. Type in the very first date you may have created the file and the very last date. Then click the Find Now button. Look at the list offered from that search. Hopefully one of those file or folder names will jog your memory.

How Do You Install a New Program?

Kids: Call your folks! Installation isn't hard, but you should make sure your parents do this, so they can make decisions (like, if the program is a hog, and wants to take over your hard disk).

If the program you want to install has a little icon on the box that says, "Designed for Windows 95," then installation is a snap. Just pop in the CD-ROM or the installation disk; a little Wizard, minus the hat and wand, appears. The Wizard asks you a bunch of questions, mostly expecting you to click the Next button. After you tell the Wizard what it wants to know, the program's installation program runs automatically.

If the new program was not specifically designed for Windows 95, you need to click the Start button and glide up to Run. The Run dialog box appears. In the Open box type the letter of the drive in which you want to install the program, followed by a colon, backslash, and what ever magic words (usually install, install.exe, setup, or setup.exe) the manual says you need to type here. Then click OK and follow the instructions of the installation program.

Can You Add Programs to the Start Menu?

If you use a program a lot, you may want to just add it to the Start menu and save yourself a lot of clicking. The easiest way to get that program on the Start menu is to drag the program's icon right onto the Start button. But if that doesn't work for some reason, try this longer way:

1. **Click the Start button and glide up to Settings.**
2. **Click Taskbar.**
3. **Select the Start Menu Programs' tab.**
4. **Click Add.**
5. **Click Browse.**
6. **Look for the program you want to add to the Start menu and double-click the program name.**
7. **Click Next.**
8. **Double-click Start Menu.**
9. **Type in a name for the program.**
10. **Click Finish.**

Now every time you want to use the program you'll find it waiting in the Start menu, like an old friend.

How Do You Neaten Up All Those Icons?

Clean your room! Straighten out your closet! Neaten up those drawers in your desk! Does just the thought of accomplishing all this send shivers up your spine and make you instantly exhausted? Luckily, when you've made a mess of the icons in a window such as those of My Computer, you can line them all up in jiffy. Just pull down the View menu and choose Line Up Icons. Those icons will snap to attention and form neat rows faster than you can say whose-it, what's-it. Everything in life should be this easy.

How Do You Change the Name of a File or Folder?

Sick of the name you originally gave a file or folder? Windows 95 gives you several ways to get started with renaming them:

- ✔ **Click the file or folder to highlight it and select Rename from the File menu.**
- ✔ **Click the file or folder and press the F2 key.**
- ✔ **Click the file or folder, wait a few seconds, and then click the file-name again.**

After you do one of these things, the name is highlighted inside a box, and a blinking cursor appears right after the name. The blinking cursor tells you that the name of the file or folder is ready and waiting for you to rename it. Type in the new name and then click anywhere outside of the text box. And, voilà! Your file or folder has a spankin' brand-new name.

Only change the name of files or folders that you have created. If you rename a file or folder used by one of your programs, you may not be able to start that program the next time you want to use it.

How Do You Copy a File onto a Floppy Disk?

If you want to bring home some files that you started at work or at school (or vice versa), you need to copy those files onto a floppy disk. A floppy disk is one of those small 3.5-inch disks encased in a hard plastic shell; it is only floppy on the inside, where the flimsy plastic records your information.

First make sure that you have a floppy disk in your disk drive. Like so many tasks in Windows 95 there are several ways to copy a file onto a floppy. Here are two of the fastest and easiest:

✔ **The drag and drop method:** Double-click the My Computer icon so you see all the drives on your computer. Now double-click the C drive, then the folder that contains the file you want to copy. Arrange the two windows side by side, so you can see the A drive icon in one, and the file in the other window. Point your mouse at the file you want to copy, hold down the mouse button, and drag it onto the floppy drive's icon. (This drive is almost always the A drive.)

✔ **The menu method:** Click the name of the file you want to copy. Then pull down the File menu and select Send To. A drop-down menu appears with suggestions for your file's destination. Click the floppy drive (usually A), which instantly sends a copy of your file to the disk in your floppy drive.

If you forget to put a floppy disk in your disk drive, Windows 95 honks you an annoying little sound and pops up a nasty little note telling you what a lughead you are.

How Do You Copy a Floppy Disk?

There are many reasons you may want to copy a floppy. We won't go into what most of those reasons are, but sometimes it's nice just to have a back-up of a precious disk. Usually you are taking the information from an original disk and putting that onto a blank disk. The odd thing is you sometimes have to keep swapping disks, as Windows sucks up information from the original, then spits it out onto the new disk (the duplicate).

When you want to experience the thrill of copying a floppy disk, just follow these steps:

1. **Put the floppy that you want to copy into the floppy drive.**

   Double-click the My Computer icon and then double-click the icon of the drive that contains that floppy (probably A).

2. **Choose File⇨Copy Disk.**

   The Copy Disk dialog box appears, with the Copy From list on the left, and the Copy To space on the right.

3. **In the Copy From list, click the drive that has the floppy in it.**

4. **Click the drive that you want to copy the floppy to, and then click Start.**

   Windows 95 whirls a bit. You are asked to remove the original and put in the blank disk you want to copy onto, and so on, until the official copying procedure is done

5. **When all is done, click Close.**

Do You Have Any Room Left on Your Hard Disk?

After you add all those games and neat programs to your computer, you'll find that you can never be too rich or have too much computer memory.

To find out how much memory you have left on your hard disk, right-click the hard disk's icon and select Properties from the shortcut menu that appears. You see a window that tells you how much used and free space you have. (For those of us who are numerically challenged, the window also offers a colorful pie chart with this information on it.)

Chapter 13

Oof! Ouch! The Ten Most Common Error Messages and What to Do about Them

. . . .

In This Chapter

▶ A:\ is not accessible. The device is not ready

▶ Cannot find this file

▶ Destination disk drive is full

▶ This filename is not valid

▶ Not enough memory

▶ Open with

▶ There was an error printing to LPT1

▶ Deleting this file will make it impossible to run this program

▶ Unable to locate the server

▶ Windows 95 wasn't properly shut down

. . . .

*Y*ou know kids who can never admit they're wrong? They're always blaming everyone else for whatever happens. Windows 95 is like that, in a way.

Whenever Windows 95 breaks down or gets in trouble, or gets confused, it beeps at you and puts up what Microsoft calls an error message — as if to say, "You idiot, we were doing just fine until you goofed." Well, sometimes that's all there is to it. You goofed. But a lot of times, the problem is not your fault.

The real problem is that some of the messages that come up seem to be written in a different language. From the way these messages are written, you may never know what's really gone wrong, or how to fix it.

In this chapter, we translate the ten most common messages. We also show you what to do next, to get out of trouble.

A:\ is not accessible. The device is not ready

Meaning: Nonsense. The A drive — the one you use for floppy disks —is probably still there and still working. In other words, it is accessible. And it is probably ready to go. This message is just one of those stupid phrases programmers write when what they really mean, "Uh, the computer couldn't find a disk in the drive. Did you put one in?"

What's really wrong: You forgot to put a disk in the drive. Or you put in a disk that started life on a Macintosh computer. Or you put in a disk that isn't formatted — that is, prepared to be read or written on.

To fix it: Put your disk in the drive and then click Retry.

Note: If the disk needs to be formatted, Windows 95 will probably invite you to do so. If this is a new disk, go ahead. If you think the disk may have valuable info on it, do not allow Windows 95 to format it again, because formatting wipes out that information.

Cannot find this file

Meaning: You may have started a program and chosen a document from the bottom of the File menu — something you created and saved in this program. But now the program can't find the file. Or you double-clicked a document's icon and got this message.

What's really wrong: You may have moved the file or deleted it.

To fix it: You have to find the file yourself. Choose File⇨Open and click the Find Now or Browse button. Locate the file, then select it, and click Open.

Or if you can't find it that way, choose Start⇨Find⇨Files and Folders and type in what the file was named, or just click the Browse button and look around.

Destination disk drive is full

Meaning: Okay, so you have been trying to put one or more files on a floppy disk or your hard disk — that's the destination disk. Of course, the disk drive itself is not full, because it is just a hollow cabinet that surrounds the disk, but the disk may be full. So you have run out of space on a disk. Not to worry.

What's really wrong: You don't have enough room to put everything on that disk. Perhaps other files on the disk are taking up a lot of room. Or maybe the file you were trying to put on the disk is bigger than the disk. (Oops!)

To fix it: If you are copying to a floppy disk, remove the first disk, put in a freshly formatted, completely empty disk, and then click Continue. If that doesn't work, make sure that the file you are copying is not bigger than 1.44 Megabytes (the total space available on a floppy disk). If it is, go back to the original program, open the document, and carve it into smaller pieces, saving each in a different document. That way, you can save several smaller documents on one disk, and the rest on another disk.

If you are trying to copy a program, you can't do this divide-and-conquer trick; you will have to use software that shrinks, or compresses, the program file, because you have no way to carve it up into pieces, or to put the pieces back together again later. Go on the Web and search for PKZip shareware at `www.pkware.com`, and then use that to compress the file. Compressing shrinks a file so it can be copied; once you get to the new location, like another hard disk, you can double-click the compressed file, and it will expand into the original size again.

If you were copying to a hard disk when you got this message, you have to clear junk off the hard disk. Time to call your parents. You don't want to take responsibility for wiping out the software they use to do their work.

 Look first for any programs you don't use and get rid of them by choosing Start⇨Control Panel⇨Add/Remove Programs. Then delete files that have the extension BAK, for backup, or TMP for temporary files, if the date is, well, more than a year or so old.

This filename is not valid

Meaning: You thought up a perfectly good name for a file, but Windows 95 choked on it. If Windows lets you use this name, it knows that later it would get so confused it would fall down on its knees and yell "Uncle!" So instead of just saying it can't accept the name, it makes you feel like you've done something illegal.

What's really wrong: You probably used one of the punctuation marks that Windows 95 uses to keep track of its own stuff. Don't try to put any of the following characters into a filename, or you'll get this message again: /, \, *, |, <, >, ?, and ".

To fix it: Rewrite the file's name without any of those characters.

Not enough memory

Meaning: To keep working, Windows 95 needs more room inside the part of the computer that remembers whatever you are working on. Techie alert: We call this part of the computer the random-access memory (RAM).

What's really wrong: You may have opened up too many programs at once, or too many windows, because each one takes up a certain amount of memory. And you need more memory (you always do).

To fix it: Do the following four things to free up some space:

🖙 Close every window you don't need to keep open.

🖙 If you have a giant graphic as wallpaper, get rid of it, by using the Display Properties dialog box. Choose Start⇨Settings⇨Control Panel and double-click Display to call up the Display Properties dialog box.

🖙 If you just copied a big picture or chunk of text to the Clipboard, copy something small — a word or two — so that it goes onto the Clipboard, instead.

🖙 Right-click the Recycle Bin and select Empty Recycle Bin.

Make sure you aren't loading unnecessary programs into memory when you start the computer. To check, click Start⇨Programs⇨Start Up. If you see any programs you can do without, remove them by clicking Start⇨Settings⇨Control Panel, then double-clicking Add/Remove Programs, and on the Start tab, deleting the unnecessary programs. (You aren't destroying the programs, just saying you don't want them in memory every time you start the computer.) If you have less than 16MB of RAM, consider getting more. (Check with your dealer about how much you can add to your machine.)

Also, because your computer likes to store some of its information on your hard disk, as if it were in RAM, clear at least 10 percent of your hard disk. In My Computer, select the C drive, then right-click it, to see the Properties dialog box. Compare the free space to the space that has already been used to store stuff.

1. **Choose Start⇨Settings⇨Control Panel.**

2. **Double-click the System icon.**

3. **On the System Properties dialog box, click the Performance tab, and on that page, click the Virtual Memory button.**

4. **Make sure that the option Let Windows Manage My Virtual Memory Settings is checked, and then click OK twice, to put away the Control Panel.**

To free up more hard disk space, save everything and close every program. Then choose Start⇨Accessories⇨SystemTools⇨Disk Defragmenter. Run this little program to neaten up the hard disk, putting together bits and pieces of files so that there aren't fragments lying all over; when one file is stored in one place, it takes less room.

Open with

Meaning: You double-clicked a file, but Windows 95 doesn't know what program to use to open that file. For once, Windows is asking you for advice.

What's really wrong: The file may not have one of those secret three-letter extensions, like .doc, or .txt, that Windows 95 uses to identify the program that created the file, or a program that could open the file.

To fix it: Choose one of the programs listed in the box, to see whether that program can open the file. When you find a program that works, do your work, and then save the file. If you are ever asked again, select that program, and click the box marked Always Use This Program to Open This File.

There was an error printing to LPT1

Meaning: You tried to print, but the printer didn't respond.

What's really wrong: Maybe the printer isn't on. Or if it is on, maybe the cables got jostled. Or if the cables are secure, maybe someone bumped the Online button, taking the printer "offline," that is, making it ignore messages from your computer. Why would you want a button that does this? Well, it's just an accident of history. Too boring to go into.

To fix it: Make sure the printer is turned on, and that the cables are tightly connected. If your printer has an Online button, make sure that it is on. Then click Retry.

Deleting this file will make it impossible to run this program

Meaning: You're trying to delete a file that's necessary for some program, or you're trying to wipe out the program itself. Time to pause and think.

What's really wrong: Windows keeps tabs on which files are really necessary for programs, and for most programs, Windows also keeps a little list of other files it uses, when it runs. If you wipe out one of those files, or the program, well, you can't run the program. And because so many people did this by mistake, Microsoft warns you. Good idea.

To fix it: If you are sure you want to get rid of this file, just go ahead. But if you are uncertain, stop right here by clicking Cancel. Then check the file by right-clicking its name and choosing Properties.

Unable to locate the server

Meaning: This only happens to you when you're connected to the Internet, or in the process of connecting to your first Web site of the day. Your browser hasn't been able to get to the page you typed or pasted into the address box.

What's really wrong: Perhaps you mistyped the address. If not, the server — the computer that serves up the Web page you were hoping to look at — may have been overwhelmed with thousands of people all trying to use it at once. Or the server is broken. Or the people who run the site just moved that page from one place to another without telling you. And so on.

To fix it: Retype the address. Be careful to type capital letters wherever they appear. Get those slashes going the right way. Then press Enter.

Windows 95 wasn't properly shut down

Meaning: Not much. Probably nothing much has been harmed. Oh, unless you forgot to save your work before you turned the computer off.

What's really wrong: You probably turned the power off without going through the orderly shutdown you're supposed to. Sometimes you have to power off like that, because a program has crashed so badly it froze everything on the screen, and refused to listen to anything you typed or clicked.

To fix it: Next time you finish a session, choose Start⇨Shut Down and then select one of the options in the dialog box that appears.

Chapter 14

Ten Useful and Fun Web Sites for Windows' Families

In This Chapter

▶ Online help for Windows 95

▶ Finding what you need

▶ The yuckiest site alive, or dead

▶ Teen talk

▶ All together now

▶ Sick in body, perhaps, but no way in mind

▶ Go on a virtual field trip

▶ Visit a museum

▶ Let's talk

▶ Getting a new job

Surfing the Web for fun and information is simply amazing. In the old days, like a few years ago, you had to schlepp to the library to do all of your research and there simply wasn't any interactive places on your computer where you could go for fun, to share ideas or simply to chat. Well, what a difference a few years makes!

Unfortunately, Web sites tend to come and go rather frequently. Some sites are created and then abandoned — we call these sites "cob Webs." All of the Web sites listed in this section have been around for awhile and had a good head of steam going when we wrote this book. However, you never know what can happen, so consider yourself warned.

Online Help for Windows 95

```
http://microsoft.com/support
```

Okay, so you think you'll live forever and you'll also never need to ask Microsoft a question about Windows 95. Maybe you're right, but given the quirky nature of computers, their operating systems, and everything else in-between, you may want to jot down the Microsoft support Web address.

Some support is free, especially in the form of frequently asked questions, but a lot of the help isn't free. If something's gonna cost ya, the fees are all clearly spelled out.

Yahoo!: Finding What You Need

```
www.yahoo.com
```

One of the best places for people to start their search for just about any-thing on the Web is at Yahoo!. Divided into helpful categories, Yahoo! makes it easy to find almost anything.

Yahoo! was so successful that it spawned Yahooligans (`www.yahooligans.com`), which is a Web guide just for kids. Like its parent, searches are made easy by clicking on a category, such as computers, games, or homework.

Yuckiest Site on the Internet — Alive or Dead

```
www.nj.com/yucky
```

Let's face it, some people think various bodily functions are gross — others think they're hysterical. Whichever group you fall into, all your secret questions, like the ones you never find the answers to in school, will be revealed on the Yuckiest Site on the Internet. Don't let the title fool you, this is actually a scientific page with a sense of humor. This is where you can find covered, in great detail, the answers to such burning questions as, What's that gunk in my eye? Why does my stomach gurgle? What causes boogers, belches, and bad breath? When you're finished with your intellectual pursuits, you can chat with other yucky enthusiasts by leaving notes for them on the message board.

TeenVoice = Teen Talk

www.teenvoice.com

Created by a teen for teens, TeenVoice is refreshingly free of nagging ads. Instead, it's chock full of great stuff. There are loads of areas to browse through, and each area brings up some more cool paths to follow. For example, you find 13 areas in the Things 2 Do Places 2 Go section from mall events, to movie info, to concerts, and even a section called Cheap Stuff 2 Do. Join the chat forums or just browse through the info. Either way, it's a must-see for any teen.

Bonus.com: Leave the Searching to Them

http://bonus.com

What if you didn't have to spend a lot of time searching through the Web to find fun sites just for kids? What if there was one site that did the searching for you? Well, there is one and its name is Bonus.com.

The editors of Bonus.com continually surf the Net looking for outstanding puzzles, games, trivia, and educational activities and puts links to them all in one spot that's safe and secure — Bonus.com doesn't link to anything outside of the site itself.

Convomania

www.mania.apple.com

Convomania is specifically for kids who are disabled or are seriously or chronically ill. These kids talk straight to each other, leaving messages or posting questions on a bulletin board. Convomania also invites kids to make a jigsaw puzzle doctor or write lyrics for the What Bugs You? section. As Convomania says, it's for "kids who are sick and tired of being sick and tired."

Discovery Channel: Go on a Virtual Field Trip

www.discovery.com

Like many of the shows on the Discovery TV Channel, their Web site is a potpourri of places, people, and things from anytime B.C. up to the present. Each month the Discovery team goes to an exotic place sending back wonderful digital pictures of their adventure. You can post your questions to the explorers or ask for more clarification on a topic they've talked about. One month they're excavating dinosaur bones in Mongolia's Gobi Desert, and another they're scuba diving around the Galapagos Islands.

After you've dug up as much info as you want, you can also follow the clues to figure out the day's Mystery Guest, who is always someone famous from history.

Smithsonian Institute: Visit a Museum

www.si.edu/newstart.htm

Have to write a research paper or maybe you'd just like to browse through an exhibit of Egyptian mummies? Look no further. On the Smithsonian Institute's Web site, you find areas devoted to the most frequently asked questions (FAQs) at the Institute. You can also tour fascinating exhibits — like the one about the Information Age that shows a slide show of devices from Samuel Morse's original telegraph built in 1827 up to the digital CD-ROM — or search for an amazingly wide variety of topics. You can even find out whether the Smithsonian is planning a visit to your area.

Family Education Network: Let's Talk

www.familyeducation.com

A wonderful site brimming with info is the Family Education Network. This is the place to find thoughtful articles on everything from finding quality child care to tips on how to react to a lousy report card without losing your cool. There's expert advice on a wide range of topics, such as potty training, heat rash, and scary movies. The number of resources is immense, including those for homeschooling parents and parents of older kids.

Parents with children who have special needs will find the Search and Respond section especially rewarding because they can talk to other parents, sharing ideas and resources.

A nice plus to this site is that it lets local schools put up their own site for free so parents can communicate with their child's school online.

The Monster Board: Getting a New Job

www.monsterboard.com

Want to read about a prospective employer before you even fill out a job application? Then log onto The Monster Board, one of the largest job sites on the Web. There are over 50,000 jobs listed here with about 4 percent dedicated to technological openings and the rest offering a potpourri of jobs. We found listings for a women's lacrosse coach in Boston, Massachuetts, and a posting for a forest manager in Bend, Oregon.

And, in case you were wondering, the job searches are not limited to just the 9 to 5 kind. There's a section for those of you who want to be their own boss with tips on how to find a franchise that suits your talents and how to finance your dream.

But The Monster Board is not just a job hotline. It also offers relocation services, online job fairs, and extensive employer profiles. One thing we didn't find, unfortunately, was a listing for summer jobs for teens.

Part V
Appendixes

In this part . . .

Welcome to information central. In this part, we tell you everything you need to know about the CD that comes with this book. We also let you in on how to fix some common problems that people have with Windows 95. And if that isn't enough, we also throw in a glossary that tells you what those nerdy-sounding words really mean.

Appendix A

Um, It Won't Work the Way I Want It to Work

. . . .

In This Chapter

▶ Preparing to call Microsoft technical support

▶ Checking to see if your machine has what it takes to run Windows 95

▶ Bringing your computer back to life with a start-up disk

▶ Solving the most common problems

▶ Solving more complicated problems

▶ Dealing with stuff that isn't really a problem, but just really bugs you

. . . .

Hold the Phone! You're on with Microsoft Technical Support

You're right in the middle of working on something cool and your screen freezes, or you hear this annoying beeping sound. You see an error message that looks like it must have been written by either a geek or a Martian. Angry? Frustrated? Sure! But before you reach for that phone and call a technical support person at Microsoft, read through this appendix and Chapter 13 and see if you can find the solution to your problem. If you do decide to call Microsoft's technical support at 425-635-7000, you should browse through this section first to find out about the numbers you need to have on hand and where to find them.

Bet you thought that because your operating system is called Windows 95, there is only one version of the operating system — that came out in 1995. Wrong! There's the preview version that actually came out *before* the official launching. (This version was laden with bugs, but it gave developers something to work with and computer journalists something to write about.) The official version of Windows 95 hit the shelves in August, 1995 with the subtlety of a jackhammer. November 1996 brought along a new version, packaged with Internet Explorer. A little while later a fourth version came out which you probably don't have because it can only be loaded onto an empty machine (meaning you can't use this fourth version as an upgrade, but if your computer is brand-new, then you're probably using this newest version).

To find out some info you need before you speak to a technical support person, just follow these steps:

1. **Right-click the My Computer icon.**

2. **Click Properties.**

   The System Properties dialog box appears, as shown in Figure A-1.

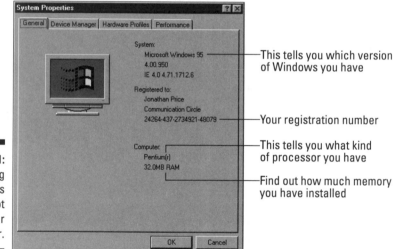

Figure A-1: This dialog box tells you a lot about your computer.

Right under the line that says Microsoft Windows 95 you see a line with a lot of numbers. Check out the letter after the 4.00.950 number. What the techies on the phone will want to know is whether or not there's a letter after these numbers.

This window also tells you what kind of processor or chip you have on your computer, how much memory is installed, and your registration number. You should have all this info handy just in case they need it over in the technical support office when you call.

3. **Write down the information you need and click OK.**

If you see the letter "A" after 4.00.950 or no letter at all, you have the original version of Windows 95 installed on your computer.

Does Your Machine Have the Power to Run Windows 95?

According to the box, Windows 95 runs just fine on a computer with a 386 processor or chip. Technically, this is true, if you don't want to play any games. Even a computer with 486 processor will have problems running Windows 95 unless it has tons of RAM.

Quite simply, Windows 95 runs best on a Pentium-equipped PC. You can also find out what kind of processor you have running on your computer by going to the System Properties dialog box (refer to Figure A-1 and the previous section).

So, why do we bring this up? Well, if you're trying to run programs with a lot of animation, graphics, or video, you need lots of memory (at least 16MB of RAM). If you have less than that, you may want to consider buying some more RAM. You can also find out how much RAM you have running on your computer by going to the System Properties dialog box (refer to Figure A-1).

Aaaachew! What to do If You Get a Virus

Sad but true is the fact that if you download a nasty little virus from the Internet or if your system crashes, strange (and sometimes unwelcome things) can happen to your computer. This is a disaster because Windows 95 uses the hard drive to start itself up. If this happens, don't call a doctor; install your start-up disk and Windows 95 will be as good as new.

But first you have to create a start-up disk when Windows 95 is healthy:

1. **Choose Start⇨Settings⇨Control Panel.**

   The Control Panel window appears.

2. **Double-click the Add/Remove Programs icon.**

   This brings up the Add/Remove Programs Properties dialog box, as shown in Figure A-2.

3. **Click the start-up Disk tab.**

4. **Click the Create Disk button.**

   A dialog box asks you to label a blank disk as your start-up disk and install it in your disk drive.

   If you used a CD-ROM to install Windows 95, and you now have it in the CD-ROM drive, you won't get this message, so just skip to Step 6.

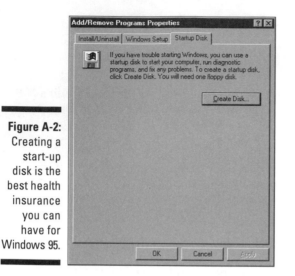

Figure A-2:
Creating a
start-up
disk is the
best health
insurance
you can
have for
Windows 95.

5. Insert the disk and click OK.

Soon you get a message asking you to insert a disk in drive A, as shown in Figure A-3.

Make life easy on yourself and select a formatted, empty disk. It will save you the time of deleting files to make room for the information that goes on the start-up disk.

6. Insert the disk and click OK.

When the start-up disk has been created, Windows 95 takes you back to the Add/Remove Programs Properties dialog box.

7. Click Cancel, which takes you back to the Control Panel.

8. Choose File⇔Close.

9. Take out the disk and put it in a safe place.

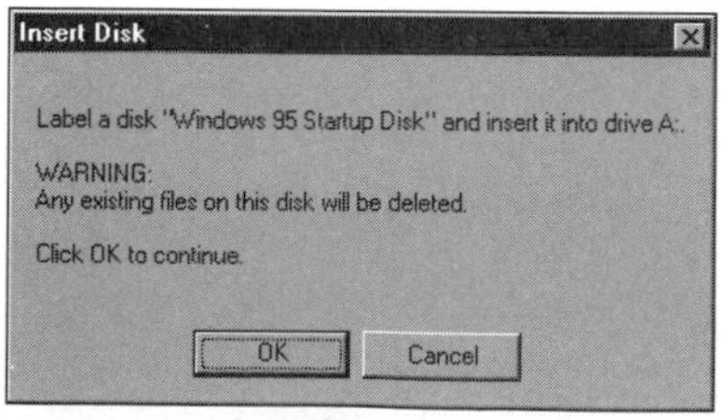

Figure A-3:
Inserting a
disk in the A
drive.

Getting Help for Common Problems

If this were a perfect world and Windows 95 a perfect operating system, this troubleshooting guide wouldn't be necessary. But because stuff happens, let's take a look at some of the most irritating, but easy-to-fix problems you may encounter.

Yikes! Get me outta here

This is mainly for gamers, but this could happen when you're using any program.

You've been playing the same game for hours and you're fed up with it. Most games make exiting a one-click, easy thing to do. But some only let you quit after reaching certain levels. When you want to take a nosedive but there's no visible way to quit, hang on and try one of these methods:

- Click the X in the upper-right corner of the program's window (if there is one).
- Hold down the Alt key, press the F4 key, and click OK.
- Try pressing the Esc key at the upper-left corner of most keyboards. This usually is the "pause" button on games and brings up options — one of which may be Quit or Exit.

Never quit Windows 95 or any program by simply turning off your computer. This can totally mess up your computer, not to mention the program you were using. To shut down your computer in Windows 95, click the Start button, choose the Shut Down command, and click OK in the box that appears. Depending on your PC, Windows may turn off the computer's power automatically, or tell you "You may safely turn off your computer."

Nothing's moving

Occasionally, everything is working just fine on your computer and suddenly, for no known reason, it just freezes up. No matter what you do, menus don't open, buttons won't squish, and you click and click and click and nothing happens.

Here are some ways to defrost your screen. We start with the least offensive way to your computer all the way to harshest, so try these remedies in order:

- ✔ Press the Esc key twice.

- ✔ Press the Alt, Control, and Delete keys all at once. This brings up the End Task window, which shows you all the programs that are running on your computer at the time of the freeze. The program that caused the freeze will probably have the words "Not responding" next to its name. To turn off that misbehaving program, select its name by clicking the program's name with your mouse or (if your mouse button is still frozen), use the arrow and Tab keys to select the item and the End Task button. After you have control again, save what work you can in your programs and restart Windows — the computer gets a bit shaky after closing a program like this, and more freezes could follow until you restart.

- ✔ Press your computer's Reset button, which forces Windows 95 to start up all over again.

And if all else fails, turn off your computer. Wait a few minutes then turn it back on.

I can't find my pointer

When you suddenly can't find your pointer, the cord that attaches your mouse to the keyboard is probably loose. Check it. If the cord has become detached, plug it in and restart your computer.

Sometimes your mouse can misbehave and not roll as smoothly as it once did because it's full of gunk, like dog hairs, lint from your sweater, or even little gooey patches of dried soda. If you turn over your mouse and find any gunk in it, that means it's time to clean it.

1. **Turn the mouse upside down so the roller ball is facing up.**

2. **Remove the cover around the roller ball. (Some just require that you unscrew it. But if you're unsure, ask your mom or dad to help you.)**

3. **Dip a cotton swab in a little isopropyl alcohol (or just water if you're desperate).**

   You may want to help your kids with this part of the process because it involves a trip to the medicine cabinet.

4. **Rub the cotton swab on the roller ball until all the gunk comes off and let the roller ball dry.**

5. **Replace the roller ball and its cover.**

You may also want to check your mouse pad to see if it's dirty. If it is, replace it.

If you just bought a new mouse, Windows 95 may not recognize the new brand yet. Here are steps to introduce Windows 95 to your mouse. The problem with the following steps is that some of you may not be able to use your mouse at all to do the steps — duh! The mouse doesn't work! No problem — you can use the keyboard for awhile to command the computer.

1. **Choose Start➪Settings➪Control Panel.**

   If the mouse pointer won't move, hold down the Ctrl key and press the Esc key to open the Start menu. Use your up, down, and right arrow keys to select Settings, and press Enter when you have Control Panel selected.

2. **In the Control Panels window, double-click the Add New Hardware icon. The Add New Hardware Wizard appears.**

   If you're using a keyboard, press the Tab key until the Add New Hardware icon is selected, and then press the Enter key.

3. **Click Next.**

   At this point, Windows 95 may display a list of computer parts.

   To make it easy, you can tell Windows to automatically detect your new hardware, as shown in Figure A-4, or you can select it from the list of parts.

Figure A-4:
Let
Windows 95
do the
searching.

A message may appear that tells you what to do if Windows seems to stop working while searching for your mouse. Click the Next button to start the search.

After a few moments of the computer's whirring, Windows hopefully tells you what mouse you have and installs the right software for it to work. Follow the steps on-screen.

Some mice come with a disk containing the software the mouse needs to work with Windows. If Windows asks you for that disk, insert it in your PC.

After Windows has finishing preparing your mouse, you should restart your computer.

You can't find a program or file

Okay, so you got mad at your computer or you got bored waiting on hold when you called Technical Support and you started clicking away with your mouse and, poof! your program disappeared. When the smoke clears away you can get it back by following these steps:

1. **Bring your pointer down to the bottom of the screen where the taskbar lies.**

2. **Click the program's button on the taskbar.**

If you were working with a program, and you can't find it on the taskbar, just choose Start⇨Documents. A list of the most recent files you worked with appears, as shown in Figure A-5.

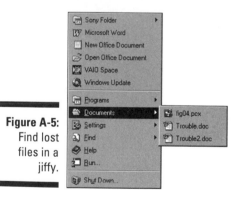

Figure A-5:
Find lost
files in a
jiffy.

3. **Click the file from the Documents list to open it.**

Taskbar missing? Press the Ctrl key and the Esc key at the same time.

You don't have a mouse with a right button

If you have a mouse with just one big button instead of two, you can accomplish all of the right-mouse button functions by pressing the Ctrl and Shift keys at the same time you press the mouse button you have.

The computer says you don't have enough memory

Worst-case scenario here is that you need to buy more memory to run your basic everyday stuff. Hopefully, one of these suggestions can give your computer a cheaper memory boost:

- ✔ If you have a lot of windows open, try closing all of them except the program windows that you're working with.
- ✔ If you have a bunch of tiny icons in the Notify area in the right part of the Toolbar (where the clock or speaker icons appear), turn off the items you don't need.
- ✔ Empty the Clipboard. A quick way to practically empty the Clipboard is to highlight and copy one word. This way only one little word is on the Clipboard. For other ways, see Chapter 6.
- ✔ Change your wallpaper to a one-color background.
- ✔ Restart your computer by choosing Start⇨Shut Down and selecting Restart your computer.

Choose Start⇨Help and look for the Help system's Memory Troubleshooter guide to give you more hints on how to conserve memory:

1. **Choose Start⇨Help.**

    The Help Topics Window appears.

2. **Double-click Troubleshooting.**

    A list of topics appears, as shown in Figure A-6.

3. **Click If you run out of memory.**

4. **Explore the various topics by clicking the appropriate icons.**

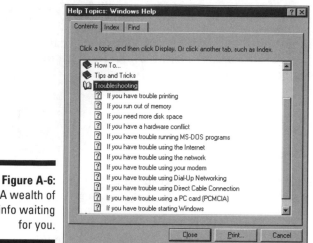

Figure A-6:
A wealth of info waiting for you.

You're having printing problems

Sometimes you put a lot of effort into creating a document, and then it just won't print out. You know there's a problem when you see the dialog box in Figure A-7 appear on your screen.

Figure A-7:
This dialog box tells you that you have a printing problem.

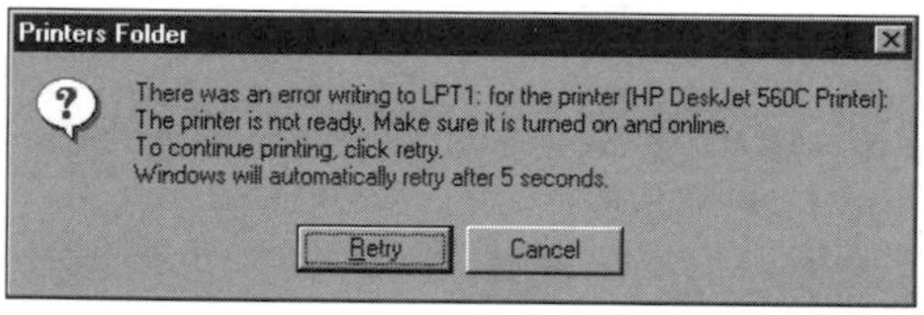

Try these solutions if you encounter some problems:

- ✔ Check to see whether your printer is turned on.

- ✔ Make sure there's paper in the printer.

- ✔ Lightly jiggle the cable connecting the printer to the PC; make sure it is securely connected on both printer and computer.

- ✔ Go to the Troubleshooting section in the help guide and click the If you have trouble printing icon. You see the help window shown in Figure A-8.

Figure A-8:
The
Windows 95
Trouble-
shooting
window
helps you
solve your
printing
problems.

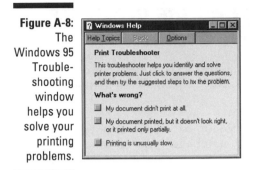

✔ Be patient. Sometimes the computer just needs a lot of time to get everything to the printer. This is especially true if you are printing a page with a lot of graphics on it.

Sometimes it's your printer and not Windows 95 that's the culprit. If you think that's the case, check the manual that came with your printer or call your printer's manufacturer for technical support.

Saving difficulties

Some nasty little error messages appear when you attempt to stow away your masterpieces. But don't worry, most of them are easy to fix. Consult Chapter 13 for tips and hints on what to do when you see any of the following error messages:

✔ This filename is not valid

✔ Destination disk drive is full

✔ A:/ is not accessible

You try to print your screen, but nothing happens!

Sometimes even the neatest little doodads don't work properly — even the Print Screen key. Because Windows 95 software and hardware developers can be a little 'creative' with their designs, not everyone gets the same thing, so try these quick fixes and see what happens:

✔ Press the Alt key while pressing the Print Screen key.

✔ Press the Shift key while pressing the Print Screen key.

How come I didn't get all the programs Windows 95 said came with it?

Unless there's been a mistake at the Windows 95 factory, the programs that you can't find from your Programs menu are probably hiding, waiting to be installed.

Before you get all mad wondering why Windows 95 just doesn't go and install everything at once, remember that not everyone has a lot of hard drive space. This way Windows 95 only installs the must-have items and lets you install the rest if hard drive space permits and if you truly want them. So, if you want to install some other neat little items, you have to do it yourself:

1. **Choose Start⇨Settings⇨Control Panel.**

2. **Double-click the Add/Remove Programs icon.**

3. **Click the Windows Setup tab.**

4. **In the Windows Setup tab, check the programs that you want to install, as shown in Figure A-9.**

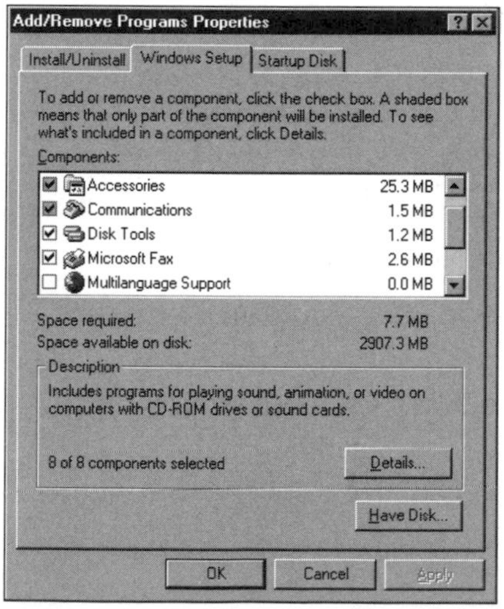

Figure A-9:
Check the
programs
you want to
install.

Screenshot caption shows: Add/Remove Programs Properties dialog with Windows Setup tab selected.

Components listed:
- Accessories — 25.3 MB
- Communications — 1.5 MB
- Disk Tools — 1.2 MB
- Microsoft Fax — 2.6 MB
- Multilanguage Support — 0.0 MB

Space required: 7.7 MB
Space available on disk: 2907.3 MB

Description: Includes programs for playing sound, animation, or video on computers with CD-ROM drives or sound cards.

8 of 8 components selected

Fixing Things that Really Bug You

It's okay. You don't have to like everything about Windows 95. Here are some common areas that can drive you up the wall.

Getting rid of a dialog box — quickly

Press the Esc key, and the dialog box closes automatically. Keep pressing the Esc key until the boxes are gone.

If you want to quickly move through a familiar round of dialog boxes, just keep clicking the Tab key until you come to the right one.

Scrolling through files and documents takes so long!

Yup, so why do it? Instead, try one of the following ways of getting around without scrolling:

- ✔ If you want to get to the last few files in a folder or to the end of a lengthy document, press the Ctrl and End keys.
- ✔ If you're at the bottom and want to get to the top, press the Ctrl and Home keys.

You're sick of the standard beeps and boops

An individualist, eh? You can erase any standard sound and add some of your own if your computer has a sound card installed. Just follow these steps:

1. **Choose Start⇨Settings⇨Control Panel.**
2. **Double-click the Sounds icon, which brings up the Sounds Properties dialog box.**
3. **Select the item from the Event list box that you want to either add or change a sound for.**
4. **Scroll through the Name drop-down list box to see a list of available sounds, as shown in Figure A-10.**

   Click the Preview button to hear the sounds.
5. **Click OK.**

How can I find out about some cool tips?

Those sneaky little devils at Microsoft added a file just for you. It's actually not so hard to find, once you know it's there:

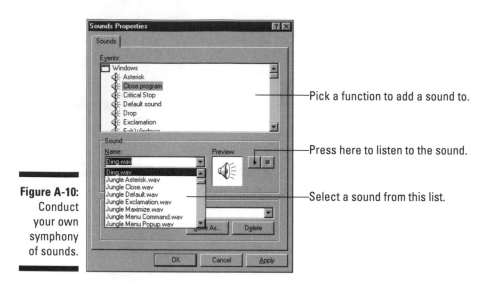

Figure A-10:
Conduct
your own
symphony
of sounds.

Pick a function to add a sound to.

Press here to listen to the sound.

Select a sound from this list.

1. **Double-click the My Computer icon.**

2. **Double-click the Windows folder.**

3. **Double-click the file Tips.txt. which brings up the tips file as seen in Figure A-11.**

Now that you found the tips file, why not print it out by choosing File⇨Print?

For a kind of Windows 95 tip of the day, log onto the Internet and type in the address www.winmag.com/win95/mtm.

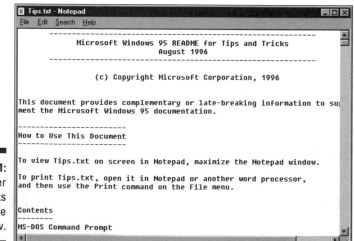

Figure A-11:
Discover
the secrets
that the
pros know.

Appendix B
About the CD-ROM

● ●

In This Chapter

▶ Knowing what you need to work the CD-ROM

▶ Exploring the programs on the CD-ROM

● ●

*W*e put tons of cool, fun stuff on the CD-ROM that comes with this book. Turn to this appendix when you want to crack open that CD-ROM and start exploring.

System Requirements

Make sure that your computer meets the minimum system requirements listed below. If your computer doesn't match up to most of these requirements, you may have problems using the contents of the CD:

- ✔ A PC with a 486 or faster processor
- ✔ Microsoft Windows 95
- ✔ At least 16MB of total RAM installed on your computer. For best performance, because many of these demos have several graphics and sounds and require a lot of memory, we recommend 32MB of RAM installed. With less than 32MB, you will notice that the demos run slowly, and they may overload your system.
- ✔ At least 15MB of hard drive space available to install all the software from this CD. (You'll need less space if you don't install every program.)
- ✔ A CD-ROM drive — double-speed (2x) or faster
- ✔ A sound card. (Not necessary to run the program, only needed to hear it.)

✔ A monitor capable of displaying at least 256 colors or grayscale.

Many of the demos on the CD-ROM are designed to run on a monitor set at 256 color resolution. To check your monitor's settings, just right-click on your Windows desktop and click on Properties in the menu that pops up. The Display Properties window appears. Click on the Settings tab. Your color resolution setting appears in the Color palette box. If your monitor is not set for 256 Color, click on the drop-down list arrow and select 256 Color. Then restart your computer to make the new setting take effect.

Most of the demos still run even if your monitor is not set to 256 colors, but you may notice that the pictures look static-y, and the colors may not look right.

The Logical Journey of the Zoombinis is the only demo that will not run if your monitor is not set to 256 colors.

✔ A modem with a speed of at least 14,400 bps

If you need more information on the basics, check out *PCs For Dummies,* 4th Edition, by Dan Gookin and *Windows 95 For Dummies,* 2nd Edition, by Andy Rathbone, both published by IDG Books Worldwide, Inc.

How to Use the CD

To install the items from the CD to your hard drive, follow these steps:

1. **Insert the CD into your computer's CD-ROM drive.**

2. **Click the Start button and click Run.**

3. **In the dialog box that appears, type** D:\SETUP.EXE.

   Most of you probably have your CD-ROM drive listed as drive D. Type in the proper drive letter if your CD-ROM drive uses a different letter.

4. **Click OK.**

   A license agreement window appears.

5. **Read through the license agreement, nod your head, and then click the Accept button. After you click Accept, you'll never be bothered by the License Agreement window again.**

   From here, the CD interface appears. The CD interface is a little program that shows you what is on the CD and coordinates installing the programs and running the demos. The interface basically lets you click a button or two to make things happen.

6. **The first screen you see is the Welcome screen. Click anywhere on this screen to enter the interface.**

   Now you are getting to the action. This next screen lists categories for the software on the CD.

7. **To view the items within a category, just click the category's name.**

   A list of programs in the category appears.

8. **For more information about a program, click the program's name.**

   Read the information that appears. Sometimes a program requires you to do a few tricks on your computer first, and this screen tells you where to go for that information, if necessary.

9. **To run the demo or install the program, click the appropriate button. If you don't want to install the program, click the Go Back button to return to the previous screen.**

   You can always return to the previous screen by clicking the Go Back button. This allows you to browse the different categories and products and decide what you want to install.

   After you click an install button, the CD interface drops to the background while the CD begins running the demo or installing the program you chose.

10. **To install other items, repeat Steps 7, 8, and 9.**

11. **After you install the programs, click the Quit button to close the interface.**

    You can eject the CD now. Carefully place it back in the plastic jacket of the book for safekeeping.

To run the demos, or to use the Betty Crocker program, you need to keep the CD inside your CD-ROM drive when you are trying out the demo or running the program. This is a good thing. Otherwise, the program ends up taking up a lot of your hard drive space.

What You'll Find

The CD-ROM that comes with this book is so full of great software that we almost couldn't fit it all on that flat little disk! Here's a summary of the software on this CD.

Edutainment programs for kids

Edutainment is a cross between entertainment and education. The programs you find on this portion of the CD-ROM make you laugh, and they also help you discover a few new things along the way.

Elmo's Preschool Deluxe

From Creative Wonders; Ages 3 to 5

At D:\ELMOS\RUN\ELMO.EXE on the CD

Elmo brings a lot of his Sesame Street Muppet friends along to introduce preschoolers to letters, numbers, shapes, colors, and even logic and thinking skills. Parents can adjust the learning level so the program can modify itself as the child's knowledge increases.

Visit Creative Wonders' Web site for more information about this program and others at www.creativewonders.com.

When you start this demo, it may change the resolution of your computer's monitor. When the demo stops, your monitor returns to its original settings, but the interface window may appear in the top-left corner of a white screen. To return the window to its original appearance, just minimize it by clicking on the Minimize button in the upper-right corner of the window. Then restore it from the Windows taskbar by clicking on the WIN95KP.EXE button. When the interface window pops back up, it should appear correctly.

This demo runs right from the interface; there is nothing installed to your computer. To stop the demo at any time, press the ALT+F4 buttons on your keyboard.

Living Books Sampler

From Broderbund; Ages 3 to 7

At D:\LBOOKS\DEMO32.EXE on the CD

Dr. Seuss's zany familiar characters Sam-I-Am and the Cat in the Hat, and Mercer Mayer's Little Critter and Grandma come to vibrant life in the interactive storybooks "Green Eggs and Ham," "The Cat In the Hat," and "Just Grandma and Me."

Filled with point-and-click activities for the beginning reader, these programs can be "read" over and over again, just like their hardcover predecessors. Even pre-readers can play along while the story is read to them.

These titles are some of the very best examples of interactive storybooks on the market today. As a bonus from Broderbund, this Living Books demo also introduces you to not just the abovementioned titles but many others as well.

Visit Broderbund's Web site at www.Broderbund.com for more information about these and other programs.

This demo runs right from the interface; there is nothing installed to your computer. To stop the demo at any time, press the CTRL+Q buttons on your keyboard.

Orly's Draw-A-Story

From Broderbund; Ages 5 to 10

At D:\ORLYS\ORLYDEMO.EXE on the CD

Orly is a cute little Jamaican girl who invites kids to come along with her as she tells various stories about her life. Kids can illustrate her stories or create new ones themselves. When they finish, they can play their stories back in a video-like format.

This is one of the most creative and innovative programs around. Visit Broderbund's Web site for more information about this program and others at www.broderbund.com.

This demo runs right from the interface; there is nothing installed to your computer. To stop the demo at any time, press the ESC button on your keyboard.

Madeline Classroom Companion: 1st and 2nd Grade

From Creative Wonders; Ages 5 to 7

At D:\MCC12\MAD_FS.EXE on the CD

This program follows the spunky Madeline through a variety of adventures. While the program covers all the basics for this age group, including Spanish and French phrases, the program places a heavy emphasis on art and creativity. Parents can easily track their child's progress, and they may find that many of the activities on this CD are similar to the ones used in the classroom.

Visit Creative Wonders' Web site for more information about this program and others at www.creativewonders.com.

This demo runs right from the interface; there is nothing installed to your computer. To stop the demo at any time, press the ESC button on your keyboard.

Schoolhouse Rock! 1st & 2nd Grade Essentials

From Creative Wonders; Ages 6 to 8

At D:\SHR12\SHR12.EXE on the CD

This program is mostly a repackaging of the successful Math Rock, Grammar Rock, America Rock, and Exploration Station programs. It covers a wide range of subjects (with a slight tilt towards history, geography, and science) and despite the title, is very worthwhile for older kids up to 4th grade.

Visit Creative Wonders' Web site for more information about this program and others at www.creativewonders.com.

This demo runs right from the interface; there is nothing installed to your computer. Clicking on the demo screens jumps you ahead to the closing screens, which is handy if you want to leave the demo, but not if you were just trying to select something on the screen.

3D Atlas 98

From Creative Wonders; Ages 8 and up

At D:\ATLAS98\3D98DEMO.EXE on the CD

Good for those "country" reports or finding out about a new location, 3D Atlas is a colorful, fact-filled alternative to flat paper atlases. Use the clickable-3D globe to explore weather patterns, political climates, and geographical wonders of the world. Narrated videos complete the multimedia-enriched package.

Visit Creative Wonders' Web site for more information about this program and others at www.creativewonders.com.

This demo runs right from the interface; there is nothing installed to your computer. To stop the demo at any time, press the ESC button on your keyboard.

Schoolhouse Rock! 1st - 4th Grade Math Essentials

From Creative Wonders; Ages 6 to 10

At D:\SHR14\SHRM14.EXE on the CD

Join Lucky Seven Sampson in his adventures through Funky Numberland. Following Lucky on his journey, kids encounter lots of math activities, through arcade, maze, and concentration-type games which are sprinkled throughout the program.

A nice plus is that kids can print out the math activities if someone else in the family needs to use the computer.

Visit Creative Wonders' Web site for more information about this program and others at www.creativewonders.com.

This demo runs right from the interface; there is nothing installed to your computer. Clicking on the demo screens jumps you ahead to the closing screens, which is handy if you want to leave the demo, but not if you were just trying to select something on the screen.

Mighty Math Demo
From Edmark; Ages 12 to 15

At D:\MTYMATH\EDMARK.EXE on the CD

In Astro Algebra, kids take charge of the spaceship, Algebra Centauri, to answer distress signals from the galaxy. Along the way, they make calculations, take measurements, and plot graphs using algebraic concepts.

Teens can use the Grow Slide so the journey steps up as they master each level. And parents, if you forgot a lot of those algebra terms from junior high, Astro Algebra has a section, just for parents, that reviews alien sounding terms.

This demo from Edmark also provides information about other Mighty Math programs for students. Visit Edmark's Web site for more information about this program and others at www.edmark.com.

This demo runs right from the interface; there is nothing installed to your computer. To stop the demo at any time, press the ESC button on your keyboard.

Logical Journey of the Zoombinis
From Broderbund; Ages 8 to 12

At D:\ZOOMDEMO\ZOOMBINI.EXE on the CD

Puzzle solvers delight in the exploits of the Zoombinis who have to figure out a way to travel through all sorts of dangers on their way to find a new homeland. By the time kids have completed this wonderful game, they get exposure to data analysis, graphing, algebraic thinking, and a host of other problem solving skills.

Visit Broderbund's Web site for more information about this program and others at www.broderbund.com.

Your monitor must be set to 256 color resolution to run this demo. To check your monitor's settings, just right-click on your Windows desktop and click on Properties in the menu that pops up. The Display Properties window appears. Click on the Settings tab. Your color resolution setting appears in the Color palette box. If your monitor is not set for 256 Color, click on the drop-down list arrow and select 256 Color. Then restart your computer for the new setting to take effect.

This demo runs right from the interface; there is nothing installed to your computer. To stop the demo at any time, press the ESC button on your keyboard.

Higher Score for the SAT/ACT

From Kaplan; Ages 14 to 18

At D:\KAPLAN\DEMOWIN.EXE on the CD

This is the soup-to-nuts course of SAT and ACT preparation. But getting ready for this all important pre-college step isn't all that's included on this program. You get links to college Web sites, Newsweek's Guide to Colleges, scholarship info, and even video tips on how to prepare for the interview.

Visit Kaplan's Web site for more information about this program and others at www.kaplan.com.

This demo runs right from the interface; there is nothing installed to your computer. To stop the demo at any time, press the ESC button on your keyboard.

Not for Mom and Dad only

Officially, these programs fall into the home software category. Unofficially, they make weekends more fun.

Betty Crocker Cookbook

From Lifestyle Software Group; All ages

At D:\BCOOK\SETUP.EXE on the CD

Plan birthday parties, holiday meals, and a week's worth of dinners all from this program. Have a fussy eater in your house? Just type in a few favorite ingredients and this cookbook comes up with a plethora of recipes.

Visit Lifestyle Group's Web site for more information about this program and others at www.lifeware.com/index.html.

After you install the demo, you can run it by choosing Start⇨Programs⇨ Lifestyle Software Group menus and clicking on Betty Crocker's New Cookbook Demo. You need to keep the CD in your CD-ROM drive to use this program.

HomeBuyer 2.0

From Stratosphere Publishing

At D:\HOMEBUY2\HOME200.EXE on the CD

Along with death and taxes, buying a home is one of the most stressful times in one's life. This program takes a lot of the anxiety out of the process by demystifying many real estate terms. The program gives you easy fill-in-the-blank forms to find just the right mortgage for you. Would a 30 year mortgage at $7^1/_2$ percent be better than a 20 year at 8 percent? And just how much of a mortgage will you be able to qualify for? You can find all the answers in this friendly program.

Visit Stratosphere's Web site for more information about this program and others at www.stratopub.com.

After you install the demo, you can run it by choosing Start⇨Programs⇨ HomeBuyer menus and clicking on HomeBuyer.

LandDesigner 3D 4.5

From Sierra Home

At D:\LD3D45\LD_DEMO.EXE on the CD

Got a problem spot where nothing will grow? Or maybe you want to figure out how to keep the front yard blooming with color all year round. You may even want to create a total landscaping plan for your whole property, complete with an irrigation layout and 3D drawings on how your plan will look 5, 10, or even 15 years from now. Everything you need, excluding a green thumb, comes with this program.

Visit Sierra's Web site for more information about this program and others at www.sierra.com.

This demo runs right from the interface; there is nothing installed to your computer. To stop the demo at any time, press the ESC button on your keyboard.

If You've Got Problems (Of the CD Kind)

We tried our best to compile programs that work on most computers with the minimum system requirements. Alas, your computer may differ, and some programs may not work properly for some reason.

The two likeliest problems are that you don't have enough memory (RAM) for the programs you want to use, or you have other programs running that are affecting installation or running of a program. If you get error messages like `Not enough memory` or `Setup cannot continue`, try one or more of these methods and then try using the software again:

- Many of the demo programs on this CD require a great deal of memory from your computer. If you find that your system is having trouble running the demos through the CD interface, you can try running the demos directly from the CD. Each description in this appendix includes the address for the demo file. To run a demo from the CD, just click Start⇨Run and then type the address in the Open textbox and click OK.

- Turn off any anti-virus software that you have on your computer. Installers sometimes mimic virus activity and may make your computer incorrectly believe that it is being infected by a virus.

- Close all running programs. The more programs you're running, the less memory is available to other programs. Installers also typically update files and programs. So if you keep other programs running, installation may not work properly.

- Have your local computer store add more RAM to your computer. This is, admittedly, a drastic and somewhat expensive step. However, adding more memory can really help the speed of your computer and allow more programs to run at the same time. This may include closing the CD interface and running a product's installation program from Windows Explorer.

If you still have trouble with installing the items from the CD, please call the IDG Books Worldwide Customer Service phone number: 800-762-2974 (outside the U.S.: 317-596-5430).

Appendix C
An A-to-Z of Nerdisms

• •

accessory: A little program that helps out around the computer. Think of it as adding something to Windows 95 the way your belt accessorizes your outfit. Most accessories are also known as *applets,* that is, miniature applications. You can locate all accessories by clicking Start, pointing to Accessories, and then pointing at a topic to see individual accessories.

applet: A little program. So small and amusing it can't be called an application, like great big office programs. Paint and WordPad are applets, as are most of the programs listed under Accessories, in your Start menu.

application: A program. The idea is that the program applies the computer's resources to something useful.

backing up: Putting the car in reverse, and . . . no, no! This means making a copy of your important files, just in case something bad happens to the original file (like you accidentally throw it away or your baby brother decides to mess with it).

clicking and double-clicking: Pressing the left mouse button once, quickly, and letting go — that's clicking. Double-clicking means doing the same thing twice in a row, very quickly. You click to select something, or choose an option. You double-click a file to open it.

clip art: Art designed to be bought and used in your own documents to liven them up. Named after the pictures that designers used to scissor out of magazines to use in their work. You usually have to pay for clip art, but once you have paid for it, you can use it on your own projects as often as you want. You can't use it on any project you sell, though, and you may not be legally allowed to publish the art on a Web site.

Clipboard: A place in the computer's memory where you can store stuff you've copied or cut, while deciding what to do with it. When you choose to paste, the computer places the contents of the Clipboard at the spot where you click. The Clipboard can only hold one thing at a time, so if you copy A, then B, and then paste, you will get B.

Control Panel: A collection of tools for adjusting settings in Windows 95, installing or removing hardware or software, and changing the way your screen looks (and the way your mouse and keyboard act).

crash: You don't hear a big crash, but you may feel like it. The computer screen freezes up. Nothing you do makes any difference. The system goes dead. That's a crash. Best to call your folks, and ask them to restart the computer, if they can.

cursor (No swearing!): The flashing vertical bar that shows you where what you type will appear in a word processing program or in a text box in a dialog box.

defaults (It's not your fault): The standard settings for things like margins, spacing, and other types of formatting are called the defaults because Windows 95 uses those settings if you don't bother to change them. These settings are, then, used "in default." It does sound as if you are being blamed, doesn't it?

desktop (It's vertical): Your screen, which you can imagine as your desktop because it contains all your work materials, plus your Recycle Bin. What? You don't put the trash can on your desk? Well, obviously, you haven't visited Microsoft's offices.

directories and folders: These are big files that hold other files, sort of the way a manila folder holds a bunch of letters. A directory is a folder and vice versa. (Microsoft used to call these things directories, but is gradually coming around to calling them folders, because people understand the idea a little better.)

display: The screen. You can control the display through the Display icon in the Control Panel.

document: Something you create in a program, such as a letter, a painting, or a budget. Its electronic form is a file. When you print the document, it appears on paper as hard copy.

dragging: Pulling some object from one place to another on the screen. You point at it, press the left mouse button and hold it down, move the pointer to the new location, and then release the mouse button. The object zips into the new location.

driver: A program that nudges, or drives, a piece of hardware, such as your printer, modem, or sound card. You have to have a driver or else the hardware just sits there and stares at you.

execute: To run a program. Why? Because you are telling the computer to carry out a set of commands, that is, to execute the instructions. Programs have a file extension of .exe.

FAQ: (Stands for Frequently Asked Questions.) Really not just the questions; the answers, too. An acronym developed on Web sites — the old hands had to answer the same questions over and over, and got tired of answering them individually. They said, "OK, here are all the dumb questions you beginners ask along with the answers, so don't bother us anymore."

file: Any collection of information with a name. Examples include that letter to your Uncle Mo, a program, a driver program, and bits and pieces of information your program has to keep around for future use.

file extension: At the end of any filename you see a dot followed by three lowercase letters. Those letters tell you what kind of program made the file, or what kind of file it is. For example, if you save a WordPad file as a Word 6 document, it has the extension .doc (for document), and if you save a file you find as a Web page, it has the extension .htm (for html), meaning it is in the Hypertext Markup Language.

font: A set of letters, numbers, and punctuation marks all in a particular style. Arial and Times New Roman are typical fonts in Windows 95; each one represents text, but each has its own look. To install or examine a font, use the Fonts icon in the Control Panel.

function key: One of the F keys that run along the top of your keyboard. Each program assigns a different action (or function) to each F key; but essentially, pressing an F key has the same effect as choosing a command from a menu.

GIF: (Stands for Graphic Image Format.) A format used in a lot of pictures shown on the World Wide Web. Good for graphics that have solid blocks of color. Not so hot for photos (try JPEG for those).

hot key: A key or keys that you can use in various combinations to issue a command, rather than using your mouse and the menu. Looking at the menu, you see keyboard shortcuts to the right of some commands. These shortcuts usually involve pressing two keys at once to issue the command. Some programs that enable you to create additional shortcuts are also called hot keys.

icon: A picture representing a file, a program, or an action you can take. Hover your pointer over the icon and its label appears, in case you want to see what the heck it is.

interface: The look and feel of Windows 95 and its programs. The components that you can control, such as icons, windows, dialog boxes, backgrounds, bars, and buttons. Behind the interface lies the code that makes the program do stuff, but all you can see and touch is the interface. You adjust the interface of Windows 95 with the Control Panel.

Internet: The network of networks, tying your computer to all the other computers around the world. Like a gigantic phone system for electronic mail. Home of the World Wide Web, where you can look at pictures, view videos, listen to sounds, and click to jump from one Web site to another.

ISP: (Stands for Internet service provider, a company or organization that lets you connect to the Internet, usually for a fee.) You call the ISP from your computer; your call comes into their computer, and their computer passes it along to the Internet, bringing back the response from the Web site out on the Internet.

JPEG: The file format of the Joint Photographic Experts Group, who designed this format to reproduce photographs well on the Web. In Windows, the file extension is usually .jpg. But you may see it as .jpeg if the photo comes from some other operating system.

launch: To start a program or start Windows 95.

link: A button, text, or picture that, when clicked, takes you to another piece of information. When you click a link on a Web page, you go to another place on that page, or to another page. You "link" to the other spot.

load: To put into the computer's memory. For example, when you tell Windows you want to start a program, Windows loads the program into the computer's memory. Then, if you want to open a file to work on, Windows loads that file into memory, as well.

maximize: To make a window as big as it can be. (Double-click the title bar or click the Maximize button at the top-right corner of the window.)

memory: We forget. No, we get confused. There are two kinds of memory. One is deep inside your computer, and is called RAM (Random-Access Memory) because you have random access to it, meaning you can dip into it almost anywhere, without having to start at A and go to B and then C, and so on. The computer uses RAM to think. That's why you want a lot of RAM. Thirty-two megabytes of RAM makes Windows 95 hum. If you want to edit full-color pictures or video, though, you need 64 megabytes, minimum. But as soon as you turn off the computer, RAM forgets what it was doing. To store your ideas for years, you need a storage place such as a floppy disk or a hard disk, where you can save files, turn off the power, and find that the files are still okay the next day when you turn on the power again. That's long-term memory, and it's measured in gigabytes these days. With 2 gigabytes you can add a bunch of games, maybe even two dozen games, before you run out of space.

MIDI: (Stands for Musical Instrument Digital Interface.) A standard for musical instruments that rely on the computer, or musical programs that run on the computer. Thanks to MIDI, you can use your computer to compose a song, and then have the computer play it for you. Or you can use a MIDI connector to take music from a real instrument and record it on your computer, change it any way you like (on the computer), and play the new version.

minimize: To shrink a window. If the window contains a document, it becomes an icon within the program's workspace. If the window is itself a program, or a window showing the contents of your computer, the window shrinks to an icon on the taskbar. (Click the button with the minus sign, near the window's top-right corner, to minimize the window.)

monitor: The computer screen and the whole box that holds it.

MSN: (Stands for Microsoft Network.) A way of connecting with the World Wide Web, and a service on the Web, provided by Microsoft.

network: What connects two or more computers so that they can talk to each other. May involve cables, phone lines, satellite hookups, or what not.

operating system: The super-program that allows all other programs to run on the computer. Windows 95 is the operating system on the PC and performs chores for other programs, such as opening them, saving files, and sending stuff to the printer.

path: The trail leading to a file. You start at the top, with the name of the drive, then the names of folders containing the file, and end with the name of the file. For example, if you have the file Zebra.doc in the Zoo folder inside the Animal folder on the C: drive (usually the hard disk) the path leading to the file would be: `C:\Animals\Zoo\Zebra.doc`.

pattern: A regular design made of lines, and sometimes colors and shades. You can choose different patterns for the background of your screen, and in Paint, you can fill a shape like a rectangle with a pattern such as cross-hatching.

RAM: Random-Access Memory, the kind of memory that lives inside your computer as long as the power is on, but dies when you power off. The computer uses RAM to calculate, doing its thinking there.

Recycle Bin: The trash. Drag a file you don't want over to the Recycle Bin and throw it away. The file can still be salvaged; that is, taken out of the trash, until you actually choose to empty the Recycle Bin. Then it's really thrown away, and only programs such as Norton Utilities or First Aid can — maybe — get it back.

saving: Storing your work on the computer's hard disk or on a floppy disk, in electronic form, such as a file.

shortcut: A Windows 95 icon that stands for a file, program, or whatever. The shortcut is not the real thing; it just points to the real thing. That's why the icon has that funny little arrow at the bottom.

shut down: The orderly way to finish your computing session. On the Start menu, you choose Shut Down, and then in the dialog box that appears, click Yes to confirm that you want to shut down the computer. Only turn off the computer when you get the message on-screen that it is safe to power off.

Start menu: The menu that pops up when you click the Start button. It enables you to start a program, open a document, adjust settings, find something, get help, run a program, or shut down.

taskbar: The bar that runs along the bottom or down the side of the screen, showing the Start button at one end, plus some status info at the other. The taskbar has buttons for every currently active program and any windows, minimized or not.

toolbar: A strip of icons, each icon giving you a shortcut to an action within a program. Toolbars usually appear below the menu bar in a program, but some also appear on the left or at the bottom of the program window.

URL: (Stands for Uniform Resource Locator.) Jargon for the Web address of a Web page. The URL is a locator in that it helps the Internet computers locate a page on a site; the page is a kind of resource. The Internet requires uniformity, or else it would fall apart, so the URL approach is universal and uniform.

wallpaper: Any image that you use as the background for your screen.

web browser: The software that you use to tour the World Wide Web. Internet Explorer is Microsoft's web browser; and Microsoft Network uses Internet Explorer to display its own pages, as well as to jump to other locations on the Web. Netscape offers its own web browser, called Netscape Communicator.

World Wide Web: The jazzy, multimedia part of the Internet, complete with pictures, videos, sounds, and text (with buttons you click to jump around).

window: An on-screen frame for information you want to look at or work on.

zoom: To magnify, as when you zoom in; or to shrink, as when you zoom out.

Index

• *Symbols* •

* (asterisk), 166
@ (at sign), 248
\ (backslash), 257
: (colon), 257
. (dot), 212–213
/ (forward slash), 166, 213
- (minus sign), 129, 155–156, 166
+ (plus sign), 129, 166, 243

• *Numbers* •

3D Atlas 98 (Creative Wonders), 294
3D Home Architect (Broderbund),
    191–192
3D Home Interiors (Broderbund), 192

• *A* •

"A;\ is not accessible. The device is not
    ready" error message, 262, 285
About the CD, 289–298
Accessibility Options icon, 89, 96–98

accessing
  the Control Panel, 19, 88–90
  Explorer, 128
  files in WordPad, 157–158
  files on the CD, 291
  help, 39–41, 45–46, 67, 283
  My Computer, 16–17, 44, 129
  sound files, 23–25
  version information, 276
accessories
  basic description of, 21, 147–170
  Calculator, 55, 147, 166–169
  CD Player, 181–184
  FreeCell, 176–177
  Hearts, 172–174
  Media Player, 21–26, 31, 43
  Minesweeper, 177–178
  Notepad, 26–28, 30, 42–43, 48–49, 51
  Paint, 93, 147, 156, 160–166
  Solitaire, 174
  WordPad, 54–62, 66–68, 112–118, 124,
    135, 147, 150–159, 219–220
Accessories dialog box, 118
Accessories menu, 21, 26
Active Desktop. *See also* desktop
  basic description of, I-1–I-32
  Control Panel settings for, I-13
  selecting, I-4–I-6
Active Desktop Gallery Web site,
    I-18–I-19
active window, 63, 65, 75–76, 78
Add Favorites dialog box, 222–223
addition/subtraction, 167–168
Add New Hardware Wizard, 281

Add To Favorites command, 222
Add/Remove Programs icon, 90, 118
Add/Remove Programs Properties
    dialog box, 118, 148–149, 264,
    277–278, 286
Adobe PageMill, 211
Adorable Downloadable Dog
    Screensavers Web site, 197
Airbrush tool, 125, 162
Alliance for Technology Access Web
    site, 104
Always Use This Program to Open This
    File option, 265
America Online
  basic description of, 245–248
  chat, I-3, 250–252
  e-mail, 226, 248–250
  installing, 246
  Microsoft Network and, comparison
    of, 230
Appearance tab, 63, 77–78, 93–95
Apple Computer, 55
applets, 148, 229
Apply button, 74–75, 92, 94
Arkenstone Web site, 97
Arrange By command, 47
Arrange Icons command, 225
arrow keys, 62
ASCII (American Standard Code for
    Information Interchange), 153
asterisk (*), 166, 263
at sign (@), 248
audio. See also sound
  CDs, playing, 25, 178–184
  recording, 184–186
Augmentative Communications Consult-
    ants Web site, 104
Auto hide check box, 38–39

• B •

Back button, 218, 236, 237
Background tab, 91–92
backgrounds (wallpaper), 166, 264,
    283, 304
  creating your own, 15, 92–95
  settings for, 91–95
backslash (\), 257, 263
backups
  basic description of, 229
  on floppy disks, 144–145
Best of Breed – The American Kennel
    Club's Multimedia Guide to Dogs
    (Macmillian Digital Hybrid), 197
Betty Crocker Cookbook (Lifestyle
    Software), 195, 291, 296–297
bitmaps, 163–164. See also graphics
board games, 198
boldface font, 155. See also fonts
Bonus.com Web site, 269
borders, 62–63, 80
Broderbund Web site, 293, 295–296
Browse button, 93
browsers. See also Internet Explorer
    browser
  basic description of, 304
  Netscape browsers, 211
  Web surfing with, 209–228
Brush tool, 161
BTW (By The Way), 251
bulletin boards, 242–245
buttons. See also buttons (listed by
    name)
  basic description of, 54–63
  clicking, with the mouse, 57–58
  command buttons, 74–75

buttons (listed by name). *See also*
    buttons
  Apply button, 74–75, 92, 94
  Back button, 218, 236, 237
  Browse button, 93
  Cancel button, 74–75
  Channels button, 219
  Chat button, I-29
  Chat Search button, 240
  Close button, 61–62, 54, 76, 129
  Communicate button, 238
  Copy button, 121
  Create Disk button, 277
  Cut button, 116
  Eject button, 24, 186
  Enable Ratings button, 235
  End Task button, 280
  Essential button, 236, 238
  Fast Forward button, 24, 186
  Find button, 238
  Find Now button, 256
  Forward button, I-24, 218, 237
  Go Back button, 291
  Go back to previous mark button, 24
  Go to next mark button, 24
  Help button, 74–75, 238
  Help Topics button, 40
  History button, 219, 225
  Home button, 218
  Join the Chat button, 240
  Leave the Chat button, 240
  List Chats button, 250
  Mark the beginning of a selection
    button, 24
  Mark the end of a selection button, 24
  Maximize button, 54, 59–61
  Minimize button, 42–43, 48, 54,
    59–61, 76
  Next button, 257
  Notify America Online button, 251
  Open button, 24
  Play button, 24, 25, 184, 185, 186, 187

  Preview button, 98, 107
  Print button, 219, 220
  question mark button, 237
  Read button, 249
  Receive button, I-24, 227, 228
  Refresh button, 218, 238
  Reset button, 280
  Restore button, 60–61
  Rewind button, 24, 186
  Save button, 29, 48
  Search button, 219, 220
  Send button, I-24, 227, 228
  Set Name button, 182
  Start button, 15, 20, 35–37, 88, 255–256
  Stop button, 24, 26, 184, 185, 218,
    236–237
  Support and Member Services
    button, 238
  Total time the sound will play
    button, 24
bytes, 47

• C •

caches, 218, 236
Calculator
  accessing, 166
  basic description of, 147, 166–169
  launching, 55
cameras, 201
Cancel button, 74–75
Cancel Printing command, 43
"Cannot find this file" error
    message, 262
capitalization, 27
cascading menus, 21
CD (*Windows 95 For Kids and Parents*)
  About the CD, 289–298
  files, accessing, 291
  files, installing, 290–291, 298

problems with, troubleshooting, 298
software on, summary of, 291–298
system requirements, 289–290
CD Player, 181–184
CD-ROM(s). *See also* CD (*Windows 95 For Kids and Parents*)
audio, playing, 25, 178–184
drives, opening, 13
storage space on, 143
Windows 95 installation CD, 11–12, 148, 231, 232
Center for Applied Technology Web site, 104
Channel Guide, I-10
channels
basic description of, 236
selecting, 239
using, I-11, I-19–I-21
Channels button, 219
chat
with America Online, I-3, 250–252
with Microsoft Network, I-3, 237, 239–241
subjects, selecting, 240–241, 250–251
Windows 98 and, I-3
Chat button, I-29
Chat Central, 240–241
Chat Search button, 240
check boxes, 74
Claris Works, 198
clicking, basic description of, 229
clip art. *See also* graphics
adding, 125–126
basic description of, 229
bitmap format for, 163
Clipboard
basic description of, 114–121, 229
copying graphics to, 156
memory usage and, 264, 283
pasting clip art from, 126
viewing the contents of, 118–120

Close button, 61–62, 54, 76, 129
closing
dialog boxes, 41, 287
games, 279
the Help dialog box, 41
colon (:), 257
color(s)
of links, 234
monitors, 290
in Paint, 161, 163–164, 165
palettes, 95, 97, 161, 163–164, 290, 296
resolution, 290, 296
schemes, selecting, 93–94
of text, 155
of the title bar, 78
Color Palette tool, 161, 163–164
Comic Chat mode, 241
command buttons, 74–75
commands (listed by name)
Add To Favorites command, 222
Arrange By command, 47
Arrange Icons command, 225
Cancel Printing command, 43
Compose Mail command, 248
Copy command, 121
Copy Disk command, 259
Cut command, 115, 138
Deck command, 174
Delete command, 140
Details command, 46
Edit Play List command, 182
Edit Your Online Profile command, 252
Folder Options command, I-5
Format command, 143
FreeCell command, 176–177
Line Up Icons command, 258
List command, 46
Minesweeper command, 177
Open command, 115, 158, 184, 262
Options command, 233, 235
Organize Favorites list command, 222

Page Setup command, 156–157
Print command, 28, 159, 227, 250
Read Mail command, 226
Rename command, 140, 258
Replace command, 157
Run command, I-17, 19, 41, 257, 290, 298
Save As command, 29, 48, 152–153, 185
Save command, 29, 48, 93, 152
Select All command, 138, 165
Send To command, 144, 259
Shut Down command, 31, 266, 279
Time/Date command, 27
Undo command, 123–125, 164
Undo Tile command, 84
Volume Control command, 24–25
Communicate button, 238
Compose Mail command, 248
compression, of files, 263
computer(s). *See also* hardware
date/time settings for, 89
magazines, 205
schedules for using, 30
turning on/off, 12–14, 30–31, 266
Confirm Delete dialog box, 140–141
Connect To dialog box, 215
Content Advisor, 235
Content Advisor dialog box, 235
Contents tab, 39–41, 67
Control Panel
accessibility options in, 89, 96–97
accessing, 19, 88–90
Add/Remove Programs feature, 118, 148–149, 264, 277–278, 286
basic description of, 38, 88–90, 229
color scheme settings, 93–94
display settings, 76–78, 90, 91–93, 98–99
installing programs with, 118, 148–149, 264, 277–278, 286
mouse settings, 57–58, 102–103

screen saver settings, 98–99
settings for visually-impaired individuals in, 89, 96–97
updating the contents of, I-11–I-15
window border settings in, 62–63
Convomania Web site, 269
cookies, 231–232
cooking software, 195, 291, 296–297
Copy button, 121
Copy command, 121
Copy Disk command, 259
Copy Disk dialog box, 259
Copy From list, 259
copying
basic description of, 111, 219–220
error messages when, 262–263
to floppy disks, 144–145, 258–259
graphics, 156, 165
Corel clip art collections, 126
country codes, 213
crashes. *See also* errors
basic description of, 300
viruses and, 277–278
Create Disk button, 277
Creative Wonders Web site, 292, 293, 294, 295
Current Call tab, I-30
cursor(s). *See also* mouse; pointers
basic description of, 300
blinking, 258
missing, 280–281
selecting text with, 112
Customer Service, IDG Books Worldwide, 298
Cut button, 116
Cut command, 115, 138
Cut icon, 122
cutting
basic description of, 111, 120–121
graphics, 165
moving documents/folders by, 138

• D •

date(s). *See also* time
  entering, into documents, 27
  last modified, for files, 47, 256
  listing files by, 47
  searching for files by, 256
  /time settings, for your computer, 89
Date Modified tab, 256
decimal system, 169
Deck command, 174
Delete command, 140
deleting. *See also* Recycle Bin
  data on floppy disks, 49
  error messages when, 265–266
  files/folders, 49, 140, 265–266
  text, 113–114, 124
"Deleting this file will make it impossible
    to run this program" error message,
    265–266
demos. *See also* software
  on the CD, summary of, 291–298
  running, 291, 296
  starting, 292
  stopping, 296
desktop. *See also* Active Desktop
  background (wallpaper), 15, 92–95,
    166, 264, 283, 304
  basic description of, 15, 33–52, 88, 301
  finding missing windows on, 81–82
  icons, 15, 16–19, 50–51, 95
"Destination disk drive is full" error
    message, 262–263, 285
Details command, 46
Details window, 46–47
Dial-Up Networking, 129, 231
dialog boxes
  basic description of, 70–75
  check boxes in, 74
  closing, 41, 287

  command buttons in, 74–75
  list boxes in, 72–74
  text boxes in, 71–72
DIPs, 179
Direct Memory Access channels, 179
DirectorShow 2 standards, I-31
Directory tab, I-29
DIRECTV satellite service, I-32
Disc Settings dialog box, 182
Discovery Channel: Go on a Virtual Field
    Trip Web site, 270
Disk tab, 277
diskette(s)
  copying data to, 144–145, 258–259
  copying data on, 259
  deleting the contents of, 49
  error messages and, 262–263
  formatting, 142–144, 262
  icon, in My Computer, 44
  preformatted, 142
  start-up disks, 277–278
Display icon, 63, 77, 89, 91, 93–95, 97, 98
Display Properties dialog box, I-12–I-13,
    I-15, 77, 91, 93–99, 264, 290, 296
division, 167–168
documents. *See also* files
  basic description of, 301
  moving, 138–139
  opening, with the Start menu, 37
  scrolling through, 287
  selecting, 135–138
Documents menu, 37, 282
dogs, 197–198
Don Johnston Web site, 104
DOS (Disk Operating System), 136
dot (.), 212–213
double-clicking, 299
double quotes ("), 263
downloading Web pages, 236
dpi (dots per inch), 100

drag-and-drop
  copying files with, 259
  moving documents/folders with, 138–140
drop-down list boxes, 73–74

• *E* •

echo effects, 185–186
Edit menu
  Copy command, 121
  Cut command, 115, 138
  Paste command, 115, 116, 121, 138, 165
  Replace command, 157
  Select All command, 138, 165
  Time/Date command, 27
  Undo command, 123–125, 164
Edit Play List command, 182
Edit Your Online Profile command, 252
Edmark Web site, 104, 295
Eject button, 24, 186
elevators, 69–70
Elliott, Allison, 190
Ellipse (Oval) tool, 162
Elmo's Preschool Deluxe, 292
e-mail (electronic mail)
  addresses, 248–249
  with America Online, 226, 248–250
  basic description of, 226–228
  Control Panel settings for, 90
  Inbox and, 34
  with Microsoft Network, 237
  with Microsoft Outlook Express, I-22–I-27
  reading, I-24, 226–227, 249–250
  sending, I-24–I-26, 227–228, 249
  Windows 98 and, I-2, I-22–I-27
  writing, 227, 249

emoticons, 155–156
Enable Ratings button, 235
encyclopedias, 203
End Task button, 280
Eraser tool, 162
error(s). *See also* crashes
  "A;\ is not accessible. The device is not ready" error message, 262, 285
  basic description of, 251–266
  "Cannot find this file" error message, 262
  "Deleting this file will make it impossible to run this program" error message, 265–266
  "Destination disk drive is full" error message, 262–263, 285
  "Not enough memory" error message, 264–265, 298
  "Open with" error message, 265
  "Setup cannot continue" error message, 298
  spelling errors, correcting, 157
  "There was an error printing to LPT1" error message, 265
  "This filename is not valid" error message, 263, 285
  "Unable to locate the server" error message, 266
Essential button, 236, 238
Expert Diet (Expert Software), 199
Explorer
  accessing, 128
  basic description of, 128–129
  creating folders in, 132
  deleting files/folders from, 140
  My Computer and, comparison of, 130–131
  playing music and, 179
  replacement of the File Manager by, 19
  Windows 98 and, I-2, I-22

• F •

F2F (Face to Face), 251
family albums, 199, 201–202
Family Education Network Web site, 270–271
FamilyPC Web site, 205
FAQs (Frequently Asked Questions), 301
Fast Forward button, 24, 186
Favorites list
  basic description of, 222–225
  organizing, 224–225
  Windows 98 and, I-10–I-11, I-21
file(s). *See also* documents; filenames
  basic description of, 301
  on the CD, accessing, 291
  on the CD, installing, 290–291
  compression of, 263
  Control Panel settings for, I-12–I-13
  dragging, onto the desktop, 51
  finding, 50–51, 131–132, 256
  formats, 47, 153
  last modified dates for, 47, 256
  listing/viewing, 46–47
  protecting, 133–135
  scrolling through, 287
  size, 47
filenames. *See also* file extensions
  allowable characters for, 133
  changing, 140, 258
  invalid, 263, 285
file extensions
  basic description of, 159, 301
  BMP, 163
  DOC, 159
  hiding, I-14
  RTF, 159
  TXT, 48, 159
File Manager, 19, 128, 131

File menu
  Copy Disk command, 259
  Delete command, 140
  Format command, 143
  Open command, 115, 158, 184, 262
  Page Setup command, 156–157
  Print command, 28, 159, 227
  Rename command, 140, 258
  Save As command, 29
  Save command, 29, 48, 93, 152
  Send To command, 259
finance software, 192–193, 297
Find All Files dialog box, 131–132, 256
Find button, 238
Find dialog box, 50–51
Find Now button, 256
Find People dialog box, I-16
Find tab, 39–40
finding items
  with the Microsoft Network Find area, 237, 241–245
  with the Windows Find feature, I-16, 50–51, 131–132, 256, 262
First Aid, 124
fitness software, 199
floppy disk(s)
  copying data to, 144–145, 258–259
  copying data on, 259
  deleting the contents of, 49
  error messages and, 262–263
  formatting, 142–144, 262
  icon, in My Computer, 44
  preformatted, 142
  start-up disks, 277–278
folder(s)
  basic description of, 16–19, 132–133, 301
  Control Panel settings for, I-12–I-13
  creating, 132–135
  creating icons for, I-10

finding, 50–51, 256
moving, 138–139
opening/closing, 129
protecting, 30, 133–135
renaming, 140, 258
saving documents in, 29
selecting, 135–138
viewing, 17, 129
Folder Options command, I-5
Folder Options dialog box, I-5–I-6, I-14
font(s). *See also* text
  basic description of, 100–102, 301
  Control Panel settings for, 99–102
  size, 95, 97, 102, 153–154
  viewing, 101
Format command, 143
Format dialog box, 142, 143
Format menu, 101
Forward button, I-24, 218, 237
forward slash (/), 166, 213, 263
FreeCell command, 176–177
freezes, handling, 279–280. *See also*
  crashes
FrontPage Express (Microsoft), 211

• *G* •

games
  basic description of, 171–188
  board games, 198
  exiting, 279
  FreeCell, 176–177
  Hearts, 172–174
  Minesweeper, 177–178
  Solitaire, 174
Games menu
  Deck command, 174
  FreeCell command, 176
  Minesweeper command, 177
  Scrabble, 198

gardening software, 193–194, 297
General tab, 234, 235
gigabytes, 47
GMTA (Great Minds Think Alike), 251
Go Back button, 291
Go back to previous mark button, 24
Go to next mark button, 24
Gookin, Dan, 290
graphics. *See also* photographs
  background, 15, 92–95, 166, 264,
    283, 304
  clip art, 125–126, 163, 229
  copying, 156, 165
  inserting, in WordPad documents, 156
  saving, 166
  scanning, 201
  selecting, 112–113
Great Software For Kids & Parents
  (Miranker and Elliott), 190
Guided Tour (Microsoft Network), 232

• *H* •

hard disk. *See also* memory
  displaying available memory informa-
    tion for, 260
  freeing up space on, 264–265
  icon, 17, 44, 260
  Shut Down and, 31
  sound made by, 13
hardware. *See also* mouse
  adding new, 281
  detection, 281
  hard disk, 13, 17, 31, 44, 260, 264–265
  Plug and Play feture and, 179–180
  processors, 11–12, 276–277, 289
  sound cards, I-27, 12, 13, 105–106, 180,
    287, 289
Hearts, 172–174

help
   accessing, 39–41, 45–46, 67, 283
   closing, 41
   Keep Help on Top option for, 41
   Memory Troubleshooter guide,
      283–284
   for Microsoft Network, 237
   for toolbars, 67
   for Windows 98, I-16–I-17
Help button, 74–75, 238
Help dialog box, 39–41
Help menu, 67
Help Topics button, 40
hiding
   file extensions, I-14
   taskbar, 38, 40
   windows, 42–43
Higher Score for the SAT/ACT
   (Kaplan), 296
highlighting. *See also* selecting
   information in text boxes, 71–72
   the title bar, 64
History button, 219, 225
History List, 225
home(s)
   computing, 190
   financing, 192–193, 297
Home button, 218
HomeBuyer (Stratosphere), 193, 297
HomePage (Claris), 211
Homework Wizard, 203
HTTP (HyperText Transfer Protocol),
   212, 216
hyperlinks. *See also* URLs (Uniform
   Resource Locators)
   basic description of, 302
   Windows 98 and, I-8, I-11

• I •

IBM (International Business
   Machines), 203
icon(s)
   basic description of, 13, 301
   Control Panel settings for, I-12–I-13
   creating, I-9–I-10
   dragging, 49
   in the Notify Area, 43
   organizing, 257–258
   selecting, 136–138
   size settings for, 28, 129, 225
   used in this book, 4–5
   Windows 98 and, I-8–I-13
IDG Books Worldwide
   Customer Service, 298
   Web site, 216–217
images
   background, 15, 92–95, 166, 264, 283,
      304
   clip art, 125–126, 163, 229
   copying, 156, 165
   inserting, in WordPad documents, 156
   saving, 166
   scanning, 201
   selecting, 112–113
IMHO (In My Humble Opinion), 251
Inactive Title Bar option, 78
Inbox, 18, 34
Index tab, 39–40, 67
installation
   of CD files, 290–291, 298
   of Microsoft Network, 231
   of new programs, 118, 148–149, 264,
      277–278, 286
   of sound cards, 180
   from Windows 95 installation CD,
      11–12, 148, 231, 232

Instant Messages, 252
Intellitools Web site, 104
interior design software, 191–192
Internet Explorer browser
  getting ready to use, 213–214
  icon, 214, 215–216
  launching, I-8, 34, 214–216
  Microsoft Network and, 230, 231,
    232, 237
  versions of, 213–214
  Web surfing with, 209–228
Internet icon, 18, 34, 90
invalid filenames, 263, 285
ISPs (Internet service providers),
    210, 212
  basic description of, 302
  making arrangements with, 231
italic font, 155. *See also* fonts

• J •

Join the Chat button, 240

• K •

Kaplan Web site, 296
Keep Help on Top option, 41
keyboard(s)
  basic description of, 26–27
  Control Panel settings, 103–104
  icon, 89, 103
  protecting, from liquids and dirt, 27
  repeat rates, 103–104
Keyboard Properties dialog box,
    103–104
KidDesk Family Edition (Edmark), 30
kilobytes, 47
Kodak, 201

• L •

LandDesigner (Sierra Home),
    193–195, 297
Leave the Chat button, 240
left-handed mouse setup, 57–58
left-arrow character (<), 263
Let Windows Manage My Virtual
    Memory Settings option, 264
license agreement, 290
Lifestyle Software Group, 296–297
Line Up Icons command, 258
lines, starting new, 27
links. *See also* URLs (Uniform Resource
    Locators)
  basic description of, 302
  Windows 98 and, I-8, I-11
list boxes
  in dialog boxes, 72–73
  drop-down, 73–74
  selecting items from, 73
List command, 46
List Chats button, 250
List view, 46
Living Books Sampler (Broderbund),
    292–293
Logical Journey of the Zoombinis
    (Broderbund), 295–296
LOL (Laughing Out Loud), 251
lurkers, 240

• M •

Macintosh, 19, 55
Madeline Classroom Companion: 1st
    and 2nd Grade Web site, 293
Magnifier tool, 164
Mail icon, 90

Mail menu
  Compose Mail command, 248
  Read Mail command, 226
margins, setting, 156
Mark the beginning of a selection
    button, 24
Mark the end of a selection button, 24
MasterClips clip art collection, 126
MasterSeries clip art collection, 126
Maximize button, 54, 59–61
Media Player, 21–26, 31, 43
megabytes, 47
Member Profiles, 252
memory. *See also* RAM (random-access
    memory)
  basic description of, 302
  caches, 218, 236
  Clipboard and, 264, 283
  conserving, 283–284
  displaying available, 260, 276
  error messages, 264–265, 283–284, 298
  freeing up, 264–265, 298
  Recycle Bin and, 141
  requirements, 289
  virtual, 264
menu(s)
  bar, 54, 65–66
  basic description of, 22–25
  cascading menus, 21
  icons on, changing the size of, 38
  making selections from, 22–23, 65–66
  right-pointing triangles on, 36–37
microphones, I-27, 30
microprocessors
  displaying information about your, 276
  recommended, 11–12, 277, 289
Microsoft FrontPage Express, 211
Microsoft Mail Postoffice icon, 90
Microsoft Net Meeting, I-27–I-31

Microsoft Network (MSN)
  basic description of, 34, 229–245, 303
  chat, I-3, 237, 239–241
  customizing, 233–234
  e-mail, 237
  icon, 18, 237
  installing, 231
  navigating with, 234–238
  parental controls with, 235
  setting up, 230–232
  visiting newsgroups with, I-26
Microsoft Outlook Express
  basic description of, I-22–I-27,
    226–228
  printing e-mail with, 227
  sending e-mail with, 222–228
  writing e-mail with, 227
Microsoft Web site, 216
Microsoft Word for Windows, 70, 133,
    135, 153, 158–159
Microsoft Works, 198
MIDI (Musical Instrument Digital Inter-
    face), 186–187, 303
Mighty Math Demo (Edmark), 295
Minesweeper, 177–178
Minesweeper command, 177
Minimize button, 42–43, 48, 54, 59–61, 76
minus sign (-), 129, 155–156, 166
Miranker, Cathy, 190
modem(s)
  basic description of, 210
  logging on and, 246, 247
  speeds, 236, 290
Modems For Dummies (Rathbone), 210
Mohta, Viraf, I-3, 203
monitor(s). *See also* screens
  basic description of, 303
  resolution, 95, 292, 296
  settings, 95–96
  system requirements and, 290
  turning on/off, 12, 31

Monster Board Web site, 271
Mosaic Web browser, 211
Motion tab, 103
mouse. *See also* cursors
    basic description for, 14
    cleaning, 280
    clicking/double-clicking, I-7–I-8, 16,
        56–58
    Control Panel settings for, 57–58,
        102–103
    left-handed setup for, 57–58
    missing pointer problems, 280–281
    navigating the World Wide Web with,
        216–217
    pad, 280
    pointer trails, 103
    scrolling with, 69–70
    without a right button, 283
Mouse Properties dialog box, 102–103
Multimedia icon, 90, 105
Multimedia Properties dialog box,
    105–106
multiplication, 167–168
music, playing, 23–25, 178–187
My Briefcase, 18, 35, 129, 130
My Computer
    accessing, 16–17, 44, 129
    basic description of, 16–18, 34, 44–47,
        129–131
    copying files in, 259
    creating folders and, 132
    deleting files/folders in, 140
    Explorer and, comparison of, 130–131
    icon, 16, 18, 44
    moving documents/folders in, 138–139
    organizing icons in, 258
    Windows 98 and, I-2, I-6, I-20–I-22
My Documents, I-11, 35, 129–130, 132

• *N* •

navigating
    in Microsoft Network, 234–238
    without scrolling, 232, 287
Net Meeting, I-27–I-31
Netscape Communicator, 211
Netscape Navigator, 211
Netscape Web site, 211
Network dialog box, 135
Network Neighborhood, 18, 90
New Message icon, 245
news services, 239
newsgroups, I-26–I-26, 237, 245
Next button, 257
Norton Utilities, 124
"Not enough memory" error message,
    264–265, 298
Notepad
    creating a computer-usage schedule
        with, 30
    creating files with, 48–49
    finding, with the Find dialog box, 51
    minimizing, to a button on the taskbar,
        42–43
    opening, 26, 27
    printing documents with, 27–28
Notepad.exe, 51
Notify America Online button, 251
Notify area, 35, 43, 283
NTSC (National TV System
    Committee), I-31
numeric keypad, 27, 68
NutriBase Personal Nutrition Manager
    (Cybersoft), 199
nutrition software, 199

• O •

On Stage area (Microsoft Network), 238–239
Online Help for Windows 95 Web site, 268
on/off switches, 12–14, 30–31
Open button, 24
Open command, 115, 158, 184, 262
Open dialog box, 23–24, 158, 184
opening
  the Control Panel, 19, 88–90
  Explorer, 128
  files, error messages and, 265
  files in WordPad, 157–158
  files on the CD, 291
  help, 39–41, 45–46, 67, 283
  My Computer, 16–17, 44, 129
  sound files, 23–25
Options command, 233, 235
Options dialog box, I-30, 233–234
Organize Favorites dialog box, 222
Organize Favorites list command, 222
Orly's Draw-A-Story (Broderbund), 293
Outlook Express
  basic description of, I-22–I-27, 226–228
  printing e-mail with, 227
  sending e-mail with, 222–228
  writing e-mail with, 227

• P •

Page Setup command, 156–157
PageMill (Adobe), 211
Paint, 93, 147, 156, 160–166
Paint Bucket tool, 162
palettes, color, 95, 97, 161, 163–164, 290, 296

parental controls, 235, 252
party invitation software, 199–200
passwords. *See also* security
  America Online and, 246–247
  Control Panel settings for, 90
  for files/folders, 124–135
  parental controls and, 235
  for starting Internet Explorer browser, 215, 216
pasting
  basic description of, 111, 115–118, 120–121
  graphics, 165
  with the Paste command, 115, 116, 121, 138, 165
  text, 219–220
PCs For Dummies, 4th Edition (Gookin), 290
Pencil tool, 161, 165
Performance tab, 264
Photo Creations (Creative Wonders), 201–202
PhotoDisc clip art collection, 126
photographs. *See also* graphics
  clip art, 126
  making family albums from, 199, 201–202
pipe symbol (│), 263
PKZip, 263
Play button, 24, 25, 184, 185, 186, 187
Play Lists, 181–184
Plug and Play, 179–180
plus sign (+), 129, 166, 243
pointer(s). *See also* cursors
  missing, 280–281
  trails, 103
Preview button, 98, 107
Print Artist (Sierra On-Line), 199, 200
Print button, 219, 220
Print command, 28, 159, 227, 250
Print dialog box, 101, 159, 219–220

Print icon, 245
printer(s). *See also* printing
  cables, 284
  Control Panel settings for, I-12
  problems with, 284
  turning on/off, 28, 31
printing. *See also* printers
  basic description of, 27–28
  bulletin board messages, 245
  e-mail messages, 227, 250, 265
  fonts, 101–102
  with the Print command, 28, 159,
    227, 250
  problems, 284–285
  software, 199–202
  Web pages, 219–220
  WordPad documents, 158–159
  your screen, 285
processors
  displaying information about your, 276
  recommended, 11–12, 277, 289
programs
  adding, to the Start menu, 257
  finding, 256, 282
  installing, 118, 148–149, 264,
    277–278, 286
  opening multiple, 26
Programs menu, 21, 26, 36
Publisher's Toolbox, 126

• Q •

question mark (?), 237, 263
question mark button, 237
Quick View, I-2
Quicken, 193
quotes, 263

• R •

RAM (random-access memory). *See also*
    memory
  adding more, to your computer, 298
  basic description of, 302, 303
  requirements, 11–12, 277, 289
  shortages, 264–265, 298
Rathbone, Andy, I-1, 290
Rathbone, Tina, 210
ratings systems, 235
Ratings tab, 235
Read button, 249
Read Mail command, 226
reading e-mail, I-24, 226–227, 249–250
Receive button, I-24, 227, 228
Recreational Software Advisory
    Council, 235
Rectangle tool, 162
Recycle Bin
  basic description of, 18, 34, 47–50, 303
  dragging data to, 49–50, 140–141
  emptying, 49, 50, 124, 141, 264
  icon, in the Explorer, 129, 130
  memory usage and, 264
  selecting data to send to, 135–138
  viewing the contents of, 49–50
  Windows 98 and, I-10
Recycle Bin icon, 18, 49
Refresh button, 218, 238
registration numbers, 276
Rename command, 140, 258
Replace command, 157
Report Wizard, 204
Reset button, 280
resolution, 292
Restore button, 60–61
Rewind button, 24, 186

right-arrow character (>), 263
R. J. Cooper Web site, 104
Rolling Stones, 10
ROTF (Rolling On The Floor), 251
RTF (Rich Text Format), 153, 158, 159
ruler
  basic description of, 67–68
  location of, 54
Run command, I-17, 19, 41, 257, 290, 298
Run dialog box, 257

• *S* •

San Francisco SPCA Web site, 197
satellite hookups, 210
Save button, 29, 48
Save As command, 29, 48, 152–153, 185
Save As dialog box, 29, 48, 152–153, 185
Save command, 29, 48, 93, 152
saving
  bulletin board messages, 245
  color schemes, 95
  error messages when, 285
  files, 28, 48, 151–154, 285, 304
  graphics, 93, 166
  with the Save As command, 29, 48,
    152–153, 185
  with the Save command, 29, 48, 93, 152
  sounds, 185
scanning images, 201
schedules, for using the computer, 30
school reports, 202–203
Schoolhouse Rock! 1st & 2nd Grade
    Essentials (Creative
Wonders), 294
Schoolhouse Rock! 1st – 4th Grade Math
    Essentials (Creative Wonders),
    294–295

science Web sites, 295
Scientific View, 168–169
Scrabble, 198
Scraps icon, 122–123
screen(s). *See also* monitors
  names, 246–247
  printing, 285
  resolution, 95, 292, 296
  savers, 98–99
  settings, 57–58, 95–96
Screen Saver tab, 98–99
scrolling
  basic description of, 45, 68–70
  through bulletin board messages, 243
  in drop-down list boxes, 73–74
  navigating without, 287
Search button, 219, 220
search engines, 221–222
security. *See also* passwords
  America Online and, 251–252
  Internet Explorer browser and,
    215, 216
  Microsoft Network and, 234–235
Security tab, 234–235
Select All command, 138, 165
Select tool, 162
selecting. *See also* highlighting
  documents, 135–138
  folders, 135–138
  graphics, 112–113
  text, 111–112
selection rectangle, 137
Send button, I-24, 227, 228
Send To command, 144, 259
servers
  basic description of, 211
  error messages and, 266
Set Name button, 182
Set Windows Password dialog box, 135

Settings menu, I-11–I-12, 37–38
Settings tab, 95–97, 296
setup
  error messages and, 298
  protecting, 133–135
  with the Windows Setup tab,
    148–149, 286
Sherlock Bones Web site, 197
Shut Down
  after changing settings in the Control
    Panel, 97
  basic description of, 30–31, 41–42, 304
  error messages and, 266
  using screen savers instead of, 99
  using the Shut Down command, 31,
    266, 279
  with Windows 98, I-17
Sierra Home Web site, 297
Smithsonian Institute Web site, 270
snail mail, 226
software. *See also* demos
  buying, online, 205
  on the CD, summary of, 291–298
  cooking software, 195, 291, 296–297
  edutainment software, 292–296
  for family projects, 190, 199, 201–202
  finance software, 192–193, 297
  fitness software, 199
  gardening software, 193–194, 297
  interior design software, 191–192
  nutrition software, 199
  printing software, 199–202
  school software, 202–203
  sharing, 189–206
  sports software, 198–199
  testing, 205
  travel software, 204–205
  updates, I-11, I-15
Solitaire, 174–175

sound. *See also* audio
  alerts, 98
  cards, I-27, 12, 13, 105–106, 180,
    287, 289
  files, finding, 107
  files, opening, 23–25
  MIDI (Musical Instrument Digital
    Interface), 186–187, 303
  recording, 184–186
  schemes, 287–288
  settings for, I-12, I-14, 105–107,
    287–288
  speakers and, I-27, 12–13, 25, 31, 43
  volume control, 24–25, 43, 105–106
Sound Properties dialog box, I-12, I-14,
    106–107, 287
Sound Recorder, 184–186
Sound tab, 98
space bar, 13
speakers, I-27, 12–13, 25, 31, 43
Speed tab, 103
spelling errors, correcting, 157
sports software, 198–199
Star (Free-form select) tool, 162
Start button. *See also* Start menu
  basic description of, 20, 36–37, 88,
    255–256
  location of, 15, 35–36
Start menu. *See also* Start button
  accessing Help with, 39–41
  adding programs to, 257
  basic description of, 304
  launching programs from, 20–21,
    26, 256
  as a new feature of Windows 95, 19
  opening documents with, 37
  Run feature, 257, 290, 298
  settings for, I-12, 37–38
  Shut Down feature, I-17, 30–31, 41–42,
    97, 99, 266, 279, 304
  Windows 98 and, I-2, I-10–I-17

status bar, 54, 68
Stop button, 24, 26, 184, 185, 218, 236–237
Straight Line tool, 162
Stratosphere Web site, 297
Support and Member Services button, 238
switch programs, 104
System Properties dialog box, 264, 276, 277
system requirements, for the CD, 289–290

• T •

tabs
  Appearance tab, 63, 77–78, 93–95
  Background tab, 91–92
  basic description of, 71
  Contents tab, 39–41, 67
  Current Call tab, I-30
  Date Modified tab, 256
  Directory tab, I-29
  Disk tab, 277
  Find tab, 39–40
  General tab, 234, 235
  Index tab, 39–40, 67
  Motion tab, 103
  Performance tab, 264
  Ratings tab, 235
  Screen Saver tab, 98–99
  Security tab, 234–235
  Settings tab, 95–97, 296
  Sound tab, 98
  Speed tab, 103
  Topics tab, 67
  Video tab, I-30–I-31
  Windows Setup tab, 148–149, 286

task list, 35
taskbar
  basic description of, 15, 19, 35–43, 88
  changing window displays with, 82–85
  Control Panel settings for, I-12
  customizing, 38
  displaying, 282
  finding lost, 35, 282
  hiding, 38, 40
  location of, 36, 54
  minimizing a program to a button on, 42–43, 59–60
  programs missing from, 282
  right-clicking, 82–83
  Windows 98 and, I-8–I-12, I-14
Taskbar and Start Menu dialog box, I-14
Taskbar Properties dialog box, 38
technical support
  America Online, 246
  information you will need when contacting, 276
  Microsoft, 275–276
TeenVoice - Teen Talk Web site, 269
television, watching, I-3, I-31–I-32, 10–11
testing software, 205
text. *See also* fonts
  boxes, in dialog boxes, 71–72
  copying and pasting, 115–118, 120–121
  deleting, 113–114, 124
  labeling graphics with, in Paint, 164
  selecting, 111–112
Text Document file format, 153, 158, 159
Text tool, 164
3D Atlas 98 (Creative Wonders), 294
3D Home Architect (Broderbund), 191–192
3D Home Interiors (Broderbund), 192
Thunderbeam Web site, 205
tic marks, 68

tiling windows, 83–85
time. *See also* dates
  of day, in the Notify Area, 43
  entering, into documents, 27
  settings, for your computer, 89
Time/Date command, 27
Tip of the Day, 14
tips files, 288
title bars, 54, 64–65, 78, 79
toggle switches, 104
Toilet Train Your Cat Web site, 197
toolbar(s). *See also* buttons
    (listed by name)
  accessing Help for, 67
  adding, to the taskbar, I-8–I-9
  basic description of, 66–67
  customizing, 234
  Internet Explorer browser, 217–219
  Microsoft Network, 234–238
Topics tab, 67
Total time the sound will play button, 24
tour, of Windows 95, 14
travel software, 204–205
TripMaker (Rand McNally), 204–205
troubleshooting guide, 279–288.
    See also help
True Type fonts, 100–101. *See also* fonts
TTFN (Ta Ta For Now), 251
typos, correcting, 27

updates, I-11, I-15
URLs (Uniform Resource Locators),
    212–213, 236, 266, 304. *See also* links
User name field, 135
user profiles, setting up, 133–135

• *V* •

version information, accessing, 276
video, I-27–I-31, 97, 186–187
Video for Windows, I-27
Video tab, I-30–I-31
videophones, I-3, I-27–I-31
View menu
  Arrange By command, 47
  Details command, 46
  Folder Options command, I-5
  Line Up Icons command, 258
  List command, 46
virtual memory, 264
viruses, handling, 277–278
visually-impaired individuals, 89, 96–97
voice messages, leaving, 30
volume control, 24–25, 43, 105–106
Volume Control command, 24–25

• *U* •

"Unable to locate the server" error
    message, 266
underlined font, 155. *See also* fonts
Undo command, 123–125, 164
Undo Tile command, 84

• *W* •

wallpaper, 15, 92–95, 166, 264, 283, 304
WDM 2 standards, I-31
Web browsers. *See also* Internet Ex-
    plorer browser
  basic description of, 304
  Mosaic Web browser, 211
  Netscape browsers, 211
  Web surfing with, 209–228

Web sites. *See also* Web sites (listed by name)
  recommended, 267–272
  searching for, 203, 220–222
Web sites (listed by name)
  Active Desktop Gallery Web site, I-18–I-19
  Adorable Downloadable Dog Screensavers Web site, 197
  Alliance for Technology Access Web site, 104
  Arkenstone Web site, 97
  Augmentative Communications Consultants Web site, 104
  Bonus.com Web site, 269
  Broderbund Web site, 293, 295–296
  Center for Applied Technology Web site, 104
  Convomania Web site, 269
  Discovery Channel: Go on a Virtual Field Trip Web site, 270
  Don Johnston Web site, 104
  Edmark Web site, 104, 295
  Family Education Network Web site, 270–271
  FamilyPC Web site, 205
  Intellitools Web site, 104
  Kaplan Web site, 296
  Madeline Classroom Companion: 1st and 2nd Grade Web site, 293
  Microsoft Web site, 216
  Monster Board Web site, 271
  Netscape Web site, 211
  Online Help for Windows 95 Web site, 268
  R. J. Cooper Web site, 104
  San Francisco SPCA Web site, 197
  Sherlock Bones Web site, 197
  Sierra Home Web site, 297
  Smithsonian Institute Web site, 270
  Stratosphere Web site, 297
  TeenVoice - Teen Talk Web site, 269
  Thunderbeam Web site, 205
  Toilet Train Your Cat Web site, 197
  Yahoo! Web site, 268
  Yahooligans! Web site, 268
  Yuckiest Site on the Internet – Alive or Dead Web site, 268–269
whiteboard, I-3, I-29–I-30
window(s)
  active, 63, 65, 75–76, 78
  basic description of, 53–86, 304
  borders, 62–63
  cascading, 82–83, 84
  finding missing, 81–82
  hiding, 42–43
  laying out, 82–85
  minimizing/maximizing, 42–43, 48, 58–62, 76
  moving, 79
  opening multiple, 80–81
  resizing, 79–80
  restoring, 43, 60–61
  special settings for, 76–78
  switching, 78
  tiling, 83–85
Windows 3.1 (Microsoft), 19, 128, 131
Windows 95 For Dummies, 2nd Edition (Rathbone), 290
Windows 95 installation CD, 11–12, 148, 231, 232
Windows 98 (Microsoft)
  basic description of, I-1–I-32
  browsing with, I-20–I-22
  getting your computer ready for, I-1
  new features of, I-2–I-3
Windows 98 For Dummies (Rathbone), I-32

Windows Setup tab, 148–149, 286
Wizards, 203–204, 256–257
Word for Windows (Microsoft), 70, 133,
    135, 153, 158–159
WordPad
  basic description of, 54–62, 147,
    150–159
  cut and paste with, 115–118
  deleting text in, 113–114
  launching, 55, 56, 66–67, 150–151
  password-protection and, 135
  pasting text into, 219–220
  ruler, 67–68
  selecting text in, 112
  toolbar/buttons, 66–67
  using the Undo command in, 124
workspace, 54
World Book Encyclopedia, 203
World Wide Web. *See also* Web sites
  basic description of, 304
  printing pages from, 219–220
  surfing, 209–228
World Wide Web For Kids and Parents
    (Mohta), I-3, 203

• *X* •

Xerox Palo Alto Research Center, 55

• *Y* •

Yahoo! Web site, 268
Yahooligans! Web site, 268
Yuckiest Site on the Internet – Alive or
    Dead Web site, 268–269

IDG Books Worldwide, Inc., End-User License Agreement

READ THIS. You should carefully read these terms and conditions before opening the software packet(s) included with this book ("Book"). This is a license agreement ("Agreement") between you and IDG Books Worldwide, Inc. ("IDGB"). By opening the accompanying software packet(s), you acknowledge that you have read and accept the following terms and conditions. If you do not agree and do not want to be bound by such terms and conditions, promptly return the Book and the unopened software packet(s) to the place you obtained them for a full refund.

1. **License Grant.** IDGB grants to you (either an individual or entity) a nonexclusive license to use one copy of the enclosed software program(s) (collectively, the "Software") solely for your own personal or business purposes on a single computer (whether a standard computer or a workstation component of a multiuser network). The Software is in use on a computer when it is loaded into temporary memory (RAM) or installed into permanent memory (hard disk, CD-ROM, or other storage device). IDGB reserves all rights not expressly granted herein.

2. **Ownership.** IDGB is the owner of all right, title, and interest, including copyright, in and to the compilation of the Software recorded on the disk(s) or CD-ROM ("Software Media"). Copyright to the individual programs recorded on the Software Media is owned by the author or other authorized copyright owner of each program. Ownership of the Software and all proprietary rights relating thereto remain with IDGB and its licensers.

3. **Restrictions on Use and Transfer.**

   (a) You may only (i) make one copy of the Software for backup or archival purposes, or (ii) transfer the Software to a single hard disk, provided that you keep the original for backup or archival purposes. You may not (i) rent or lease the Software, (ii) copy or reproduce the Software through a LAN or other network system or through any computer subscriber system or bulletin-board system, or (iii) modify, adapt, or create derivative works based on the Software.

   (b) You may not reverse engineer, decompile, or disassemble the Software. You may transfer the Software and user documentation on a permanent basis, provided that the transferee agrees to accept the terms and conditions of this Agreement and you retain no copies. If the Software is an update or has been updated, any transfer must include the most recent update and all prior versions.

4. **Restrictions on Use of Individual Programs.** You must follow the individual requirements and restrictions detailed for each individual program in Appendix B of this Book. These limitations are also contained in the individual license agreements recorded on the Software Media. These limitations may include a requirement that after using the program for a specified period of time, the user must pay a registration fee or discontinue use. By opening the Software packet(s), you will be agreeing to abide by the licenses and restrictions for these individual programs that are detailed in Appendix B and on the Software Media. None of the material on this Software Media or listed in this Book may ever be redistributed, in original or modified form, for commercial purposes.

5. **Limited Warranty.**

   (a) IDGB warrants that the Software and Software Media are free from defects in materials and workmanship under normal use for a period of sixty (60) days from the date of purchase of this Book. If IDGB receives notification within the warranty period of defects in materials or workmanship, IDGB will replace the defective Software Media.

   (b) **IDGB AND THE AUTHORS OF THE BOOK DISCLAIM ALL OTHER WARRANTIES, EXPRESS OR IMPLIED, INCLUDING WITHOUT LIMITATION IMPLIED WARRANTIES OF MERCHANTABILITY AND FITNESS FOR A PARTICULAR PURPOSE, WITH RESPECT TO THE SOFTWARE, THE PROGRAMS, THE SOURCE CODE CONTAINED THEREIN, AND/OR THE TECHNIQUES DESCRIBED IN THIS BOOK. IDGB DOES NOT WARRANT THAT THE FUNCTIONS CONTAINED IN THE SOFTWARE WILL MEET YOUR REQUIREMENTS OR THAT THE OPERATION OF THE SOFTWARE WILL BE ERROR FREE.**

   (c) This limited warranty gives you specific legal rights, and you may have other rights that vary from jurisdiction to jurisdiction.

6. **Remedies.**

   (a) IDGB's entire liability and your exclusive remedy for defects in materials and workmanship shall be limited to replacement of the Software Media, which may be returned to IDGB with a copy of your receipt at the following address: Software Media Fulfillment Department, Attn.: *Windows 95 For Kids & Parents,* IDG Books Worldwide, Inc., 7260 Shadeland Station, Ste. 100, Indianapolis, IN 46256, or call 800-762-2974. Please allow three to four weeks for delivery. This Limited Warranty is void if failure of the Software Media has resulted from accident, abuse, or misapplication. Any replacement Software Media will be warranted for the remainder of the original warranty period or thirty (30) days, whichever is longer.

   (b) In no event shall IDGB or the authors be liable for any damages whatsoever (including without limitation damages for loss of business profits, business interruption, loss of business information, or any other pecuniary loss) arising from the use of or inability to use the Book or the Software, even if IDGB has been advised of the possibility of such damages.

   (c) Because some jurisdictions do not allow the exclusion or limitation of liability for consequential or incidental damages, the above limitation or exclusion may not apply to you.

7. **U.S. Government Restricted Rights.** Use, duplication, or disclosure of the Software by the U.S. Government is subject to restrictions stated in paragraph (c)(1)(ii) of the Rights in Technical Data and Computer Software clause of DFARS 252.227-7013, and in subparagraphs (a) through (d) of the Commercial Computer–Restricted Rights clause at FAR 52.227-19, and in similar clauses in the NASA FAR supplement, when applicable.

8. **General.** This Agreement constitutes the entire understanding of the parties and revokes and supersedes all prior agreements, oral or written, between them and may not be modified or amended except in a writing signed by both parties hereto that specifically refers to this Agreement. This Agreement shall take precedence over any other documents that may be in conflict herewith. If any one or more provisions contained in this Agreement are held by any court or tribunal to be invalid, illegal, or otherwise unenforceable, each and every other provision shall remain in full force and effect.

Installation Instructions

• •

*T*o install the items from the CD to your hard drive, follow these steps:

1. **Insert the CD into your computer's CD-ROM drive.**

2. **Click the Start button and click Run.**

3. **In the dialog box that appears, type** `D:\SETUP.EXE`.

   Most of you probably have your CD-ROM drive listed as drive D under My Computer. Type in the proper drive letter if your CD-ROM drive uses a different letter.

4. **Click OK.**

   A license agreement window appears.

5. **If you want to use the CD, read through the license agreement, nod your head, and then click the Accept button. After you click Accept, you'll never be bothered by the License Agreement window again.**

   From here, the CD interface appears. The CD interface is a little program that shows you what is on the CD and coordinates installing the programs and running the demos. The interface basically lets you click a button or two to make things happen.

YOUR ONLINE RESOURCE

WWW.DUMMIES.COM

Discover Dummies Online!

The Dummies Web Site is your fun and friendly online resource for the latest information about ...*For Dummies*® books and your favorite topics. The Web site is the place to communicate with us, exchange ideas with other ...*For Dummies* readers, chat with authors, and have fun!

Ten Fun and Useful Things You Can Do at www.dummies.com

1. Win free ...*For Dummies* books and more!
2. Register your book and be entered in a prize drawing.
3. Meet your favorite authors through the IDG Books Author Chat Series.
4. Exchange helpful information with other ...*For Dummies* readers.
5. Discover other great ...*For Dummies* books you must have!
6. Purchase Dummieswear™ exclusively from our Web site.
7. Buy ...*For Dummies* books online.
8. Talk to us. Make comments, ask questions, get answers!
9. Download free software.
10. Find additional useful resources from authors.

Link directly to these ten fun and useful things at **http://www.dummies.com/10useful**

WWW.DUMMIES.COM

For other technology titles from IDG Books Worldwide, go to **www.idgbooks.com**

Not on the Web yet? It's easy to get started with *Dummies 101*®: *The Internet For Windows*® *95* or *The Internet For Dummies*,® 4th Edition, at local retailers everywhere.

IDG BOOKS WORLDWIDE

Find other ...*For Dummies* books on these topics:
Business • Career • Databases • Food & Beverage • Games • Gardening • Graphics • Hardware
Health & Fitness • Internet and the World Wide Web • Networking • Office Suites
Operating Systems • Personal Finance • Pets • Programming • Recreation • Sports
Spreadsheets • Teacher Resources • Test Prep • Word Processing

IDG BOOKS WORLDWIDE BOOK REGISTRATION

We want to hear from you!

Register This Book and Win!

Visit **http://my2cents.dummies.com** to register this book and tell us how you liked it!

- Get entered in our monthly prize giveaway.

- Give us feedback about this book — tell us what you like best, what you like least, or maybe what you'd like to ask the author and us to change!

- Let us know any other *...For Dummies*® topics that interest you.

Your feedback helps us determine what books to publish, tells us what coverage to add as we revise our books, and lets us know whether we're meeting your needs as a *...For Dummies* reader. You're our most valuable resource, and what you have to say is important to us!

Not on the Web yet? It's easy to get started with *Dummies 101*®: *The Internet For Windows*® *95* or *The Internet For Dummies*,® 4th Edition, at local retailers everywhere.

Or let us know what you think by sending us a letter at the following address:

...For Dummies Book Registration
Dummies Press
7260 Shadeland Station, Suite 100
Indianapolis, IN 46256-3945
Fax 317-596-5498

BUSINESS AND
GENERAL
REFERENCE
BOOK SERIES
FROM IDG

COMPUTER
BOOK SERIES
FROM IDG